THE CHANGING IMAGE OF THE CITY

Janet R. Daly-Bednarek

The Changing
Image of the City

Planning for Downtown

Omaha, 1945–1973

University of Nebraska Press

Lincoln & London

The paper in this book meets the
minimum requirements of American National
Standard for Information Sciences –
Permanence of Paper for Printed Library Materials,
ANSI Z39.48-1984.

Library of Congress Cataloging in Publication Data
Daly-Bednarek, Janet (Janet R.), 1959-
The changing image of the city: planning for downtown
Omaha, 1945-1973 / Janet R. Daly-Bednarek.
p.   cm.
Includes bibliographical references (p.   ), and index.
ISBN 0-8032-1692-0 (alk. paper)
1. City planning – Nebraska – Omaha – History –
20th century.
2. Central business districts – Nebraska – Omaha –
Planning – History – 20th century.
3. Urban renewal – Nebraska – Omaha –
History – 20th century.   I. Title.
HT168.N343D35 1992
307.1′216′09782254 – dc20
91-42758 CIP

Contents

Illustrations

Following page 148

Tables

Acknowledgments

I would like to thank my mentor at Creighton University, Dr. Dennis N. Mihelich, for giving me my first view of what being a historian really means. He also unfailingly told me the book would be a good idea, even as I doubted it myself. I must also thank Dr. Samuel P. Hays of the University of Pittsburgh. He pushed me to my intellectual limits yet allowed me the freedom to stay out there and see how far I could go. He gave me plenty of rope but made sure I never hanged myself. The other members of my dissertation committee—Drs. Van Beck Hall, Ted Muller, Moe Coleman, and Joe White—also deserve a word of thanks for putting up with me while I made my mad dash toward graduation. A fellow Pitt student, Chris Hogan, spent many hours proofreading the manuscript back in the days before I could afford a word-processing program with a spelling checker. And I must thank the computer technician who converted my files once I had the new program and machine, thereby rescuing my manuscript from megabyte oblivion. My colleagues at the Office of the Air Force Historian have been very supportive, offering their sincere congratulations at every milestone during the past year or so.

My parents always encouraged me to push myself and become everything of which I was capable. My brothers, John and Joe, always cheered me on, even when I was something of a pain. Without my family, I couldn't have done this.

Finally, although he is a relative newcomer to this project, I have to thank my husband, Mike. He nagged me just enough to make sure I finished, provided a great deal of much-welcomed computer expertise, and sat on the floor a couple of nights cautiously tearing apart the hundreds of pages of fanfold paper so I could mail the final manuscript to the publisher. Such devotion is rare and precious.

Of course the content and the interpretation are mine, and for them I accept full responsibility.

ONE

New Ideas and Changing Images

The post–World War II years were a time of dramatic change in cities throughout the United States. Central cities decayed, losing industry, population, and hope, while suburban fringes blossomed as young families sought the green-lawned havens of single-family dwellings in which they could live the American Dream. Even the Sunbelt Cities of the South and West, fabled for their dramatic expansion, experienced growing pains as demands for services escalated beyond the limits of municipal financing. Urban advocates and critics alike declared that the United States was the victim of an urban crisis. Some even confidently predicted the death of the American city.

Reflecting national trends, Omaha, Nebraska, went through a number of remarkable transformations. It grew in both physical size and population. The economic base shifted from a dominance of meat and grain processing, transportation, and wholesaling to a dominance of retailing, finance, government, and services. Omahans became more educated, more white collar. In Omaha as elsewhere, the downtown, once the city's shining glory, withered as expansive shopping malls thrived, fed by their natural ally the automobile.

Beyond the real and serious problems of Omaha and other urban areas, however, another transformation took place: a change in the image of the city. City planners in the immediate postwar years, at both the local and national levels, viewed the city primarily as a place to work, a place that functioned to hold industry and jobs. Consequently, city plans focused

I

heavily on infrastructure improvements and on enhancing efficiency. Years of decline in traditional industries, together with the dawn of the service economy, gradually forced a redefinition of the city. The new service economy and the amenities-oriented middle class it created made demands far different from those expressed earlier; efficiency was no longer the key. By and large, the new service industries did not need better streets and sewers to do business. They sought a business environment that provided not just a favorable economic climate, but an exciting and vibrant living environment. The educated and mobile individuals involved in the service economy demanded cultural and recreational amenities; they wanted a sophisticated ambience as well as a congenial tax structure. The new attitudes prompted a redefinition of the city as a place in which to live, a place that provided the ambience and amenities now in demand. In that spirit, Omaha's planners and boosters responded in the late 1960s and reshaped its image to accommodate their perception of the changed attitudes.

Nationally, much of the planning and boosting activity of the postwar years focused on downtowns and waterfronts. At first, the assumption that a downtown would continue in its traditional role as the center of business, retail activity, and industry underlay planning proposals. Planners emphasized infrastructure improvements and face-lift projects to maintain the center-place status. They defined waterfronts largely in terms of their commercial value as highways for goods; cities used rivers flowing past them as convenient sewers. Gradually, as both the role of the downtown and the image of the city changed, proposals for downtowns began to reflect new ideas. Once planners accepted downtown's new role as an office, entertainment, and cultural center, they called for projects that would create the demanded cultural and recreational amenities and ambience sought by the new middle class. The image of the waterfront changed as it came to be valued as an environmental and recreational amenity. Such changes were evident in professional planning journals, in books and articles written by planning experts, and in the types of projects cities undertook.

City planning in Omaha between 1945 and 1973 endured a similar transformation. The issue became one of determining the relationship between changes in general planning theory and developments at the local level. The task would have been simple if new planning ideas merely succeeded old ones in patterns of clear-cut transitions or if a relatively few like-minded planning theorists were able to convince all local planners to accept their ideas and local planners in turn were able to sell those ideas to all interested parties. Neither was the case, however, so the problem became twofold: how to describe the course of changes in planning thought and how to describe the ways in which elite planners could transmit their ideas to local planners and various community groups interested in planning.

A study of planning ideas and activity in Omaha indicated that the simple transition models mentioned above did not apply to the developments taking place. No identifiable watershed in planning thought appeared; the process was gradual and incremental. Omaha planners did not look to experts and then follow their advice. In fact, until the early 1960s, they were reluctant to turn to outsiders. When they latched on to popular planning notions, they did so selectively, choosing only those ideas that fit their perception of problems and their image of the city. The evidence suggested, therefore, that when describing the relationship between changes in experts' ideas and developments at the local level, it was best to think of planning as involving groups operating at three independent yet related levels: elite experts, local planners-practitioners, and various constituencies interested in solving problems in their localities. Each level had its own perspective on problems and its own image of the city, so each devised its own solutions.

The elite experts articulated most, if not all, of the highly developed ideas about city planning. They came from a variety of disciplines, including architecture, engineering, journalism, landscape architecture, and the social sciences, and at any given time a significant number of them might hold certain planning ideas up as standards. They might argue over the precise details, yet they would broadly agree on the essential elements. Over time, however, individual experts introduced new ideas. Some were dismissed immediately, but others persisted and challenged the standard notions. Gradually, if they proved successful, the new ideas displaced older ones. The result was a change in the overall content of planning ideas. It was not necessarily dramatic and it did not arrive as a whole, but, rather, as the cumulative contribution of many thoughts and themes from people in the disciplines that supplied planning experts. Thus no individual or small group of experts was responsible for the change. Instead, a large number of

3

people contributed, and over time the elite gradually switched from emphasizing one set of standard ideas to stressing another.

Planning experts responded to broad changes in the urban context.
Decentralization, which produced sprawling suburbs and decaying downtowns, created new problems that required new solutions. The transformation from an industrial-commercial economy to a service economy created a
variety of planning issues because the service enterprises' technical requirements were different from those of older industries. Rising urban groups,
especially the new amenities-oriented middle class, demanded not only
more and better services but also a quality environment with an urban
ambience, plus cultural and recreational facilities. Planners therefore needed
to address both the changed structure of cities and their new concerns.

While the experts shaped general planning thought, local planners-
practitioners and constituency groups also participated in the planning
process. In fact, they were the most crucial element in determining the
projects that would be undertaken in a given locality. Because of their
training or their interest in planning, they were exposed to the experts'
ideas, with the planners looking to the experts and the constituencies
looking to both local and expert planners for ideas. Some of the contact
was made directly through conferences, short-term consulting trips, and
other forms of personal and professional communication (letters, journals,
books). A good deal of it came indirectly, not from talking to the experts,
but from observing what other cities did. Selective imitation, which involved adopting projects viewed as the current fashion in city planning, was
a significant factor in the process. Further, in their contact with experts,
neither group accepted the ideas of any one expert or group of experts as a
whole. Rather, they selected the ideas that best fit their own perceptions of
their cities' problems and images.

As did the experts, local planners came from a variety of disciplines. In
fact, as a group they were noted for their heterogeneity. Unlike many
experts, however, they probably were involved primarily in the day-to-day
operations of city planning. When they looked to experts in their fields for
ideas, unless they were the steadfast disciples of one of them, they were
likely to draw ideas from several. What they selected depended on their
background, where they were working and for whom. For example, a local

4

planner trained primarily as a landscape architect would tend to consider ideas from experts in that field. A planner in a rapidly growing southwestern city might consider ideas different from those of a planner employed in an older, declining city in the Northeast. Further, as minor experts in their own right, local planners likely modified the ideas they selected on the basis of their own practical experiences. And very often they based their own ideas on local conditions and needs.

The multitude of constituency groups interested in planning constituted the final level. In many ways they were the pivotal element because they probably were making the planning decisions. They ranged from housers (those interested in public-housing reform) to boosters (usually civic-minded businessmen interested in promoting the image of their city) to real-estate interests, park enthusiasts, construction and engineering interests, beautifiers, and politicians, to name a few. Any city might have one or (more likely) many such groups involved in planning and decision making. One or two groups might have dominated, but more than likely a number of groups competed to set the civic planning agenda. They, too, demonstrated selectivity in the planning ideas upon which they drew. The composition of the groups determined, in large part, which ideas they chose. If housers dominated, they tended to select ideas meeting their goals. Boosters and real-estate interests, on the other hand, undoubtedly selected quite different ideas that reflected their quite different goals. The types of groups making the planning decisions therefore determined what kinds of projects were undertaken.

The connection between planning and boosting proved to be another key element. Both aimed to promote growth and development, but especially in regard to certain large-scale projects, booster goals provided the rationale for many planning initiatives. Auditoriums, civic centers, streets and boulevards, parks, airports, and new city halls frequently were designed to meet both the desire of boosters to put their city's best foot forward and the technical requirements of planners. Boosters used the planning process to demonstrate their city's energy and up-to-date nature. They remained keenly aware of what business and industry looked for. When efficiency was important, they pushed for infrastructure improvements that enhanced it. As service businesses and industries began looking more for quality-of-life factors, such as cultural and recreational amenities, boosters gradually shifted their emphasis and worked to give such projects priority in planning schemes.

The constituency groups' perceptions of problems and their image of the city further influenced choices. A redefinition of the problems and a reshaping of the image in light of broad social, economic, and demographic changes therefore was another factor that caused shifts in planning strategies at that level. The local changes were similar to those seen at the expert planners' level yet did not merely reflect them. The locals took cues from the experts but continued to select only ideas that met their goals and fit their image of their city. For example, not every city participated in urban renewal or applied to the Great Society's model-city program. Neither did every city build extensive public-housing projects or construct superblocks and megastructures. At any given time, a number of planning and boosting ideas—both old and new—were available. Local individuals chose those that best fit their circumstances and goals.

The connection between city-planning experts and national trends and local individuals making planning decisions was frequently indirect and to some extent tenuous, but there were cases in which acknowledged experts directly shaped planning. For example, Edmund Bacon of Philadelphia and Robert Moses of New York certainly exerted much influence in their respective cities. More frequently, however, especially when one moves beyond events in the nation's twenty to thirty largest cities, local individuals making planning decisions probably did so with little direct or at most periodic expert advice.

When a city participated in a planning initiative, it was not simply a matter of reflecting a national trend or deferring to experts. Rather, choices were made that depended to a large extent on local circumstances. For instance, cities neither rejected old ideas nor accepted new ones at a uniform rate, but that is not to argue that each city represented a unique case. The choices made fell into broad categories. For example, housers in one city tended to make decisions similar to those made by housers in another. The same was true for boosters, real-estate interests, and beautifiers.

It was important, therefore, to view planning as operating on those three related yet independent levels. Within each level, changes occurred as individuals made choices and responded to the broad social and economic transformations at work reshaping the American city. Communication between the levels also involved a matter of choices. At the local level the choices depended on the individuals and groups involved, local conditions, and, perhaps most important, the image of the city held by those making the planning decisions. As long as the planners and constituency groups viewed their cities in traditional terms, their decisions were intended to meet the needs of commercial or industrial interests. So they concentrated on maintaining efficiency, focused on basic infrastructure improvements, and tried to maintain the downtown and waterfront in their traditional roles. By the 1960s most cities had undergone significant social and economic changes as the service economy replaced the traditional commercial and industrial economy. Expert planners, local planners, and constituency groups all needed time to comprehend the extent and meaning of the transformations. The experts were the first to express new ideas. Gradually, those operating at the local level recognized changes in their cities and shifted their priorities to meet the needs of the service economy and of the new downtown and waterfront. Then they chose planning ideas that met their new goals of creating urban ambience and providing a wide variety of cultural and recreational amenities.

Planning: The State of the Profession

Throughout the postwar period, perhaps *eclectic* best described the city-planning profession. According to its chronicler, Mel Scott, it suffered from a persistent shortage of trained practitioners and from an inability to define a precise course of study for aspiring planners. For these reasons, expert planners and local practitioners came from many fields, including landscape architecture, engineering, architecture, and even journalism and the social sciences. A number of acknowledged experts were not planners per se but critics of what planners were doing. Furthermore, planning theorists, because of the complexity of their subject, invited the participation of individuals from other fields. Not surprisingly, therefore, the planning profession witnessed a number of internal divisions.

Mel Scott's detailed study of city planning identified several divisions within the profession, the most basic of which was between "actionists"

7

and what might be called revisionists. The actionists, comprised of "planning directors, consultants and heads of federal and state agencies concerned with urban programs," held that the answers to urban problems lay in stronger governmental action, improvement in administration and better relations between planners and policymakers. This group supported existing policies and the "familiar constructs" of planning theory. The revisionists reacted to the changing city structure by proposing extensive research. Comprised of "professors of city planning, directors of academic research institutes, heads of foundations interested in urban problems, and writers and critics in the field of human environment," they thought planning assumptions needed reexamination and proposed research touching on nearly all factors involving planning. Hence the division basically involved those wishing to work within the existing framework and those wishing to take off in new directions. The latter gradually gained influence, especially in universities and foundations, and planning slowly became more broadly research oriented. The process took time. For example, the call for more and better research went out in 1950, but not until 1955 did the Ford Foundation offer grant money to support it. The improvement of planning through detailed research spread even more slowly to localities. Divisions persisted and broadened in the 1960s "as planning agencies experimented with a variety of approaches and as professors in university schools of planning divided into groups with disparate interests and opposing philosophies." Individual planners reacted differently to the many urban changes they confronted, and the reactions further fragmented the profession.[1]

Also interpreted as a problem, the training and background of those acting as planners remained quite varied. Throughout the 1950s and 1960s there was a shortage of trained professional planners. Leaders at a 1958 conference acknowledged "more than 250 planning jobs" left vacant because there were no trained planners to fill them. Despite a growing number of universities offering course work and degrees in city planning, the shortage continued well into the late 1960s. A 1968 Housing and Urban Development Department study estimated the shortage at between fifteen hundred and seventeen hundred planners. This meant that people without degrees staffed planning departments in many cities, especially smaller ones. Instead, Scott says, they held degrees in a wide variety of related fields, such as "political science, economics, geography, sociology, architecture, landscape architecture, [and] engineering."[2]

Professional planners and planning schools responded by offering workshops and special training seminars. No remedies, however, allowed the profession to keep up with the rapidly escalating demand for trained professionals that came with the expansion of urban programs at the national, state, and local levels. The private sector also recognized the value of the planners' expertise. Churches, hospitals, and universities building new facilities; developers and real-estate interests; construction and engineering firms; and foundations with large land holdings competed with governmental agencies for the planning-school graduates. Increasing the number of trained planners and thereby improving the quality of planning remained a constant concern of the profession.[3]

Planning experts blamed at least some of the failure of national planning initiatives on the "primitive state" of local planning programs. During the early 1950s, administrators of the Housing Act of 1949 found that many cities interested in slum clearance had inadequate legal and administrative mechanisms to carry out such a program. Of the first 205 applicants seeking federal funds under the act, "only 128 had official planning agencies, and only 56 of these had full-time staffs." The national government continued to encourage planning at the local, metropolitan, and state levels throughout the 1950s and 1960s, with the latter decade witnessing rapid expansion of the types of planning supported by federal grants.[4] Federal monies did not ensure, however, that personnel were available to help localities take full advantage of the opportunities provided. The profession managed to become more sophisticated by the late 1960s, but the continued shortage of trained planners remained a problem at the local level.

While planners were struggling to expand training, there was debate in the profession about the ideal content of a planner's education. Inability to agree on a standard definition of city planning, which ranged from a narrow focus on land-use patterns to an all-encompassing concern for every aspect of urban development, contributed to the problem. At the narrow end of the spectrum stood the definition of planning as expressed by John T. Howard, director of planning in Cleveland, Ohio. He "held to a conception of city planning based on an image of the city as 'a good or bad pattern of land uses and population densities, knitted into better or worse work-ability by systems of streets, utilities and public service utilities.'"[5] The result of planning activity was "a plan, or plans, for physical change and development."[6] Scott says Howard reflected the opinions of most planners, at least in the 1940s and early 1950s. In his 1954 study of the content of general plans, law professor and planner Charles Haar demonstrated that demarcating patterns of land use lay at the core of master planning. He suggested, however, that such a vision was far too narrow and that planners should broaden the scope of their activities somewhat.[7] In fact, in the 1950s a number of individuals, including the revisionists, challenged the narrow focus on physical planning. They felt planning must respond to economic and social trends, not just physical requirements.[8]

In the mid-1950s, Martin Meyerson suggested that beyond publishing a long-range plan, city planning departments should also perform a number of intermediate functions on a sustained basis. These functions included conducting marketing analyses and ongoing economic research, presenting and analyzing alternative policies, extending capital-improvement pro-gramming, and reviewing the effects of existing actions and programs.[9] It was not enough simply to establish a plan; the department needed to guide individuals making land-use decisions and help them make rational, benefi-cial choices.

By the 1960s planning professionals realized that they needed broader definitions of both the city and planning. In 1963, Melvin Webber, plan-ning professor and former editor of the profession's journal, developed the idea of the city as a complex system: "We are coming to comprehend the city as an extremely complex social system, only some aspects of which are expressed as physical buildings or as locational arrangements. . . . As the parallel, we are coming to understand that each aspect lies in a reciprocal causal relation to all others, such that each is defined by, and has meaning only with respect to, its *relations* to all others."[10]

One could no longer separate the physical city from the social, economic or political city. A city was more than buildings and infrastructure, it was the "skills and capacities of urban populations, the accumulated knowledge and wisdom of culture, and the ways in which people organized themselves for the joint conduct of their affairs."[11] Using that definition of the city, Webber declared that planners must take a more systematic approach to urban problems, arguing that planners must work with professionals in "public health, education, law enforcement, engineering, and public administration" to develop a "systematic integration of programs for improving urban communities."[12] His work indicated that planners should no longer focus only on the physical form of the city, but on "the processes that relate the interdependent aspects of the city one to another."[13]

In 1967 the American Institute of Planners adopted a broader statement of purpose. The original statement described planning as "the unified development of urban communities and their environs and of states, regions, and the nation, as expressed through determination of the comprehensive arrangement of land uses and land occupancy and the regulation thereof."[14] The new statement removed the limitation imposed by the focus on land use by eliminating that phrase and broadening, by implication, the scope of planning to "include social and economic plans and programs." The profession thus adopted "a comprehensive planning approach in which social development and economic development were integral with, but not independent of, physical development." The much broader statement of purpose further reinforced the heterogeneity of the planning profession. No one planner could possibly be an expert in all of the fields now involved in planning: social work, economics, engineering, architecture, education, and so on. Planning, therefore, had to welcome into its ranks experts from these various fields and adopt an interdisciplinary approach. Although Robert Weaver, secretary of housing and urban development under President Lyndon Johnson, proposed "a whole new order of urban expert," one who would be a trained urban generalist, the trend was toward specialization.[15]

The city planning profession that developed was heterogeneous and complex. Not surprisingly, the number and range of planning ideas put forth by experts demonstrated a similar heterogeneity. Experts from a number of fields contributed many planning ideas for the downtown and the waterfront, their research having led them to redefine the role and function of those areas. It would be impossible to explore every facet of planning thought, so this study will focus on ideas concerning the downtown and the waterfront as they appeared in planning and planning-related journals and reports.

Planning: The Ideas

Most of the new ideas for planning projects seemed to grow out of a concern for urban design. An elusive term, it emphasized man's relationships with the built environment. Cities must be constructed on an understandable human scale, but this did not rule out skyscrapers; it simply asserted that cities needed such features as identifiable landmarks and focal points so that people could feel comfortable and secure moving about within them. Planning experts coupled urban design with a renewed sense of the importance of aesthetics. Within that context there developed a number of related themes, including beautification, parks and open space, historic preservation, pedestrian ways, and, eventually, environmental, cultural, and recreational amenities.

In the late 1940s and early 1950s, plans for the downtown reflected two basic programs: clearance (through urban renewal) and infrastructure improvements, especially streets and highways. Plans assumed that if blighted areas were cleared and new structures erected and if access to the area were improved, then the downtown would continue to play its traditional center-place role. Rivers, lakes, and oceans were viewed almost as part of the infrastructure because they served as highways for bulky goods and as sewers, for most cities dumped their sewage and industrial wastes into nearby waters.

As cities underwent broad social, economic, demographic, and structural changes, downtowns and waterfronts ceased to play their traditional roles. Gradually, planning ideas adjusted to the changed circumstances. A reshaping of the general image of the city proved essential to the shift. In traditional industrial and commercial cities, downtowns and waterfronts had specific roles. As planning experts and local constituency groups came to grips with the service economy, they redefined the downtown and waterfront and gave them new and different roles. This gradual reshaping of the city's image was accompanied by new planning ideas for both areas.

For the most part, planners in the 1940s and 1950s continued to define the downtown by its traditional functions. One of the 1950s model plans clearly reflected this definition and presented the standard planning answers to the area's problems. Under the leadership of Mayors Joseph Clark and Richardson Dilworth and planner Edmund Bacon, Philadelphia developed several plans that together represented one of the most acclaimed initiatives of the decade. The plans did not deal specifically with the downtown, but the overall strategy included a center strengthened by completion of a metropolitan transportation system. Build a system allowing easy access between downtown and the growing metropolitan and regional centers and Philadelphia's downtown would continue in its traditional center-place role.[16] Also in the 1950s, Philadelphia undertook extensive clearing of blighted areas surrounding its downtown, including the environs of historic Independence Hall and the old produce and meat market on the banks of the Delaware.[17] The plans reflected two prominent solutions to downtown problems: clearance and improved access. Other standard answers included more downtown parking and transit facilities or satellite parking facilities to accommodate the anticipated increase in traffic.

Standard planning priorities for riverfronts proved more difficult to determine. A 1945 article in the *Journal of the American Institute of Planners* these "potential uses of waterfront sites":

a. Existing and potential waterborne commerce (characteristics and transportation requirements).
b. Facilities for warehousing and storage of cargo.
c. Shipbuilding and boatbuilding.
d. Marine repair facilities.
e. Supply services needing storage areas, as for bunker oil and gasoline and bunker coal.
f. Special provisions for commercial and sport fishing craft and for pleasure craft.[18]

Clearly, the image of waterfronts focused on their commercial value.

On the other hand, a shoreline plan for Los Angeles described in the same journal only one year later established an entirely different set of priorities. Its major features included beaches and boardwalks, scenic drives, recreational areas, a cultural center, a bird sanctuary, and parkways.[19] And

13

in 1948, Eero Saarinen and Dan Kiley created for Saint Louis's riverfront an award-winning design that stressed sensitivity to the historic value of the area and gave the city a direct link to its riverfront, long hidden from view by railroad tracks and trestles. However, Saint Louis did not complete the project until 1964. By that time circumstances had worked to revise the original scheme significantly; most important, the city lost its connection to the river.[20] It must also be kept in mind that cities continued dumping their sewage and industrial wastes, frequently untreated, into nearby waters well into the 1960s, and the relatively flat waterfront land often became a favored location for highway construction. One was confronted, therefore, with a complex and often contradictory vision of the proper role and use of waterfronts. Plans for improved dock and warehouse facilities conflicted with every proposal for scenic drives or parks. Both the commercial and the aesthetic values and plans to enhance one or the other found champions. Until environmental values gained credence in American life and rivers, lakes, and the ocean were freed of choking pollutants, their value as scenic and recreational amenities could not be fully realized.

In the 1950s and 1960s new themes and threads of thought entered planning discussions. They had the cumulative effect of significantly re-forming planning strategies for downtowns and waterfronts. Redefinition of downtown's role in the changing city was a major factor in the process. The realization that it had lost many of its traditional functions demanded fresh ideas, and the resulting definition and image opened the way for innovation. The other important threads of thought—urban design, beau-tification, parks and open space, malls, pedestrian ways, historic preserva-tion, and cultural and recreational amenities—did not necessarily enter planning discussions in direct response to downtown problems, with the exception of malls. Gradually, however, planners applied the ideas or their spirit to a rebuilding of the downtown that would fit its new image.

The vast amount of research conducted by planners beginning in the 1950s uncovered and detailed transitions under way in the downtown. That discovery, which many had made intuitively and which research reinforced, produced two major responses. The first emphasized the need to reinstate the downtown in its traditional role. The Philadelphia plan and many others adopted that strategy, calling for clearance and better access to shore up and maintain the downtown's traditional functions. By the early 1960s, however, other planners responded by declaring that if the downtown was becoming something quite different, then plans must recognize its new functions. As long as those who made planning decisions held a traditional view of the downtown, they continued to rely on traditional answers. Acceptance of a new definition opened the way for adoption of other planning strategies.

In 1961 the *Journal of the American Institute of Planners* devoted an entire issue to downtown problems. Two articles not only presented innovative schemes but redefined downtown's role and image. Charles Abrams harkened back to the traditional market fair as his model, while Blanche Lemco Van Ginkel emphasized the importance of creating downtowns offering a sense of urbanity and a wide range of urban activities. She argued for sensitivity to the human scale.

Abrams, a lawyer by profession, was a leading 1950s figure in city planning. His article "Downtown Decay and Revival" represented a mixture of traditional and innovative ideas that leaned toward innovation. In a traditional vein, he still saw the downtown as the ultimate center of the city, as vital to a city as the heart is to the human body. Abrams moved beyond that view to present a number of innovative ideas reflecting a new image of the downtown. He asserted that downtown must offer not only efficiency but also variety and excitement. The ancient fair provided his model, which he asserted was a progenitor of the modern downtown. Fairs not only "centralized the supply and demand for merchandise" but "brought people from long distances . . . to visit the sideshows and mix in the ferment of life." Over the centuries, new forms of doing business undermined the fair and gave birth to the modern downtown. The vast changes in city structure then threatened to condemn the downtown to the same fate the fairs encountered. To revive itself, "downtown should, in short, try to reclaim those aspects of the old fairs and markets which would bring people to it."[21] It should offer the same variety, excitement, and escape from provincialism that made the traditional fairs such vital institutions. Wrote Abrams:

> If the downtown is to live, it must be planned as a place to spend a day, not an hour, a place a suburban worker can spend an evening as well as his

working time. There should be more tea rooms, sidewalk cafes, retreats both inside department stores and outside, more use of pleasant roofs, television corners and benches. There must be more clubs that proletarians can join as a family, where each member can find something to interest him. Nearby art galleries should have more comfortable seats and should be accessible through the ground floor, rather than via the long climb past the monumental columns. There should be music rooms and more interests for the children. Universities should become adjuncts of downtown, luring adults to pleasant leisure as well as to adult education.

. . . The visitor should be saying "Let's go to the city," not "Let's go shopping in the city," for he should be thinking of the city as supplying him with a *series* of alternatives, not just a shopping tour.[22]

In at least two passages, Abrams urged planners to be more sensitive to how and why cities and downtowns live, as well as how efficiently they function. He appealed for more emphasis on providing variety and excitement as a way of answering the demands and values of at least one special breed of urbanite, the executive wife. In an interesting passage he detailed the multifaceted importance of appealing to her needs:

Few people know all the factors that make a city live today. Availability of raw materials, power, labor, orientation to the market, transportation costs, and a kindly attitude towards investment are only some of the reasons. There are also a few intangibles such as proximity to education, to officialdom and contracts, to other trades, to finance, and to centers of research. If a city is dull, the inducements of profit, subvention, and cheap labor will no longer be enough. For in the current world in which managerial know-how is a key, executives are essential to city growth, and one of the most unfaltering influences on the executive (and therefore on the location of industry) has become the executive's wife. If she is clever—and all of them are—she won't settle for a suburban house and a TV set unless there's a downtown nearby. Climate, department stores, beauty parlors, servants and cooks, a bridge club, the prospects for teenagers, bazaars and a few good friends may make the difference with this sphinx of the trade routes. "Money isn't everything," she has frequently whispered over the bread, cheese, and checkbook and the executive's decision has been made before he can say "I'll think it over." A study in depth of her motivations could yield one of the hidden secrets of industrial location.

16

Downtown is her escape from boredom, her city's oasis, and the place where she can spend the day shopping and come back with nothing but a new can opener and be happy. Variety in a city is indispensable and it is a thriving downtown that has it for her.[23]

Concluding, Abrams referred to the work of landscape architect Grady Clay and Jane Jacobs, two critics of contemporary planning who urged those involved to pay more attention to the qualities that give life to an area. In doing so, he suggested that planners look at cities in a whole new way:

The problem of how to make a city vibrate and continue vibrating has just begun to receive attention. It is a frontier question, but should challenge a profession that has paid all too much attention to the stock devices of zoning, slum demolition, and projects, and too little to the hidden secrets of what gives a city its impulse and makes people move toward life.[24]

In 1961 the issue of livability was indeed on the frontier. During the decade, however, its importance grew as it became apparent that downtowns needed to be something far more than efficient if they were to survive and thrive.

Blanche Lemco Van Ginkel, an architect and planner, wanted to create a new downtown based on its multiplicity of functions. Contemporary planning primarily sought to revive the business function, but Van Ginkel argued that planning must give proper attention to the complex activities of the downtown. Too often planners tried to separate the various functions physically, a practice that resulted in the "sterility of the civic center . . . the monumental seat of government at the climax of a sweep of open space, forbiddingly set apart from the people which it claims to serve."[25] Van Ginkel contended that

the city is as complex as man is complex. Man's needs may be reduced to the physical essentials. But the requirements of creative man are more numerous—tangible and intangible, complementary and even conflicting: to work and to rest, to give and to receive, and not successively but simultaneously—learning in teaching and destruction in creation.

The current land use terms of residential, industrial, commercial, recreational, are no more than the human terms of living, working, exchanging, resting. They each must be studied separately and assigned a proper environment and relationship, but they cannot be compartmentalized in the living city any more than in the living man. Hence at the heart of the city all the activities of man in community should exist in their highest form—not separately but in close interaction.[26]

As did Abrams, she thought planners should be more sensitive to the downtown's variety, not just its business efficiency.

Van Ginkel also suggested that planners needed a new image of the downtown. They needed to concentrate not so much on how well it functioned, but on what its vast array of functions actually were and on how to enhance them:

> The current emphasis on the CBD [the business center of the downtown] arises perhaps from the preoccupation with functioning instead of with function. The trouble with the city center is not that it does not work, but that it should perhaps be doing a different job. To the extent that it is so, form follows function and not functioning. In this context function must mean the human function of the core of the city in which there is the complexity and richness of all man's activities and aspirations.[27]

Thus both Abrams and Van Ginkel saw the downtown as a place of variety with sensitivity to the human scale. They rejected the emphasis on efficiency and business functions in favor of concern for cultural, recreational, entertainment, and leisure-time functions. Writing in 1963, George Sternlieb reinforced their arguments with results of his detailed study of downtown retailing. He did not argue so much for variety as he did for readjustment of planning strategies. Like Abrams and Van Ginkel, he stressed that planners must reevaluate their attitude toward the downtown and asserted that efforts to maintain traditional downtown retailing had failed and that planners must take a fresh approach.

As Sternlieb saw it, the various "one shot" efforts at shoring up downtown retailing—mass transit subsidies, shopping malls, superhighways, peripheral garages—failed. Even "the most fashionable cure," urban renewal, did little to improve the situation. The existing tools of planners could not reverse the "rapidly changing retail patterns" that favored the suburbs over the downtown.[28] "With very few exceptions," he concluded, "the planner must view the city's retailing function as being far more limited in the future than in the past."[29] In the spirit of that observation he made a very important point. As Abrams and Van Ginkel probably would have agreed, planners focused too much on the traditional center-place functions that the downtown was losing, undoubtedly forever, within the context of the changing structure of the city. Concluded Sternlieb: "The planner must set his eyes on the probable future rather than using as his goal the re-creation of what was, but may never be again."[30]

A 1968 study concurred with Sternlieb's assertions. John Allpass also concluded that cities no longer witnessed a "traditional center structure":[31]

It is quite obvious that for several years there has been a tendency to break through the centralized structure, first and foremost in industry, but also in wholesale and retail trade, and education. The coming structure will eventually take shape as a more even, loosely knit dispersion of urban activities over the whole urban region. . . .

. . . Planning aimed at preserving the traditional hierarchical center will be ineffective, leaving the development of the region to assemble around these big dispersing establishments, forming a casually scattered structure.[32]

By the late 1960s, and probably even earlier, planners recognized the structural changes that had redefined the role of the downtown and developed the core elements of a new image for the area. Downtown was only one of many centers, but it specifically should offer urbanites variety and excitement through cultural and recreational amenities, along with entertainment, business offices, access to government, and a wide array of services. Even before the rethinking of downtown's role, however, planners began to express new approaches to their discipline. An early and important concept was that of urban design. It was a very basic idea, and many innovations grew out of it or developed in relation to it. It was also complex because it proved to be an elusive and difficult concept to define. A concern for urban design helped create the image of the downtown as the focal point of the variety and excitement a city provided its residents. The focus was on the quality of design, but it also touched directly on the quality of life.

In 1951, Christopher Tunnard, director of the graduate program in city planning at Yale, contributed an article to the planners' journal, "Cities by

Design," in which he proposed to concentrate on what he called civic design (subsequently the concept was referred to as urban design). He offered this definition:

> What is Civic Design? If we can describe city planning as programming, administration, and land use allocation, then civic design becomes the translation of the plan into three-dimensions. Sir Patrick Abercombie, perhaps the greatest living exponent of the art, has described it as being something infinitely more difficult than architectural design; but it seems difficult only, I think, because we have had so little experience in doing it and because the problems of scale are not just architectural ones. It is as Abercombie says something more than architecture and something different from city planning as it is commonly practiced. Perhaps as a creative profession it can be described as a combination of architecture, planning principles and landscape design and a method of coordinating all the creative arts which must be given urban expression if we are to achieve an integration of art and life.[33]

Tunnard argued "for a greater role to be given the creative professions in city planning, to lift city planning out of the plane of workability and expediency on which it now rests, to change something of the surgical approach of the city planner for that of the artist." He cited both European examples and the accomplishments of nineteenth-century designers in the United States. He did not want simply to revive the earlier Municipal Art and City Beautiful movements, but to follow their examples of creative excellence.[34]

Civic design had power, Tunnard believed, to enhance life in the city, to inspire, and to foster better social relationships among urban dwellers. He did not suggest that superior design could end all urban problems, but he felt that it could strengthen the fabric of the city: "Civic Design which is so closely a part of architecture has a tremendous power, the power to move us deeply; even to evoke the highest forms of social cooperation through its appeal to the individual and to groups; and to project our most cherished national traditions." Designers must both help train and then satisfy the aesthetic sensibilities of human beings lest they "wither or become perverted." Attention to beauty by designers fostered appreciation of beauty in urban dwellers. Tunnard quoted Louis Sullivan: "If the mind feeds on beauty it will reproduce beauty. If it feeds on filth, it will reproduce filth.

The mind will inevitably reproduce what it feeds upon." Tunnard concurred, saying, "Beauty has a reality too, but only to those who acknowledge it. The possibility of beauty should be the sustenance of Civic Designers . . . beauty as a positive aim, not as a by-product of design. And it will never tolerate slums or congestion."[35]

Tunnard's vision of civic or urban design was probably too abstract and esoteric to appeal to a large number of the more practically minded city planners. In the mid-1950s, however, Kevin Lynch, associate professor of planning at the Massachussetts Institute of Technology, began championing a more realistic style of urban design. Based on research and offering practical suggestions, Lynch's ideas quickly entered the planning discourse and proved quite influential in the long run. Lynch and Alvin K. Lukashok published the results of their research on childhood memories of the city in 1956. They interviewed their subjects to determine what urban features had impressed them enough as children as to be retained in memory. Lynch and Lukashok then classified the types of memories: texture and color, play areas, hills, transport and traffic, space and the sense of crowdedness, marks of social status, associations, orientation, and neighborhoods. Their article was largely descriptive and offered only tentative conclusions. In their summary, however, the authors made an important point: "Knowledge of how people react to their physical environment, and how they invest it with emotional qualities, is quite as important as knowing the technical or economic or sociological resultants of a given form. It may be extremely useful, simply to know something of the features which seem to be most significant to people, so that these features may receive special design attention."[36]

In 1958 the American Society of Planning Officials took up the issue of urban design at its annual meeting. Lynch presented a paper in which he expanded on his earlier findings. He introduced a concept he called imageability, a quality he put at the core of urban design. In studying "the simple problem of finding one's way in the city," he discovered

that it is crucial that our visual environment be an imageable one; that is, that it be so shaped that with our human senses we can form a clear mental image of it, an image that is both vivid and coherent, whose parts are both easily recognized and also well knit. To be able to enter the door of this room, I had first to recognize the door as an entity, second to see how it related to me and to the rest of the environment, and third to attach to it the meaning of a hole for going in.

Now this quality of imageability depends on the way physical things are arranged in space, and may vary all the way from the clarity of an Italian landscape to the shifting confusion of sand dune country, or from the mighty coherence of a cathedral to the tricks of the hall of mirrors in the fun house.[37]

Attention to details of features that enhanced imageability would give cities form and unity. He described the task as "the making of an urban landscape that is sensuously vivid and coherent, that is a delight just to look at."[38]

Lynch gave final form to his ideas in his influential work *The Image of the City*, published in 1960. In it he described the city as "the powerful symbol of a complex society" that must have "strong expressive meaning." He expanded his explanation of imageability, defining it as "that quality in a physical object which gives it a high probability of evoking a strong image in any given observer. It is that shape, color, or arrangement which facilitates the making of vividly identified, powerfully structured, highly useful mental images of the environment."[39]

Lynch argued that the mobility of modern life necessitated a concern for design. As a person moved from city to city, region to region, his adjustment could be eased by attention to qualities that make cities imageable: "Good imageability in his environment would allow him to feel quickly at home in new surroundings." Furthermore, the massive changes under way within cities often left residents disoriented: "The techniques of design . . . may prove useful in maintaining a visible structure and a sense of continuity even while massive changes are occurring. Certain landmarks or nodes might be retained, thematic units of district character carried over into new construction, paths salvaged or temporarily conserved."[40]

Cities had to be more than efficient. They needed not only to move people about, but to express their dreams and aspirations. They must enhance every aspect of human life—and give themselves deeper meaning—by providing a sense of place:[41]

> True enough, we need an environment which is not simply well organized, but poetic and symbolic as well. It should speak of the individuals and

their complex society, of their aspirations and their historical tradition, of the natural setting, and of the complicated functions and movements of the city world. But clarity of structure and vividness of identity are first steps to the development of strong symbols. By appearing as a remarkable and well-knit *place*, the city could provide a ground for the clustering and organization of these meanings and associations. Such a sense of place in itself enhances every human activity that occurs there, and encourages the deposit of a memory trace.[42]

Throughout the 1960s others worked to refine the concept. Tunnard and Lynch spoke of the city in general. Others concentrated on using urban design to enhance one part of the city: the downtown. Morton Hoppenfeld, civic designer for the National Capital Planning Commission, focused on the center-city area of Philadelphia, the two-mile by one-mile heart of the city between the Delaware and Schuylkill rivers. He wrote of the need to make the area the physical manifestation of Philadelphia's image.

> The Center City is the heart of a metropolis and must be its symbol; it must evoke an image of hospitality, formality, and graciousness to all who see and use it. It must also excite the senses and reflect the nature of its being: the most intensively used two square miles of land in the region, served by miles of railroad, great expressways, subways, and helicopters. Nearly half a million people arrive here daily because this is the metropolitan control center and the major concentration of employment. Approaching the city from a distance, it looms visually as a real urban center set in a green valley. The visional expression of urbanity must pervade the Center City.[43]

Although he couched his description of the role of the city center in rather traditional terms, he clearly reflected the influence of a concern for design. He also harkened to the ideas of Abrams and Van Ginkel as he asserted that design "must help set the stage for human activity."[44]

The American Society of Planning Officials again took up urban design in 1966 in a session on "The Value of Townscape." Paul D. Spreiregen, director of urban design programs for the American Institute of Architects, and Frank Hotchkiss, vice-president of Victor Gruen Associates, offered definitions of urban design that emphasized its role in enhancing the livability of a city. Spreiregen asserted that the purpose of design was "to make the city an appropriate human habitation—not just livable, but conducive to bringing out the best that is in all of us." Hotchkiss concurred and expanded on that notion, adding that design "must recognize and express the way people will actually be living in our particular evolving society. It must grasp the emerging aspirations. It must reflect the changing social, political, economic, and moral attitudes and habits of urban man."[45]

In 1968 the society debated whether urban design was "attainable, elusive or illusionary." Although several papers admitted that achieving quality urban design was indeed a difficult goal, it should still remain a concern of planners. Hoppenfeld addressed the session and reemphasized the desirability of creating "an environment that is responsive to the needs and aspirations of people where they are and, at the same time, to evoke higher aspirations, to transcend the present, to refresh, and to change continually."[46]

Thus the concept of urban design centered on creation of a quality environment, built to human scale, in which urbanites could realize the fullness of life—a tall order made even more daunting by the general focus on the city as a whole. Urban design could, however, narrow its focus to one particular area of the city, including the downtown. Lynch and others identified certain design conventions that could be widely applied.[47] Several other new approaches to downtown planning appeared in the 1950s and 1960s, many directly or indirectly related to the concern for high-quality design, including beautification, parks and open spaces, malls, pedestrian ways, historic preservation, and a variety of amenities.

Not surprisingly, a desire for beautification of cities appeared concurrently with the arguments for urban design. Somewhat less ambitious and more focused than the latter, beautification became a national rallying cry by the middle 1960s. It took a number of forms—antilitter, progreenery, architectural excellence—yet the general thrust was aimed at making cities more pleasing and attractive. Much of it arose as a reaction against the unpleasant consequences of a federal initiative, the Interstate Highway Program. Changing values, including a desire for more aesthetically pleasing surroundings, sustained it. Beautifiers pushed for improvements everywhere: city and countryside, suburbs, the downtown.

In 1956, Thomas D. Schocken asked his fellow planners the rhetorical question "Must our cities remain ugly?" He admitted that being ugly was a problem plaguing cities but that certain technological shortcomings had priority. Yet, he argued, planners must not only focus on technical matters, they must also give due consideration to aesthetics.[48] The following year, Stephen K. Bailey and Richard T. Frost echoed Schocken's argument. In an article dealing with the problem of protecting the beauty of the countryside within a context of rapid metropolitan growth, they, too, acknowledged the priority assigned certain infrastructure needs while contending that a concern for aesthetics must somehow become part of the picture:

> In summary, the job ahead seems most pressing. It may be that other metropolitan problems—sewage disposal, transportation, water sources—will command the immediate and, in many areas, the desperate attention of those who hope to make some sense out of rapid growth. But the aesthetic or more likely non-aesthetic results of a failure to elevate beauty to public control will mar the country's natural advantages far more and far longer than all the planning for immediate needs can balance off. To the extent that aesthetics in land use continues to be ignored, the country and its posterity will suffer irreparable damage.[49]

Landscape architecture, a field closely associated with city planning, seemed to take up the issue of beautification with the most enthusiasm. The editor of its professional journal, Grady Clay, suggested formation of a national beautification organization in 1962. In "Anti-Uglies, Unite! A Proposal for an American Civic Trust," Clay described recent reactions against despoliation of the landscape by highway construction and argued that they indicated the existence of a strong base of support for beautification. He cited the 1959 freeway revolt in San Francisco and similar action in Hershey, Pennsylvania, to support his argument. He mentioned organizations already in the field—National Trust for Historic Preservation; Action, Inc.—and "potential allies," such as "garden clubs and neighborhood improvement societies." He felt that through a national umbrella organization, these groups could "rise above local partisanship, remain above self-seekers, overcome public apathy, fight uglification, and help create a more beautiful America."[50] Three years later, Clay reported significant progress, and in 1965, President Lyndon Johnson created the Task Force on Natural Beauty, which launched a nationwide campaign for beautification. The task force, and politicians, realized that such a program had "political pull," according to Clay, because it had broad public support.[51] From that point on, beautification remained a highly popular goal.

Beautification took many forms. The antilitter campaign, which gained enormous popularity, was but one of them. Johnson's program included landscape grants to help communities maintain their natural amenities. The push for beautification thus involved strong support for parks and open space. Civic-improvement agendas long had included parks. Whether as decorative ornaments, escapes from urban turmoil, or "lungs" for the city, parks figured prominently in the plans of those wishing to improve the city. Open space grew out of the parks movement. As cities sprawled into the surrounding countryside, people became concerned that uncontrolled development would despoil the country's natural amenities. In the late 1950s planning experts, among them William Whyte, Jr., of *Fortune* magazine, called for preservation of large tracts of rural land. He proposed the purchase of land for future parks and recreation areas and tighter control of development. Whyte, landscape architects, and others interested in parks and recreation successfully lobbied Congress, so the Housing Act of 1961 included a provision for the preservation and planning of open spaces. Throughout the 1960s, both parks and open spaces found steadfast and successful champions.[52]

Urban growth not only threatened the countryside but imperiled city parks as well. Highways, housing, and office developments all cut deeply into park acreage. Not surprisingly, landscape architects early on took up the cause of park preservation. Their professional journal reported the findings of the Conference on Public Parklands and Open Spaces in 1962. Convened in response to widespread encroachments on urban parks, conferees concluded that stronger measures were needed to expand and preserve parks and open spaces. They recommended more extensive metropolitan planning and tighter development controls. A Georgia landscape architect speaking of Atlanta expressed the opinion of many: that parks were vital to a city's success, that a system of parklands could make a city the envy of and an example for others.[53] They were one urban amenity that found early and extensive support.

Urban violence also seemed to threaten parks; they became havens for muggings, fights, and riots. Parkland became a battleground upon which a number of groups fought for control. Poor and minority groups, city officials looking for cheap land to develop, recreationists, and nature lovers all struggled to use parks to meet their varied needs and goals. As park acreage decreased in cities, pressure on the remaining land increased. Once again the landscape architects responded. In 1964, Grady Clay called for purchase of parkland preceding development to ensure adequate provisions for suburbia and the redesign of older city parks to meet the demands put on them.[54]

Parks also received attention within the context of a far more expansive topic, open space. Open space included traditional parks and squares, large tracts of undeveloped land on the fringes of cities, important natural features (cliffs, bluffs, waterfronts), and even the voids separating buildings in heavily built-up downtown areas. In other words, it was a very elastic term. Generally, concern focused on preservation of the countryside from urban sprawl, but downtowns and waterfronts also figured prominently in discussions, at least by the late 1960s. Speaking of such built-up areas, planning consultant Charles Eliot asserted "that cities consist of both solids and voids, and that the voids are just as important to the whole as the solids."[55] Gleaming buildings of quality design were indeed important to the image of the downtown, but Eliot insisted that planners consider the spaces between those buildings to complete the picture.

Throughout the 1960s planners and landscape architects argued on behalf of open space preservation. Most of the attention focused on large-scale plans to preserve vast tracts of countryside as parks or greenbelts to provide breaks in the face of relentless, all-consuming urban sprawl.[56] In 1965, Ann Satterthwaithe, writing in *Landscape Architecture*, argued that saving the countryside was not enough.[57] She insisted that urban open space receive concentrated attention and quoted President Lyndon Johnson, who said:

> More of our people are crowding into cities and cutting themselves off from nature. Access to beauty is denied and ancient values are destroyed. Conservation must move from nature's wilderness to the man-made wilderness of our cities. All of this requires a new conservation. We must not only protect from destruction, but we have the job of restoring what has already been destroyed—not only develop resources, but create new ones;—not only save the country-side, but yes, finally salvage the cities. It is not just the classic

conservation of protection and development. Its concern is not with nature alone, but with the total relation between man and world around him. Its object is not just man's welfare, but the dignity of his spirit.[58]

She was concerned that most open space purchases were in distant suburban areas, far from easy access by the typical urban dweller.[59]

David Lowenthal echoed Satterthwaithe's sentiments in 1968. He, too, felt that a narrow focus on wilderness preservation ignored the importance of small urban open spaces. Too often, he said, planners and park enthusiasts drew distinctions "between wild and tame, natural and artificial, countryside and metropolis."[60] They valued wild, natural, and the countryside while condemning that which they considered tame, artificial, and the metropolis. Lowenthal held that such distinctions were counterproductive, saying it was not enough to

> [hanker] after some distant and elusive paradise and abandoning all else as beyond hope. It is not only in the wilderness that we escape the tensions of civilized life; man-made environments can also be salubrious. To regard everything used as irretrievably spoiled is, moreover, to relegate the wilderness itself to a museum.
>
> City dwellers have come to believe that nature can be found only in unspoiled forests and distant mountains. But nature is in fact all around them—in their own backyards and streets, vacant lots and waterfronts. We need to foster an appreciation of nature in all its guises, humanized as well as wild, near as well as far, intimate as well as grand, transplanted as well as preserved.[61]

In 1977, August Heckscher, former director of the Twentieth Century Fund, cataloged many of the ways in which planners had incorporated open space into their designs for the central city, downtowns, and waterfronts. He described developments all over the country, ranging from small fountain squares to linear parks, plazas, and public squares; Saint Louis's memorial arch and park; Detroit's Renaissance Center; and Minneapolis's Mississippi River waterfront plan.[62] Some of them worked better than others, but all reflected the new definition of the downtown that emerged in the 1960s. Heckscher began by asking, if downtown was not what it had been, what had it then become?

The answer, made evident in the decade of the 1960s, was that downtown had a far more complex and diverse function than had earlier been acknowledged. It was a center for shopping, yes. But it was also a center for government, for the arts, for education, for voluntary institutions, for wide-ranging banking, insurance and financial services. It was a forum for the kind of human interchange required by modern business transactions. It was a magnet for tourists and conventions. It was a place where at some stage in the life cycle many people would choose to live.

These various functions, overlapping and in their physical embodiment often combined, constituted a new kind of downtown with a dense and compact spatial organization.[63]

Careful use of open spaces helped make the pieces of the new downtown fit together better.[64]

Closely related to parks and open spaces were downtown shopping malls. The first appeared as a ten-day experiment in Springfield, Oregon, in 1957. Faced with a serious economic crisis, downtown interests developed the idea of turning Springfield's main shopping street into what they called Shoppers Paradise. Four basic ideas guided the design: bypass Main Street traffic; provide convenient parking space; give pedestrians the right-of-way; and develop a shopping environment. Plans resulted in a three-block shopping mall that was closed to automobile traffic and made attractive through the use of "music, color, exhibits, landscaping, play areas for children, and benches for adults."[65] By 1964, dozens of cities in the United States and Canada followed Springfield's example. The projects were still experimental, some permanent, others designed to last a limited time.[66] Shortly thereafter, the mall idea gained wider acceptance because of two important examples of what could be done, one in Fresno, California, and the other, more important, in Minneapolis, Minnesota.

In September 1964, Fresno opened a permanent downtown shopping mall. Using urban renewal money, the city extensively redesigned twelve square blocks. The design included new "warm beige" pavement, trees, flowers, benches, pools and fountains, redwood and tile decorative panels, sculpture, and a central clock tower. The author of an article describing the mall, George Wickstead, did not proclaim it an unqualified success; he felt it needed more variety and open spaces. Merchants complained about a lack of parking, yet Wickstead described the mall as "a striking effort to re-develop a vital element in a vital city."[67]

The Fresno mall (now considered a planning disaster)[68] was an important example of early mall design, but Nicollet Mall and related projects in Minneapolis proved by far the most sophisticated and influential design of the 1960s. Designed by several planners over many years, the projects quickly became the model for revitalizing downtown. There were five phases: Gateway Center, Nicollet Mall and its transitway, the Hennepin Avenue entertainment area, the Civic Center, and the Convention Center. The centerpiece was blocks-long Nicollet Mall, described as a "linear pedestrial environment." Designed by landscape architect Lawrence Halprin, it included "a serpentine, 24′ wide transit way . . . [s]pecially designed lights, bollards, walls, planters, benches, trash receptacles, bus shelters, flower containers, pedestrian signals and pavings." Each block had a "special fountain or a unique clock to create more detail identity with the development." Halprin included trees "to define areas and break up vistas . . . to provide strong contrast in form, color and texture as well as seasonal variety."[69]

Unlike the authors of previous articles on malls, who gave them weak endorsements, Roger Martin heartily congratulated Minneapolis. He hoped its example would be followed by others cities and concluded:

> All considered, the emerging urban landscape of Minneapolis, exemplified by the Gateway Center and Nicollet Mall, is an immense improvement and will generate more quality as the public begins to realize the values of this new environment. It is this aspect, *consciousness of the value of quality*, that is the one most positive resultant of these combined design efforts. Second only to this value is the development of an *awareness on the part of the public of what new uses exterior space can provide*. For the first time we see Northerners sitting outside and absorbing the sunshine on a pleasant winter day. Thirdly, and possibly of greatest interest to landscape architects, the public has seen the *value of interweaving the natural environment and the world of pavement and structure*; bringing back an expanded sense that the urban environment can be more than merely man's creations clustered together in a man-made environment.
>
> These efforts have created the desire on the part of the public to link the

nature-dominated landscape and natural systems to the man-dominated land-scape and man-made systems.[70]

The pedestrian—something of downtown's forgotten man—stood at the center of the new concern for design, the human scale, open-space refuges, and malls. Traditional downtown planning focused mainly on the problems of the automobile: how to move it through the city and park it with maximum efficiency. Plans did not completely ignore the pedestrian, but concern for the person on foot existed largely only in relation to the automobile and its needs. In the 1960s pedestrians assumed a more promi-nent place in planning schemes. In 1962 transportation planner Robert L. Morris and consultant S. B. Zisman argued for a more systematic approach to pedestrian traffic. They held that most planning on the subject was based on subjective intuition. In the spirit of the new emphasis on research, they asserted that pedestrian traffic needed the same detailed study as that given vehicular traffic. "There is a need to think of people first," they said.[71] That concern for the pedestrian broadened throughout the decade in response to the idea of downtown as a "people place." Plans included malls, benches, fountains, walkways, parks, and other devices to make the area more amenable to the people who used it, not just the businesses and the automobiles.

Other thoughts applied to downtown and riverfront planning were more difficult to trace. Most of the concern for historic preservation; recreational, leisure-time, and cultural amenities; and a quality environ-ment originated outside the planning discipline. Private organizations and individuals undertook preservation projects independent of planning theo-ries to underpin their work; they responded to personal values, not plan-ning experts. The new amenities-oriented middle class sought various leisure-time outlets as part of and in response to their values. And the environmental movement arose from social, economic, and political forces far broader than a relatively narrow concern for more attractive and healthy cities. All of these concerns, however, eventually worked their way into and influenced city planning discourse and action.

The American Society of Planning Officials took up historic preservation in 1964. Two papers delivered at the annual meeting that year detailed

31

various aspects of the issue. The first, by Realtor John Codman of Boston, explained methods of drafting and passing historic-preservation legislation and its benefits to the community. As a Realtor, he focused primarily on its role in stabilizing and maintaining property values.[72] The second article, by attorney Albert B. Wolfe, provided a brief history of activity in the field. Private organizations, such as the Mount Vernon Ladies Association, had carried out preservation activities since the middle 1800s. The National Trust for Historic Preservation, chartered by Congress in 1949, directed most of the contemporary efforts. Privately financed, in 1964 it controlled five properties and sought to establish stronger legal protection for historically significant structures. Before World War II only two cities—Charleston, South Carolina, and New Orleans—had preservation control ordinances. By 1964 more than sixty had passed such measures. Wolfe argued that in view of the clearances carried out under urban renewal, far stronger protection was needed. His article further indicated relatively broad support for historic preservation, yet he said that "relatively few professional planners or planning officials" belonged to the National Trust.[73] Obviously, historic preservation was not an important planning priority in 1964. During the next decade, however, especially as individuals undertook small projects with great success, it became more important.

Recreational, leisure-time, and cultural amenities were also difficult to trace as planning issues. At its 1966 conference the American Society of Planning Officials dedicated a session to recreation. Papers dealt with outdoor urban recreation, new designs for city parks, and federal aid for parks and recreation.[74] Perhaps a clearer indication of its emerging priority came in 1968 when a joint conference of three landscape architect organizations took up the issue of "Planning for Leisure and Change."[75] Actions taken in various cities further indicated there was concern for cultural amenities. Both Pittsburgh and Omaha, to cite only two examples, transformed run-down, formerly ornate vaudeville-movie theaters into glittering centers for the performing arts.

Environmentalism entered the planning discourse in the early 1970s, with both planners and landscape architects taking up the issue.[76] In a 1971 article, Maynard M. Hufschmidt proposed "Environmental Quality as a Policy and Planning Objective." Among the issues he discussed was that of combining amenity and ecological values. He contended that the general public valued a more attractive, healthier, and ecologically sound environment; it demanded policies that enhanced overall environmental quality. Hufschmidt did not mention downtowns and waterfronts, but his arguments suggested a concern for such matters as air-quality control (citing as an example Pittsburgh's smoke-abatement program) for aesthetic as well as environmental reasons and the cleaning up of rivers and streams for the same reasons. He also mentioned efforts to abate the detrimental amenity effects of dumps, quarries, strip mines, billboards, and junkyards.[77] Obviously, beautification and environmental qualities were in many ways complementary goals, and they came together in identifying waterfront areas as recreational and environmental amenities. Once they had been cleared of the most choking pollutants and their banks or shores cleaned of debris, the natural beauty and desirability of waterfronts came to the fore.

By the late 1960s and early 1970s city planners had a new store of ideas upon which to draw when planning for downtowns and riverfronts. In the 1950s the main ideas centered on urban renewal, the federal highway program, and meeting the space demands of automobiles. With a new image of the downtown and waterfront as places of variety, vitality, and amenities, planners developed a different set of ideas. Gradually, urban design, beautification, parks and open space, and recreational, cultural, and environmental amenities entered planning discourse and reshaped ideas for the downtown and waterfront. Local planners eventually realized the full implications of the changes transforming their cities. Within the context of the professional debate over the image of and planning for cities, they, too, gradually reshaped their image of their city and began to draw on new planning ideas.

Omaha and the National City Planning Movement

Omaha experienced significant changes in the decades following World War II. Between 1945 and 1973, social, economic, and political changes transformed it. In the immediate postwar period the city was a commercial and food-processing center. In the 1950s its residents gloried in the fact that their hometown was both the site of the world's largest stockyards and held the title of world's largest meatpacking center. It had a part-time municipal government. Civic and business leaders shared a rather limited vision of their city and held to an intense privatism in planning, preferring to do much of it by themselves without expert help. By 1970, Omaha was more precisely a sprawling regional service center providing retailing, health, educational, financial, professional, and business services in its trade areas. Its citizens found themselves rallying around new sources of economic strength: Mutual/United of Omaha (insurance), Northwestern Bell Telephone, and Northern Natural Gas. The civic and business leadership, which changed in composition with the rise of the service economy, shared an expansive view of the city and tended to defer more to outside planning expertise. Within the context of these transformations, Omaha gradually moved toward closer connections with national planning thought.

Omaha's planners—public and private sector—were never completely out of touch with the general body of planning thought. They adopted or tried to implement any number of planning initiatives and often were in synch with national programs. For example, they immediately latched on to the national highway program in the 1950s and their plans called for megastructures and superblocks at the times those ideas were still popular. In many other ways, however, they lagged behind developments in planning thought. By the early 1960s, expert planners on the cutting edge were already redefining the city and downtown and devising plans to reflect the new definitions. Omaha's planners, however, did not accept a new image of the city and downtown until the late 1960s, when a series of economic crises forced a reevaluation of planning and boosting strategies. After that, local planners tapped into the sources of new ideas and chose to implement a number of them in their city. The ideas they selected fit their new image of the city and downtown and reflected many preferences already expressed in small ways at the local level. Further, they accepted no one model, drawing instead from a number of available models.

The composition of the local constituency groups pushing for planning also influenced the type of ideas selected. Generally, in Omaha two groups exercised the most power. Urban boosters—the chamber of commerce, real-estate and construction interests, leaders of growth-oriented businesses and institutions—enjoyed by far the most influence. Their intense

34

privatism, which diminished only slightly over time, combined with the subordinate position of city government, guaranteed them a powerful voice in establishing planning priorities. In their booster activities they shaped and articulated the image of the city. Their emphasis on growth and development prompted them to choose the planning ideas they felt would best promote that end. As long as they held a traditional vision of Omaha, they focused on traditional booster strategies. A commercial and food-processing city needed an efficiently functioning infrastructure (roads, bridges, sewers), a hard-working labor force, and a friendly tax environment. That image and these priorities shaped planning well into the middle 1960s despite the fact that social and economic changes had transformed Omaha. After 1966 and several economic crises, civic and business leaders gradually recognized and accepted the fact that Omaha was a service city. Once that realization took hold, but still operating within a booster framework, they began to adopt new ideas and strategies. A service city with a large, amenities-oriented middle-class population needed not efficiency, but an exciting and vibrant living environment that offered cultural and recreational amenities and an urban ambience.

A strong park lobby was the other significantly influential group. From the 1930s on, under the leadership of Rachael Gallagher, park proponents successfully advanced their agenda. As open space became part of the picture, they also fought for that program. They were not responsible for all that was done in those areas, but they certainly created an atmosphere conducive to such ideas. In addition, beautifiers made their priorities quite prominent. Mrs. Les Anderson and Keep Omaha Beautiful, Inc. raised public awareness of the litter problem, of the benefits of greenery, and of environmental issues. Park proponents and beautifiers both received important support from City Planning Director Alden Aust, hired in 1957. A landscape architect by training, he proved quite amenable to their goals.

Significantly, public housing enjoyed little or no support in Omaha, neither among the leadership nor the general public. Every program involving or believed to involve public housing met vocal and usually insurmountable opposition. Further, a restrictive state enabling act, combined with a strong anti-public-housing real-estate lobby and a revolt by determined small property owners, stymied urban-renewal efforts. Voters turned down the program in three elections despite considerable support from many important civic and business leaders. Omaha's downtown thus remained free of the "federal bulldozer." These circumstances gave planners in the late 1960s and early 1970s a clean slate for future projects because no ongoing urban-renewal projects stood in the way and many historic areas remained available for creative renovation. Some individuals in tune with the beautifiers did undertake historic-preservation projects, but the program did not become civic priority until the late 1970s. Thus boosters, and to a lesser degree park supporters and beautifiers, wrote most of Omaha's planning agenda throughout the postwar period.

City planning in Omaha between 1945 and 1973 fell into three broad time periods: 1945 to 1958, 1958 to 1966, and 1966 to 1973. The two plans produced during the first emphasized long-held civic priorities based on a traditional vision of the city. In fact, most of the proposed programs found their origins in the 1930s and early 1940s, when civic and business leaders scrambled to take advantage of first New Deal money and then defense spending. The so-called Blue Book Plan of 1946 and its update, the Omaha Plan of 1957, both emphasized infrastructure improvement and a face-lift approach to the still largely unrealized problems of the downtown. The Missouri River existed as a potential highway for commerce and as a sewer of last resort. Generally, plans concerning the river focused on improving it for barge traffic or in some small way alleviating the worst sources of contamination. The civic and business leaders of that day still saw their city in traditional terms. Although significant changes were under way, they were largely unrecognized or unappreciated.

While not totally isolated from national planning thought, Omaha's planners had a tenuous and indirect relationship with it. They were keenly aware of what their urban rivals were doing and sought to match them, civic auditorium for civic auditorium. The intense privatism of the civic and business leader, however, made them reluctant to seek outside expertise. They developed both plans of the era with little or no expert help. In the late 1950s, however, they did latch on to two initiatives, still relatively new, that fit their perception of the city's needs: the national highway program and urban renewal. Both programs, they felt, would maintain the downtown in its traditional center-place role. As for the river, flood control under the Pick-Sloan Plan had priority.

In the years between 1958 and 1966, there occurred important transitions in city planning thought at both the national level and in Omaha. The reshaping of many ideas, however, moved much more quickly at the national level. In Omaha, older ideas remained dominant in the formal planning process and stood at the core of the Central Omaha Plan of 1966. The Interstate Highway and urban renewal remained priorities for the downtown. As late as 1966, civic and business leaders still viewed the area in traditional terms even though broad social and economic changes already were under way. The river, which failed to meet its promise as a highway and by law was no longer to be used as a sewer, faded from view. Its traditional functions diminished; Omaha leaders developed no new ideas for it before 1966.

On a small scale and generally as the result of efforts by individuals and small groups, several new planning ideas found expression in Omaha. Civic beautifiers, historic preservationists, and supporters of cultural and recreational amenities appeared on the scene. Some began to suggest that both Omaha and its downtown had changed. Civic and business leaders came into closer contact with planning initiatives in other cities through a series of study trips, and expert planners from the Omaha-based Leo A. Daly Company, not private citizens, developed most of the Central Omaha Plan. It required the crises of the late 1960s, however, to dislodge old ideas and inspire a reshaping Omaha's image.

Three factors helped push the reshaping forward. First and most important was the nearly total collapse of the meatpacking industry. Second, between 1966 and 1973, there were a tremendous number of changes in Omaha's leadership structure. Older leaders, influential since the 1950s, retired or died, making room for new ones to rise to the top. The new blood opened the possibility for changes in attitudes and ideas, and that possibility became reality with the introduction of the third important factor, a dynamic and influential leader with fresh ideas. Eugene Leahy, elected mayor in 1969, came to office with a number of innovative ideas. Under his leadership a new image of the city was forged. Although he was not directly responsible for all that happened, he proved to be the necessary spark that ignited many of the changes.

Within the context of tremendous social and economic changes and new leadership, those involved in the planning and boosting process began to search for different ways to promote their city. It could no longer be heralded as a vigorous meatpacking center, so they needed to find other characteristics they could use to present Omaha's case to the outside world. Slowly they forged an image that reflected the growing demands for cultural and recreational amenities and the importance of ambience. As the city as a whole forged a new image, so did the downtown. Beginning in the late 1960s, boosters attempted a series of projects to give downtown Omaha a new flavor. Much in tune with what Abrams and Van Ginkel had suggested in 1961, sidewalk sales, band concerts, art fairs, new Christmas decorations, small shopping plazas, and the addition of greenery were used to reach a common goal: attract shoppers in particular and the public in general back downtown.

The formal planning proposals of the late 1960s and early 1970s reflected Omaha's new image. The melding of the new image with planning culminated in a collection of related proposals generally grouped under the collective term riverfront development. The long-neglected Missouri River proved the focal point for the revitalization efforts, not as a highway or sewer, but as a superior recreational and environmental amenity. The actual development proposal was a wide-ranging and ambitious scheme championed by Eugene Leahy that in his words sought to build a "whole new lifestyle" along the river.[78] The full project, which included a 54-mile-long park, never came to fruition. The spirit of the riverfront idea, however, inspired a number of projects that reflected the ideas of a new lifestyle and the demands made upon the city by service industries and the amenities-oriented middle class.

The centerpiece and key element in the whole scheme was construction of Central Park Mall, a one-block-wide park stretching from Sixteenth Street to the Missouri River. At the core of the park concept was the desire to give downtown Omaha an exciting urban ambience. It was an open space, an area of grass and trees and water, in the heart of the city. It was a people place for the enjoyment of those who worked downtown and those who came there seeking a vibrant urban environment. Neither the park nor any of the other so-called riverfront projects were completed by 1973. However, by that time all the projects were either under construction or at least approved, so the stage was set for the rebuilding of much of the downtown and the riverfront to reflect the new image of the city.

Omaha: How Typical?

In *The Contested City*, his well-received book on post–World War II urban America, John H. Mollenkopf argued that economic, political, and social forces had transformed America's big cities in the decades since 1930. The shift from an industrial economy to a service economy worked to diffuse urban growth, to decentralize the highly concentrated city created by the industrial economy in the nineteenth century. New institutions, such as "high-rise office buildings, government centers, cultural complexes, hospitals, and universities displaced aging factory districts, wholesale markets, and rail yards" and became the "new defining institutions within central cities." National and local politicians "constructed new political alignments and new coalitions around the framework of federal urban development programs" creating "progrowth" coalitions. These supported the use of federal urban programs to help shape, direct, and encourage urban growth. Mollenkopf concentrated primarily on the role of urban-development politics in the creation and nurturing of national political coalitions, especially the Democratic New Deal coalition.[79]

As do many—if not most—scholars who study America's cities, Mollenkopf based his analysis on the nation's largest cities, which he put in three broad categories. First, he looked at cities that had been transformed by the nineteenth-century's Industrial Revolution into "large, dense, smokey, and brawling cities" and that in the twentieth century were experiencing frequently painful changes because of the shift from an industrial economy to a service economy. Second, he focused on cities in the Southwest that "had no industry at all" but "grew up during and after World War II on new high-technology industries as well as on administrative and service activities." Third, he especially examined cities, such as Boston and San Francisco, that "may have been significant production centers between 1880 and 1930, but they also had developed strong corporate, banking, and 'third sector' activities, often because they were cultural and commercial centers before they industrialized."[80]

While his findings and generalizations may be valid for those cities, it is less clear that they could be applied *in toto* to cities that did not fit one of his three categories. Mollenkopf's general descriptions of the shape of the new service economy and its effect on cities—such as the rise of government centers, cultural complexes, hospitals, and universities and the white-collar middle-class sector it created—could perhaps be applied wherever the urban economy was a service economy, but the impact of transformation into a service economy most certainly varied depending on the size, social composition, and previous economic base of the city involved. The Omaha experience suggests that generalizations about the response of the nation's largest cities to the economic and political forces at work since 1930 cannot be applied *in toto* to explain the response of medium-sized cities. Omaha was not a nineteenth-century industrial city, nor was it a city that experienced phenomenal growth after World War II, nor did it resemble a city like Boston or San Francisco. It did not have the same level of dislocation as many of the cities studied by Mollenkopf, nor did it see the development of the same type of Democratic progrowth coalition. Furthermore, Omaha did not become a central city surrounded by autonomous suburbs as it used its power to annex adjacent areas aggressively and successfully.

In those ways, Omaha was not typical when compared with the nation's largest cities. However, its experience in the post–World War II era may be more typical of the nation's medium-sized cities. Those cities, though, have not been studied as extensively as the larger cities, so not as much is known about their growth and development since 1945. Only a more extensive study of cities in the middle of America's urban hierarchy could validate the thesis. Omaha's experience does suggest, however, that the changes in America's cities since the 1930s have been of a variegated nature and that analysis based on the experience of only the largest cities may not accurately reflect the experiences of all cities.

TWO

The Changing City: Omaha, 1945–1973

Omaha changed between 1945 and 1973. There were demographic changes, a shift in the economic base, changes in the corporate identity, and changes in the relative strength of the local government that influenced the nature of the public-private partnership. The changes, in turn, prompted gradual reconsideration of the city's image. It changed, too, reflecting movement toward the idea of the livable city, one that emphasized, not its efficiency, but its ambience and potential for enhancing the quality of life. The many transformations during the three decades under study happened concurrently, but not necessarily in synch with one another. In the end, however, they produced a city that in 1973 was quite different from what it had been in 1945 and thought differently about itself.

Demographic Changes and the Shift in the Economic Base

Omaha's population grew sluggishly during the 1930s. Thereafter, between 1940 and 1970, came three consecutive decades of respectable—if not spectacular—growth. Between 1930 and 1970, the population increased from 214,006 to 347,328, and during the period of most rapid expansion, 1950–1970, the city maintained a fairly consistent ranking among all U.S. cities (see table 1).

Growth in the black and other minority populations contributed to the overall increase, but even though the black population more than doubled

Table 1: Population and Rank

Year	Population	% Change	Rank
1930	214,006	—	—
1940	223,844	+5%	—
1950	251,117	+12%	40
1960	301,589	+20%	42
1970	347,328	+15%	41

Source: Omaha City Planning Department, "Omaha Population Study," Report No. 143 (July 1, 1965), 2; U.S. Bureau of the Census, *City and County Data Book* (Washington: Government Printing Office, 1952, 1962, 1972); Seventeenth Census of the United States, 1950, Census of the Population Census, vol. 2, *Characteristics of the Population;* Eighteenth Census of the United States, 1960, vol. 1, *Characteristics of the Population;* Nineteenth Census of the United States, 1970, vol. 1, *Characteristics of the Population.*

between 1950 and 1970, it barely accounted for 10 percent of the total population. Blacks, though, far outnumbered other minorities. That segment of the population did not reach even the 1 percent mark (see table 2). This did not mean that Omaha escaped racial strife. A small minority population did not mean peaceful coexistence and the absence of racial tension; racism and prejudice existed in Omaha as everywhere else in American society. However, because of their relatively small number, Omaha blacks were not as visibly influential as they were elsewhere. Further, they were not able to use strength of numbers to wield significant political power.

Along with the respectable population growth came a remarkable expansion of the area encompassed by the city limits. In 1950 the city covered 40.7 square miles, by 1960, 51.2 square miles, and by 1970, the total jumped to 76.6 square miles. That represented nearly a doubling of area in twenty years. As may be surmised by a juxtaposition of population and area figures, Omaha's growth depended on its ability to implement an aggressive annexation program, and it annexed territory almost from its very beginning. The first annexation came in 1857, only three years after the city

Table 2: Racial Composition

	1950	%	1960	%	1970	%
White	234,235	93.3	275,330	91.3	310,599	89.4
Black	16,311	6.5	25,155	8.3	34,431	9.9
Other	571	.2	1,113	.4	2,298	.7
Total	251,117	—	301,598	—	347,328	—

Source: U.S. Bureau of the Census, Seventeenth Census of the United States, 1950, Census of the Population Census, vol. 2, *Characteristics of the Population;* Eighteenth Census of the United States, 1960, vol. 1, *Characteristics of the Population;* Nineteenth Census of the United States, 1970, vol. 1, *Characteristics of the Population.*

was platted. After that, annexations continued in fits and starts, more aggressive after periods of rapid growth, less after periods of stagnation. No formal policy was developed, however, until the creation in 1956 of a city planning department headed by a professional planner. More than two hundred annexations carried out between 1956 and the early 1970s under that policy proved absolutely vital to Omaha's growth. The population growth pattern matched those elsewhere in the nation. Nearly all of the growth occurred in fringe areas; older eastern sections of the city lost population. The fringe areas formed a semicircle arching northwest, west, and southwest of the older sections. To grow in population, Omaha had to expand its corporate limits. Approximately eighty thousand people lived in the nearly forty square miles annexed between 1956 and 1973, representing 23 percent of the 1970 population. Moreover, those eighty thousand people also represented 83 percent of the city's total population growth since 1950. Clearly, Omaha benefited from its location in a state with one of the most liberal annexation laws in the country.[1]

The annexation program became especially aggressive after 1965 and constituted the city's major response to change. The annexations carried out between 1965 and 1970, anticipating the 1970 Census of the Population, added 30,002 citizens. In 1969 alone, an almost staggering 12,591 people came on board. The total number added between 1965 and 1970 represented 66 percent of the city's growth during the 1960s (the total does

Table 3: Annexations, 1965–1973

Year	Population Added
1965	3,737
1966	2,452
1967	9,349
1968	1,705
1969	12,591
1970	168
1971	7,460 [Millard]
1972	160
1973	430

Source: *Omaha World-Herald,* July 17, 1985; information provided by the Omaha City Planning Department. Reprinted by permission of *The World-Herald.*

not include the city of Millard, approved for annexation by the Omaha City Council in 1968 but, because of legal challenges, not added to Omaha until 1971; see table 3).[2] Annexations continued after 1973, but into the early 1980s they consisted mostly of commercial and industrial properties containing few or no residents.[3]

It was easy to see that Omaha was growing in both area and population during the postwar period. Anyone traveling around and about the city during those years saw its growth in miles upon miles of new subdivisions and industrial tracts springing up every year in what had been farm fields.

The transformation of the economic base was more intangible and thus more difficult to grasp. In the post–World War II decades, Omaha's economy shifted from commercial and food-processing dominance to service-sector dominance (see table 4). The commercial and food-processing economy consisted of three major employment sectors: manufacturing (which included food processing), transportation (which included communications and public utilities), and wholesaling. The definition of the service

Table 4: Composition of Omaha Labor Force, 1951–1970

	1951	1955	1960	1965	1970
Agriculture	9,500	7,450	7,050	6,150	6,300
% total labor	6%	4%	4%	3%	3%
Construction, Mining	7,900	7,750	10,600	10,550	12,150
% total labor	5%	4%	6%	5%	5%
Manufacturing	31,550	33,550	37,450	35,700	40,200
% total labor	18%	19%	19%	17%	17%
Transportation, Communication, Public Utilities	22,950	23,350	20,100	20,100	20,600
% total labor	13%	13%	10%	10%	10%
Wholesale	12,950	12,500	12,350	13,400	14,650
% total labor	8%	7%	6%	6%	6%
Retail	22,600	22,850	25,600	29,250	38,100
% total labor	13%	13%	13%	14%	16%
Finance, Insurance, Real Estate	10,750	12,300	13,250	14,550	16,700
% total labor	6%	7%	7%	7%	7%
Services	18,450	20,150	23,500	28,650	37,350
% total labor	11%	12%	12%	14%	16%
Government	14,000	16,100	20,150	24,050	30,050
% total labor	8%	9%	10%	12%	12%
Nonagriculture, Nonwage	17,300	17,950	18,950	17,750	17,100
% total labor	10%	10%	10%	9%	7%
Total Employment	171,250	178,450	194,400	207,600	240,700
Unemployment	3,350	4,350	5,450	7,150	7,350
% total labor	2.0%	2.4%	2.8%	3.4%	3.1%

Source: John C. Cunningham, "Education and Manpower in the Omaha SMSA" (University of Nebraska at Omaha, Center for Applied Urban Research, April 1971), 37. Estimated to nearest 50.

Table 5: Traditional Sectors

	1951	1955	1960	1965	1970 (May)
Total Employment	171,250	178,450	194,400	207,600	240,700
Manufacturing	31,550	33,550	37,450	35,700	40,200
% total labor	18%	19%	19%	17%	17%
Transportation, Communication, Public Utilities	22,950	23,350	20,100	20,100	20,600
% total labor	13%	13%	10%	10%	10%
Wholesale	12,950	12,500	12,350	13,400	14,650
% total labor	8%	7%	6%	6%	6%
Combined %	39%	39%	35%	33%	33%

Source: Cunningham, "Education and Manpower," 37.

sector has changed over the years, but for purposes of this analysis, it will consist of workers in the traditional service industries (personal, business, and professional), in retailing, and in government. In 1951 manufacturing, transportation, and wholesaling combined commanded 39 percent of Omaha's total employment. Their share dropped to 35 percent by 1960 and to 33 percent by 1970. Within that sector, manufacturing employment declined from 18 percent of the total labor force in 1951 to 17 percent in 1970; transportation fell from 13 percent to 10 percent; wholesaling dipped from 8 percent to 6 percent (see table 5). At the same time, the service sector increased its share from 32 percent in 1951 to 35 percent in 1960 and to 44 percent in 1970. Within that sector, retail employment rose from 13 percent of the total labor force in 1951 to 16 percent in 1970; services rose from 11 percent to 16 percent; government rose from 8 percent to 12 percent (see table 6). The 44 percent share held by the service sector in 1970 made it even more dominant than the commercial and food-processing sector had been in 1951.

46

Table 6: Service Sectors

	1951	1955	1960	1965	1970 (May)
Total Employment	171,250	178,450	194,400	207,600	240,700
Retail	22,600	22,850	25,600	29,250	38,100
% total labor	13%	13%	13%	14%	16%
Services	18,450	20,150	23,500	38,650	37,350
% total labor	11%	12%	12%	14%	16%
Government	14,000	16,100	20,150	24,050	30,050
% total labor	8%	9%	10%	12%	12%
Combined %	32%	34%	35%	40%	44%

Source: Cunningham, "Education and Manpower," 37.

As has been indicated, manufacturing employment declined overall (see table 5). Hit hardest was the food-processing segment (meat, dairy, grain, bakery, other), especially meatpacking. Between 1950 and 1970 the total number of workers employed in food and kindred industries fell from 18,500 to 11,830. Within that segment of the work force, the number of workers employed in meatpacking declined from 11,900 in 1950 to 7,210 in 1966. Although exact figures are not available, the number undoubtedly fell even more after 1966 as three of the so-called Big Four packers closed: Cudahy in 1967, Armour in 1968, and Swift in 1969. Wilson remained in operation until 1976. By the early 1970s the number of workers remaining in meatpacking was estimated at only 4,000.[4]

Even with the collapse of this traditional employment source the unemployment rate in the metropolitan area remained relatively stable, usually fluctuating between 2 percent and 4 percent.[5] Increased employment in the machinery and equipment manufacturing industries undoubtedly contributed to that fortunate circumstance. In 1950 only 2,100 people found employment in those fields, but by 1960 the number had risen to 7,800 and by 1970 an estimated 12,000 people were employed there (see table 7).

The increased employment in machinery and equipment manufacturing

Table 7: Manufacturing Employment

	1950	1955	1960	1966	1970
Total Manufacturing	30,200	33,550	37,450	37,200	40,038
Food, Kindred	18,500	—	17,200	13,860	11,830
% total manufacturing	61%	—	46%	—	30%
(meat)	(11,900)	—	(10,400)	(7,210)	(4,000)*
(% of Food)	(64%)	—	(60%)	—	(34%)
(% of Manufacturing)	(40%)	—	(28%)	—	(1%)
Machinery, Equipment	2,100	—	7,800	—	12,200*
% of Manufacturing	1%	—	21%	—	30%
Manufacturing % of					
Total Employment	18%	19%	19%	—	17%

*Estimate

Source: Lawrence A. Danton and Masoud Hariri, "Preliminary Projections of Growth of the Omaha SMSA to 1990" (University of Nebraska at Omaha, Center for Applied Urban Research, August 1967), 57–60; U.S. Bureau of the Census, *City and County Data Book,* 1972.

further indicated that the manufacturing mix in Omaha became more diversified and more balanced between 1950 and 1970. In 1950 food processing dominated the manufacturing sector with 61 percent of total manufacturing employment. Meatpacking employed 64 percent of those in food processing; further, its employees made up 40 percent of the total manufacturing employment. By 1960 the number of employees in food processing had fallen to 46 percent of the total. Meatpacking fell to 60 percent of the processing workers and 28 percent of the total manufacturing employment. The decline of the food-processing sector continued until 1970, when it commanded only 30 percent of the manufacturing employment. And with only an estimated four thousand workers left in meatpacking, that segment fell to only 34 percent of the food-processing total and a mere 1 percent of the manufacturing total (see table 7). Accompanying that was the relative and absolute rise in the importance of the machinery and electrical equipment sector. In 1950 it comprised less than 1 percent of the total manufacturing employment. The figure jumped to nearly 21 percent by 1960 and continued upward, reaching the 30 percent mark by 1970 to equal the percentage employed in food processing. The equity between food processing and machinery and equipment manufacturing indicated the emergence of a more diversified and balanced manufacturing base. Manufacturing maintained a rather stable position in the metropolitan economy (falling overall only 1 percent between 1950 and 1970). The internal composition of that sector, however, changed considerably (see table 7).

Transportation and wholesaling employment also declined, contributing to the overall decline of the commercial and food-processing sector. Figures breaking down employment in those areas were not available, but those that were did not indicate which products were wholesaled or what percentage of employment was tied to any one product. A full breakdown of transportation employment was available, but only for the years 1958 through 1966. Most of the difficulty in pinning down transportation employment lay in the fact that the official figures did not include railroad employees, or if they did (as the figures in tables 4 and 5 do), the number was withheld. That became problematic in studying Omaha because the Union Pacific was a major employer. The only study available that did break down transportation employment indicated an interesting trend, at least for the years 1958 through 1966. In 1958 railroads employed 49 percent of all people working in transportation, communication, and public utilities; by 1966 they employed only 41 percent of the total. Other transportation employment (trucking, bus, air) remained relatively stable (see table 8). Concurrently, other segments rose in importance. Communication employment increased from 14 percent of the total to 20 percent. Public utilities employment increased from 6 percent to 9 percent. Transportation employment overall remained the largest part of total employment in that sector, though it decreased from 80 percent of the total in 1958 to 71 percent in 1966 (see table 8).

Machinery and electrical equipment, communication, and public utilities were growth areas in the commercial and food-processing sector. In

Table 8: Transportation, Communication, Public Utilities

	1958	1962	1964	1966
Total	20500	20550	20150	20250
Railroads	9950	8850	8700	8300
% total	49%	43%	43%	41%
Motor, warehousing	3750	3650	3400	3600
% total	18%	18%	17%	18%
Other transportation	2700	2800	2650	2550
% total	13%	14%	13%	12%
Communication	2900	3700	3800	4050
% total	14%	18%	19%	20%
Other Public Utilities	1200	1500	1600	1750
% total	6%	7%	8%	9%
Transportation %	80%	75%	73%	71%

Source: Danton and Hariri, "Preliminary Projections," 57–60.

the overall metropolitan economy, however, the most significant growth was in the service sector. It came to dominate the economy, and each of its employment categories improved its position relative to total employment between 1951 and 1970. Growth in the service-sector labor force outdistanced that of the total labor force, another indication of both the relative and absolute increase of its importance. In 1970 the total labor force represented 141 percent of the 1951 total. In the traditional service area, by contrast, the 1970 total was 202 percent of 1951; in the government area the 1970 total was 215 percent of 1951; in retailing 1970 was 167 percent of 1951. By comparison, the manufacturing total in 1970 was only 127 percent of the 1951 total in that category (see table 9). In fact, the service sector added more than ten thousand jobs every five years between 1955 and 1970, representing 73 percent of all jobs added during those years.[6]

Table 9: Service, Government, Retail

	1951	1955	1960	1965	1970	% increase
Total Labor	171,250	178,450	194,400	207,600	204,700	141%
Services	18,450	20,150	23,500	28,650	37,350	202%
% total	11%	12%	12%	14%	16%	
Government	14,000	16,100	20,150	24,050	30,050*	215%
% total	8%	9%	10%	12%	12%	
Retail	22,600	22,850	25,600	29,250	38,100*	167%
% total	13%	13%	13%	14%	16%	
Services	55,050	59,100	69,250	81,950	105,500*	192%
% total	32%	33%	35%	39%	44%	

*Estimate

Source: Cunningham, "Education and Manpower," 37.

Certain interrelated factors accompanied the shift in the economic base toward service dominance. The median level of education and the percentage of both high school graduates and college graduates rose in the over-twenty-five population age group between 1950 and 1970. In 1950 the median level of education stood at 11.4 years, representing a median educational achievement level below that of high school graduates. The level of education increased dramatically during the 1950s and reached a median level of 12.0 years by 1960. It increased even more in the 1960s, standing at 12.3 by 1970. The rise in the median education level anticipated the growing percentages of high school and college graduates in the twenty-five-and-over population. In 1950, 45 percent of the adults over twenty-five had a high school diploma and 7 percent had a college degree; by 1960 the number with a high school diploma had risen to 51 percent and with a college degree to 9 percent. In 1970 the numbers stood at 61.6 percent with a high school diploma and 12.4 percent with a college degree (see table 10).

Table 10: Education

	1950	1960	1970
Median Education	11.4	12.0	12.3
High School Graduates	45%	51%	61.6%
College Graduates	7%	9%	12.4%

Source: U.S. Bureau of the Census, Seventeenth Census of the United States, 1950, *Census of the Population,* vol.2, *Characteristics of the Population;* Eighteenth Census of the United States, 1960, vol.1, *Characteristics of the Population;* Nineteenth Census of the United States, 1970, vol.1, *Characteristics of the Population.*

Concurrently, white-collar workers increased their percentage among all workers from 49.1 percent in 1960 to 54.6 percent in 1970 (figures are not available for 1950). In 1970, 24.7 percent of all workers occupied professional or managerial positions while 29.9 occupied sales or clerical positions.[7]

Changes in the Corporate Identity

The shift from a commercial-processing economy to a service economy also can be traced by examining declines, transformations, and expansions in many of the major firms involved. The stockyards and meatpacking industries declined precipitously, while grain processing changed considerably, as could be seen in the new directions taken by Nebraska Consolidated Mills (later ConAgra). The railroad industry (specific to Omaha, the Union Pacific Railroad) also underwent significant restructuring. Further significant growth occurred in the insurance, banking, finance, and real-estate category, led by two insurance companies, Mutual Benefit and Accident (Mutual of Omaha) and Woodmen of the World. Each became a prominent symbol of Omaha's emergence as an insurance center. Two other companies also moved to the forefront and became significant components of Omaha's corporate image: Northwestern Bell Telephone Company and Northern Natural Gas Company. And two individuals and their companies exerted tremendous influence, Peter Kiewit, Jr., and Leo A. Daly, Jr. Kiewit's construction company and Daly's architectural firm emerged as very powerful components of Omaha's corporate structure. Finally, retailing, government, medical, educational, and services rounded out the new image.

The stockyards and meatpacking plants in southeast Omaha rose and fell in tandem. At one time or another, Omaha had both the world's largest meatpacking center and its largest stockyards. In 1934, Wilson and Company moved some of its operations to Omaha, which meant the city had plants owned by all of the Big Four in meatpacking: Armour, Cudahy, Swift, and Wilson. In the midst of the Great Depression, it was very encouraging news. Nineteen packers operated in the city and employed nearly thirteen thousand people at the industry's peak in the mid-1950s. More than one-third of them worked for one of two companies, Armour (twenty-five hundred) or Cudahy (twenty-eight hundred). In 1957 the Omaha Chamber of Commerce declared, "Livestock is Omaha's lifeblood." The 1950s also proved to be the heyday of Union Stockyards. In the mid-1950s the yards finally surpassed those in Chicago and earned the title world's largest. They were spread over more than two hundred acres.[8]

The decline, when it arrived in the 1960s, came quickly. The arguments were familiar to any city experiencing plant closings: old, inefficient facilities and outdated labor contracts. Moreover, the structure of the meatpacking industry throughout the United States changed significantly as it decentralized. Smaller plants were built closer to a new source of livestock, the large feedlots that sprang up all over the country; the older facilities could not compete economically. The same decentralization signaled the end of dominance by the central terminal market and stockyards. As packers began buying direct from the farmer-feeder, the central stockyards became obsolete. Union Stockyards declined, yet retained its world's-largest title until 1973. It did so only because, as the marketing of livestock decentralized, no other single center grew to challenge it. In the late 1970s the stockyards, which once covered two hundred acres, were consolidated into eighty.[9]

Meatpacking was not the only food-processing industry that changed; grain processing also was restructured and reoriented. The corporate history of one of the larger Omaha firms in that field, Nebraska Consolidated

Mills, demonstrated many of the themes involved in the process. Initially, its primary business was flour milling, but in the immediate post–World War II years millers realized that flour was not a growth product. The industry already faced considerable competition from convenience foods, which cut sharply into consumer purchases of flour. Nebraska Consolidated decided the answer to the decline lay in diversification. Between the mid-1950s and the mid-1960s the company, led by President J. Allan Mactier, while expanding its flour milling operations, moved into feed (mostly cattle feed) and poultry processing. It not only expanded in the continental United States but moved into Puerto Rico and provided management know-how to mills in France and Spain. The company only briefly entered the convenience-foods market. During the post–war years it produced a convenience cake mix marketed under the Duncan Hines label. However, because the company was not oriented toward that type of consumer product, it sold the Duncan Hines division to Procter and Gamble in 1957. Even without Duncan Hines, Nebraska Consolidated was one of the five hundred largest feed and grain processors in the United States by the mid-1960s.[10] To reflect its new diversified image, the company changed its name to ConAgra in 1971.

Union Pacific Railroad also adopted a new name to reflect internal changes, reorganizing in 1969 under an umbrella holding company called Union Pacific Corporation. Diversification of corporate activities, including a previous reorganization in 1960, prompted the name change. In 1960 the railroad divided its operations into three divisions: transportation, natural resources, and land development. Initially financed by congressional land grants, it always owned a large amount of land. In the 1960 reorganization the company formed a separate division, UPland, to handle its real estate holdings more profitably. Very quickly UPland acted on a multitude of speculative real-estate schemes. By 1969 it was planning developments not only in Omaha but also in the Portland, Oregon, central business district and in Southern California, and it even announced plans to build a hotel in Las Vegas. Its vast land holdings also led it into natural-resource development, especially coal, oil, and gas. The resource division expanded rapidly as it directed the purchase of two oil companies, began a massive oil and gas exploration venture, and led the way in Alaskan natural-resources development. The transportation division handled the corporation's more traditional railroading activities.[11] Union Pacific was still "a great big rolling railroad." Dropping the word "railroad" from its corporate name in 1969, it recognized the fact that it had become far more than just a railroad; it was a real estate company, a natural-resources developer, *and* a railroad.

Meatpacking, grain processing, and railroading were easily recognized traditional Omaha industrial enterprises. Insurance, banking, finance and real estate also had deep roots in the Omaha economy, but changes in the latter fields were perhaps not as fundamental as those in the former. The insurance, banking, and real-estate sector did not increase its share of total employment dramatically. It rose from 6 percent of total employment to 7 percent between 1951 and 1955 and remained stable at 7 percent thereafter. The number of people employed increased steadily nonetheless and grew at a rate slightly higher (155 percent increase 1951 to 1970) than that of total employment (141 percent). While growth in other areas far outpaced them, insurance, banking, finance, and real estate—especially insurance—emerged as very important components of Omaha's corporate identity (see table 11).

Two companies, Mutual of Omaha/United of Omaha and Woodmen of the World, led the insurance-industry rise. Mutual was founded in Omaha and both firms had headquarters there. Both were leaders in their respective insurance fields. Mutual of Omaha, the most visibly prominent of the two, began in 1909 as the Mutual Benefit Health and Accident Association under the direction of C. C. Criss, a medical-school student, and his wife, Mabel. Very much a family business—it employed Dr. Criss's brother and father—the company grew steadily and built its first home-office building in 1939. The major expansion, however, came after World War II under the leadership of V. J. Skutt, who became president in 1949. Skutt spearheaded a rapid expansion of the company, and as a result, Mutual became the world's largest health and accident firm in the 1950s. United of Omaha (United Benefit Life Insurance Company), an affiliate of Mutual since 1926, also expanded in the 1950s and became one of the world's largest life-insurance firms. Diversification was another part of the postwar picture. In 1953, Mutual started its travel-insurance division and in a short

Table 11: Insurance, Banking, Finance, Real Estate

	Employment	% labor force
1951	10,750	6
1955	12,300	7
1960	13,2500	7
1965	14,550	7
1970	16,700	7
% increase		155

Source: Cunningham, "Education and Manpower," 37.

time the company logo could be found on insurance vending machines in airports all over the United States and in thirty-seven foreign countries.[12]

Perhaps most Americans learned of Mutual of Omaha and became familiar with its Indian head logo via the company's sponsorship of the television program "Wild Kingdom." That long-running program brought the adventures of Marlin Perkins and his various assistants into America's living rooms week after week and embedded the company name in the consciousness of the nation. Together with the ubiquitous travel-insurance machines and counters, the company and the city became intimately intertwined. The bond was cemented further as headquarters, located just west of the downtown, expanded to enlarge the company's physical presence in the city.

The skyscraper stood as the visible symbol of Omaha's other very prominent insurance firm, Woodmen of the World. The fraternal insurance organization moved its headquarters to the city in 1895. In 1911 it built the city's first skyscraper, the eighteen-story Woodmen of the World Building. Although not large by national standards, it was impressive by local ones. The company prospered and by the end of World War II, like Mutual, it laid claim to the title of world's largest in its field. Woodmen reinforced its identification with the skyscraper in the late 1960s. After being persuaded to keep its headquarters downtown, the company once again erected the city's tallest building, thirty-story Woodmen Tower, completed in 1969.[13] Again, by national standards the building was not large, but as Omaha's tallest it dominated the downtown skyline. Upon its completion, it quickly emerged as a new focal point, a new centerpiece, and a new symbol for the city and downtown.

Mutual/United and Woodmen were merely the most prominent Omaha insurance firms. In all, nearly forty had headquarters or offices in Omaha by the late 1950s. The number held steady throughout the 1960s, and their growth pushed Omaha into the front ranks of U.S. insurance centers. By the late 1960s it rivaled but never surpassed the traditional insurance centers of Hartford, Boston, and New York.[14] The city that had once prided itself on the number of cattle, hogs, and sheep it butchered gradually found a new source of civic identification in the number of life, casualty, liability, accident, and health policies sold.

The insurance industry provided one piece of the new picture of Omaha, and two other large firms headquartered there offered much of the rest. Northwestern Bell and Northern Natural Gas became extremely vital components of the local economy. Further, the top executives of both firms filled top positions in Omaha's leadership structure, joining V. J. Skutt of Mutual at the epitome of prestige and influence.

Northwestern Bell, part of the American Telephone and Telegraph system, handled telephone service in a five-state region: Nebraska, Iowa, Minnesota, and North and South Dakota. Though large from the start, Northwestern Bell grew into a regional giant in the post–World War II period. In the first five years after the war alone the company installed 492,000 telephones. By 1960 it had 2.4 million customers, a number that expanded to 3.8 million by 1970. Technical advances were concurrent with company growth. Direct-dial and long-distance service were early innovations, while satellites, microwave transmissions, and further mechanization of operations symbolized later progress. Expansion of headquarters buildings in downtown Omaha provided physical evidence of growth. In 1957 and again in 1964, Northwestern Bell constructed twelve-story additions and in 1970 completed a fifteen-story addition. In 1975 the company announced plans for a new seventeen-story headquarters building in downtown Omaha.[15]

Northwestern Bell was and is one of Omaha's largest companies, so the business and civic community naturally turned to it for leadership. It responded and three of its five presidents between 1945 and 1973, Russell J. Hopley (1942–49), A. F. Jacobson (1955–70), and Thomas S. Nurnberger, Jr. (1970–75), especially the latter two, emerged as powerful figures. Each was involved in city planning activities as they actively participated in a number of civic organizations, served on various committees, and put the prestige of their firm behind favored projects. Northwestern Bell had a particular interest in the viability of the downtown core because its corporate headquarters and a good deal of its equipment were located there.[16]

The other rising star of the post–1945 period was Northern Natural Gas. This fledgling gas and pipeline company opened its Omaha offices in 1930. Several factors hampered early growth. The very task of building long-distance, high-pressure pipelines to transport natural gas was fraught with technical difficulties. Further, people were very suspicious of the strange new product. Despite these problems, the company grew during the 1930s, aided in large part by the fact that Omaha's major meatpackers chose to use natural gas in their plants. By the 1940s, gas had won general acceptance. Concurrently, Northern, previously owned by a consortium of outside corporations, became an independent, publicly owned corporation.[17]

Newly independent, Northern Natural entered a period of rapid expansion during the 1950s. John Merriam, its dynamic young president, led the progress, ushering in an aggressive campaign to build new pipelines and seek out new customers. Moreover, Merriam felt that the growth of his company depended on growth in the region it served, so he began a long-term program to bring new industries and new customers to the Midwest. Many of the tactics he employed were rather common—advertisements, billboards, articles in business publications and so forth—but one component was unique for its time and foreshadowed many themes taken up in the late 1960s. In short, Merriam sought to build a whole new image for the region. As he explained it in an interview, "as far as the rest of the world was concerned, the Midwest was a cultural wasteland and many people passed up on the opportunity to live and work here. We were trying to overcome that negative attitude, and I think we accomplished a great deal. We publicized museums, symphonies and operas. And that made it easier to attract the people."[18] In a related effort, Earle Clark, vice-president of public relations, commissioned a number of artworks under the general heading "Living in the Northern Plains." The paintings of cultural institutions and community activities were intended to bolster the image of both the communities in the Northern Great Plains, including Omaha, and of the company. Northern thus pioneered the idea of depicting the region as a lively place to live, a booster theme taken up more generally in the late 1960s as the value of such an approach became more evident.[19]

With the business brought in by the advertisements and, more important, with diversification, Northern Natural Gas continued to grow throughout the 1960s. During those years it moved into liquid fuels and petrochemicals. Northern not only took on new enterprises, it also took on Willis Strauss as its new president in 1960 (Merriam continued as chairman of the board until 1967). Strauss, too, was a very young executive, and he continued the tradition of community service established by Merriam. He was given important roles in planning and community development throughout the 1960s and into the 1970s. He emphasized many of the same themes Merriam had used in promoting the company and the region. Together, the two corporate leaders developed a company policy of contributing to cultural, civic, educational, and charitable institutions.[20]

Omaha served as headquarters for two large privately owned concerns, each headed by a native son. Peter Kiewit, Jr., and Leo A. Daly, Jr., were Omahans and more or less contemporaries. Kiewit, born in 1900, and Daly, born in 1917, rose to the top of the power structure in tandem. Each played an increasingly important civic role throughout the postwar period. The fact that they worked in two highly related fields further strengthened the bond between the two in the public mind and in their professional lives. Kiewit was a builder and contractor; Daly was an architect.

In 1931, Kiewit assumed leadership of Peter Kiewit's Sons', Inc., founded in 1884 by his father and uncle. Shortly thereafter he reorganized the firm and in 1935 renamed it Peter Kiewit Sons' Company. From that point on, it grew rapidly and prodigiously. The growth resulted in large measure from Kiewit's ability successfully to follow and capitalize on government construction. In the 1930s and 1940s, Kiewit built numerous public-works and defense projects and in the 1950s moved into highway and freeway construction. He was so successful in the latter field that in 1966 *Fortune* labeled him "the Colossus of the Roads." Peter Kiewit Sons' held a half-billion dollars' worth of federal highway-construction contracts, more than twice the amount held by anyone else in the field. By the late 1960s, mass transit and public power facilities became part of the firm's list of construction specialties.[21]

Peter Kiewit Sons' also grew because of constant diversification. In 1943, for example, it began digging for coal on land it owned in Wyoming, the rationale being that it needed some way to keep its huge stock of equipment busy during the long winter. The spirit of diversification continued until PKS, Inc., a holding company established to organize the various firms held by Kiewit, consisted of thirty-eight subsidiary corporations involved in heavy construction, insurance, the manufacture of concrete products, ranching, coal mining, and publishing (in 1962 Kiewit bought Omaha's only daily newspaper, the *World-Herald*). By the time of his death in 1979, Peter Kiewit, Jr., was a millionaire more than a hundred times over.[22]

Leo A. Daly, Jr., seventeen years Kiewit's junior, did not take over the architectural firm founded by his father until 1952, when his father died. Even at that time the company was not a small concern; it had branch offices in three cities. The most extensive growth, however, occurred after 1952. Like Kiewit, Daly also watched government spending closely and won design contracts for highways, hospitals, schools, water-supply and power facilities, parts of the Kennedy Space Center and the underground headquarters of the Strategic Air Command. The firm also designed a wide variety of private buildings, including homes.[23]

Diversification helped the Daly company grow. It provided not only architectural services, but engineering and planning services as well. For example, it drew up master plans for downtown Sacramento, California, for Los Alamos, New Mexico, and for Half Moon Bay, California, as well as several plans for Omaha. It planned industrial and military complexes and college campuses, including Creighton University's. By 1973, Daly had offices in six U.S. cities plus Paris, Hong Kong, and Singapore and employed approximately five hundred people.[24]

Kiewit and Daly had emerged as the twin giants of the Omaha power structure by the mid-1960s. Complementary business interests, as well as common memberships in civic clubs, on committees, and on boards of trustees, brought the two together. In 1966 they shared these titles: governor of Ak-Sar-Ben (an Omaha social and civic organization), director of the Boys Club of Omaha, trustee of the Joslyn Society of Liberal Arts, and director of the Omaha Chamber of Commerce. Each sat on the board of directors of one of the city's three large banks, Kiewit at Omaha National and Daly at U.S. National.[25] The most intensely concentrated example of cooperation between the two was perhaps the Creighton University campus. Leo Daly designed and Peter Kiewit constructed many of the major buildings added to the school in the late 1950s and 1960s. Each also donated a great deal of money to the school.

As has been mentioned, much of the employment growth in metropolitan Omaha was in the retail sector. It came from a variety of sources: large national chains, regional chains, local stores with multiple outlets, and smaller stores. One store provided a lion's share of civic leadership in the retail sector: J. L. Brandeis and Sons, founded in 1889. It was the city's largest locally owned retail concern and served as the leader in retailing. Brandeis anchored Omaha's first large suburban shopping mall (Crossroads) and pioneered in building a warehouse–distribution center on the western fringe of the city. In addition to the Crossroads store, the company built outlets in three other Omaha malls, moved into neighboring Council Bluffs, Iowa, and into Lincoln and Grand Island, Nebraska, and opened small operations in several surrounding towns. By 1966, according to the local newspaper, it was the largest independent retailer between Chicago and Los Angeles. Throughout the postwar period Brandeis had an executive whose chief responsibility was representing the company in the community. From the 1930s through 1963, Edward Fitch ("E. F.") Pettis held the job. After his death, John Diesing, Pettis's former assistant, performed the task. Both were effective leaders, Diesing particularly so as he quickly advanced to a position of considerable influence. The influence of other retailers was less extensive, although a number were prominent spokespersons for the downtown. Louis Somberg, president of Natelson's, a women's clothing store, was an especially active proponent of downtown interests.[26]

Health and educational institutions represented other important growth areas in the local economy. Medical and health-related employment rose significantly during the 1960s. Two medical schools and more than a dozen hospitals helped solidify Omaha's position as a major midwestern medical center. In the mid-1960s, six of the larger hospitals (Archbishop Bergan Mercy, Bishop Clarkson Memorial, University, Nebraska Methodist, Lutheran, and Booth Memorial) announced expansion plans that resulted in the addition of 1,232 beds. Creighton University and its affiliated Saint Joseph's Hospital announced plans to build a 500-bed facility in 1970. In 1950 the number of hospital beds in Omaha stood at 2,221, by 1960 the total reached 3,003, and by 1970 there were 4,518 beds.[27]

Hospital expansion and growth in the health professions pushed employment in medical and health-related fields from 6,305 in 1959 to 13,759 in 1973, or 3 percent of the total work force in 1959 and 5 percent in 1970. Although there are no comparable data for the entire period, nonetheless the available data did point to a significant increase in health-care employment (see table 12).

Educational institutions grew apace at the elementary, secondary, and postsecondary levels. Accompaning the increase in total population was growth in the school-age population. Enrollment in elementary and secondary schools rose from 32,874 in 1950 to 89,788 in 1970. When the early members of the baby-boom generation reached their midteens in the late 1950s and early 1960s, they swelled enrollment at colleges and universities. Five colleges and universities served postwar Omaha: the Municipal University of Omaha (later the University of Nebraska at Omaha), Creighton University, the University of Nebraska Medical Center, the College of Saint Mary, and Duchesne College (closed in 1967). In 1960 total enrollment in these institutions stood at 6,416. The figure had more than doubled by 1970, when 14,501 enrolled.[29] Moreover, the expansion of higher education, coupled with the labor demands of the service economy, helped transform Omaha's demographics. The growing number of people successfully completing college and then moving into the work force raised the median level of education.

Table 12: Health Care

	Employed	% total labor
1959	6,305	3
1962	7,017	3
1964	7,887	4
1965	8,007	4
1966	8,513	4
1967	9,284	4
1968	10,173	5
1969	11,408	5
1970	11,811	5
1971	12,561	—
1972	13,157	—
1973	13,759	—

Source: U.S. Bureau of the Census, *County Business Patterns* (Washington: Government Printing Office, 1959, 1962, 1964–73). The 1959 and 1962 figures are combined county figures (Douglas, Sarpy, Pottawattamie); the 1964–73 figures are SMSA-level figures. The Omaha SMSA includes the three counties above; Cunningham, "Education and Manpower," 37.

Government, the Business Community, and the Public-Private Partnership

Local government and the business community changed in the postwar period as the public-private partnership was redefined. City hall, a weak, dependent institution headed by part-time politicians, became a stronger and more independent one headed by a full-time mayor with a professional staff. Positions on the city council remained part time—in theory, if not in practice. The corporate leadership structure also changed, mainly because of retirements or deaths, although the fortunes of various companies were factors as well. The result was a transformation of the public-private partnership. In the late 1940s and into the 1950s, the private sector almost completely dominated the relationship. In the 1960s, however, local government status and expertise rose, and by the late 1960s and early 1970s, city hall emerged as a more equal but still in many ways lesser member of the partnership.

At first glance, the growth of governmental employment might account for much of the change in the local government. Indeed, city employment did grow, but much of the growth in overall governmental employment resulted from an increase in the number of people employed by federal and state government offices in the city. Available figures indicate that between 89 percent and 92 percent of the governmental employment in the Omaha standard metropolitan statistical area, or SMSA, was in positions offered by the federal and state governments, not counting an undoubtedly small number of people employed by other municipalities in the SMSA. Omaha city employment accounted for only 8 percent to 11 percent of all governmental employment, and its growth lagged behind the overall growth rate of governmental employment. Total government employment rose 115 percent between 1951 and 1970, but city government employment increased only 68 percent. (see table 13).[30] The growth of city government therefore paled somewhat when compared with that at other levels of government. Nonetheless, the expansion was significant because it symbolized local government's emergence as a more equal member of the public-private partnership.

Omaha entered the postwar period with a part-time commission form of government that it had adopted in 1911 as part of a progressive reform effort to replace the political machine–dominated structure with one headed by civic-minded businessmen. To discourage anyone from making an elected position at city hall a full-time career, the new city charter set very low salary levels. Reformers hoped this would discourage machine candidates and encourage independent, civic-minded businessmen to run for office. Exactly how well the plan worked is beyond the scope of this study. Significantly, however, the salaries set in 1913 were still in effect in 1951.[31] Between those years, Omaha grew, making the jobs of those governing it far more difficult and complex, yet the mayors and commissioners of the late 1940s and early 1950s earned no more than their predecessors. The situation kept city government operating at a very low activity level.

Table 13: Government Employment

	Total Gov't Emp.	City Emp.	% total Gov't
1951	14,000	1,543	11
		(1950)	
1955	16,100	1,455	9
1960	20,150	1,787	9
1965	24,050	2,004	8
1970	30,050	2,591	9
% increase	115	68	

Source: U.S. Bureau of the Census, *City and County Data Book,* 1952, 1956, 1962, 1967, 1972; Cunningham, "Education and Manpower," 37.

Charter reform in the 1950s was intended to correct many of the old system's limitations; the process will be discussed at length later. Relative at this point, however, the new charter set up a strong mayor-council form of government. The mayor became a full-time city executive with a salary to match, in theory at least, his responsibilities. The council positions remained part-time jobs. Under the old system each commissioner headed a city department; the new charter provided for professionally trained and qualified department heads.[32] City hall did not become a model of modern local government overnight. The potential for change embodied in the charter reforms took more than a decade to be realized, for the private sector cast a long shadow. City hall needed to take many steps forward before coming into its own. The concurrent increases in both revenues and expenditures aided that movement.

City revenue grew throughout the postwar period, including two five-year spans of dramatic increase. It went from $7,663,000 in 1950 to $39,600,000 in 1970, a 417 percent increase. Much of the growth came in two spurts, one between 1950 and 1955 and the other between 1965 and 1970 (see table 14). During the first, revenue rose 91 percent. Two factors contributed to this. First, Omaha improved its property-tax assessment and collection system (mainly because of repeated crises in city finances). Sec-

Table 14: Revenues and Expenditures (in thousands)

	1950	1955	1960	1965	1970
City Revenues	$7,633	$14,661	$17,653	$24,119	$39,600
City Expenditures	$9,686	$13,518	$18,529	$24,054	$40,400

Source: U.S. Bureau of the Census, *City and County Data Book*, 1952, 1956, 1962, 1967, 1972.

ond, it annexed a good deal of residential property, most of it in the more affluent western areas of the city, swelling the tax rolls. The second period of sizable increase (64 percent) also depended in part on annexations. More important, however, the state legislature decided to introduce a sales tax, the first in Nebraska's one-hundred-year history, in 1967. The state later allowed cities of a specified size to levy their own sales tax above that set by the state. Omaha took advantage of the opportunity and in 1969 levied an 0.5 percent city sales tax.[33] Property taxes remained by far the most important source of revenue, yet the sales tax helped a great deal.

City expenditures grew with revenues, but the rate was lower. Revenue increased 417 percent, while expenditures rose 317 percent. The fact that expenditures began at a higher level than revenues helps to explain the discrepancy. General fiscal conservativeness was also a factor. Omaha operated with a surplus in two of the five benchmark years examined (see table 14). The biggest jump in expenditures occurred between 1965 and 1970, when they increased 68 percent. The acceleration continued during the administration of Mayor Eugene Leahy (1969–73). A very popular and persuasive mayor, Leahy pushed the city to do more and spend more. By the end of his term, expenditures had risen to seventy million dollars.[34]

Increased revenues, expenditures, strong leadership, and growth in expertise (for example, a planning department headed and staffed by professionally trained planners) combined to make city hall more equal to the business community. As city hall changed, so did the local leadership structure. The transformations were subtle, mostly tied to the career and life cycles of the men involved (Omaha's top leadership was exclusively male). The emergence of certain companies and the decline of others also played a part. No clear benchmarks appeared, perhaps because there was also a great deal of stability, yet by the early 1970s the leadership was quite different from that of the early 1950s.

There were two formal studies of Omaha's leadership structure, both undertaken by *Omaha Sun Newspapers*, the first in 1966 and the second in 1981.[35] Both studies were, in essence, lists of those men who exercised the most power and influence in the community. The 1966 study served as the focal point for the following analysis. Before 1966, the closest equivalent to a leadership list was a list of the executive committee of the Committee of '52.[36] That group, forerunner of the Omaha Industrial Foundation, was formed to give the Omaha economic development a needed push. The executive committee represented the leadership of the organization, which drew members from every segment of Omaha's economy. Most likely, those at the top of the Committee of '52 were also at or near the top of the leadership structure. The 1981 study served as a reference point for determining who was at the top in the mid-1970s. Biographical material on men listed at the top and those indicated as up and coming was used to fill out the leadership lists as well (see table 15).

Analysis of the lists yielded several interesting points. The power and influence of men at the top of older, traditional Omaha businesses gradually gave way over time. The 1952 list contained the names of the heads of Cudahy (a meatpacker), a coal company, Storz Brewery, Swanson (a food processor), and a grain company. Buyouts, mergers, the increasing rise of natural gas, and the imminent decline of meatpacking helped trim away leadership representatives from those traditional companies. A member of the Swanson family still occupied the list in 1966, but he headed Swanson Enterprises, a holding company for a diversified range of businesses. The chairman of Fairmont Foods also appeared on the 1966 list, but that company soon moved its operations out of Omaha. Of the food-processing industry, only ConAgra contributed to the leadership ranks by the mid-1970s, and it was by then involved in many new fields, some far removed from traditional flour milling.[37]

Influential throughout the period were men who held the top spots at eight corporations: Omaha National Bank,[38] First National Bank, United

Table 15: Omaha's Private Leadership, 1952–1973

PART I: 1952 LEADERSHIP LIST

Hayden W. Ahmanson	President, National American Fire
Thomas H. Ashton	Manager, Bemis Bag
*W. Dale Clark	Chairman, Omaha National Bank (retires 1962) Chairman, Omaha World-Herald Company (1962–66)
M. J. Flannigan	Kennedy and Parsons (law firm)
F. W. Hoffman	President, Cudahy Packing
†Morris E. Jacobs	President, Bozell and Jacobs (advertising)
*E. J. McNeely	President, Northwestern Bell Telephone (succeeded 1955)
†John F. Merriam	President, Northern Natural Gas (chairman, 1960)
*Ellsworth Moser	President, U.S. National Bank
Sam W. Reynolds	Vice-President, Reynolds-Updike (coal)
†V. J. Skutt	President, Mutual of Omaha
Robert H. Storz	Vice-President, Storz Brewing (sold, 1959) President, Storz Broadcasting (1964)
†Gilbert Swanson	President, C. A. Swanson and Sons (food processing) (merged, Campbell Soups, 1955)
*Fred W. Thomas	President, First National Bank
J. LeRoy Welsh	President, Butler-Welsh Grain Company
Also:	
†Melvin Bekins	President, Bekins Van and Storage
†Frank Fogarty	General Manager, WOW Radio

*Immediate successor appears on subsequent list   †Appears on subsequent list

Table 15, continued

†A. W. Gordon	President, Omaha Loan and Building
†Clarence Landen	President, Securities Acceptance Corporation

PART 2: 1966 LEADERSHIP LIST

*Morris E. Jacobs	President, Bozell and Jacobs (retires 1967)
*A. F. Jacobson	President, Northwestern Bell Telephone (succeeded 1970)
*John F. Merriam	Chairman, Northern Natural Gas (retires 1967)
†Edward Lyman	President, U.S. National Bank
†V. J. Skutt	President, Mutual of Omaha
Gilbert Swanson	President, Swanson Enterprises (dies 1968)
*John F. Davis	President, First National Bank (retires, 1967; dies 1972)
Willard D. Hosford	Vice-President, John Deere Plow
Melvin Bekins	President, Bekins Van and Storage (dies 1966)
Frank Fogarty	Vice-President, Meridith Broadcasting (retires, 1970)
A. W. Gordon	Chairman, Omaha Loan and Building
†Peter Kiewit	President, Peter Kiewit Sons'
†Leo A. Daly	President, Leo A. Daly Company
Erhard Edquist	Chairman, Fairmont Foods (company leaves)
†Willis A. Strauss	President, Northern Natural Gas (chairman, 1967)
*Edd Bailey	President, Union Pacific Railroad
Kenneth C. Holland	Former President, Carpenter Paper

*Immediate successor appears on subsequent list   †Appears on subsequent list

Richard Walker	President, Byron Reed (real estate)
Clarence Landen Also:	Chairman, General National Insurance Group
†Nick Newberry	President, Woodmen of the World (1967)
†Ed Owen	President, Paxton-Vierling Steel
†J. Allan Mactier	President, Nebraska Consolidated Mills (Con Agra)
†Charles Peebler	President, Bozell and Jacobs (1967)
†Morris Miller	President, Omaha National Bank (1962)
†Harold Andersen	President, Omaha World-Herald Company (1966)
John R. Maenner	President, Maenner Company (real estate)
N. P. ("Sandy") Dodge	President, N. P. Dodge Company (real estate)

PART 3: MID-1970S LEADERSHIP LIST

Morris Miller	President, Chairman, Omaha National Bank
Harold Andersen	President, Omaha World-Herald Company
Charles Peebler	President, Bozell and Jacobs
Thomas J. Nurnburger	President, Northwestern Bell Telephone
Edward Lyman	President, U.S. National Bank
V. J. Skutt	Chairman, CEO, Mutual of Omaha
John Lauritzen	President, First National Bank (1967)
Peter Kiewit	President, Peter Kiewit Sons'
Leo A. Daly	President, Leo A. Daly Company
Willis A. Strauss	President, Chairman, Northern Natural Gas

†Appears on subsequent list

Table 15, continued

John Kennefick	President, Union Pacific Corporation
John F. Diesing	Secretary-Treasurer, J. L. Brandies (retailer)
Nick J. Newberry	President, Woodmen of the World
Edward F. Owen	President, Paxton-Vierling Steel
J. Allan Mactier	President, ConAgra
William A. Fitzgerald	President, Commercial Federal Savings and Loan

States National Bank, Omaha World-Herald Company, Bozell and Jacobs (advertising), Northwestern Bell Telephone, Northern Natural Gas, and Mutual of Omaha. With the exception of Mutual, each corporation had at least one change in leadership. Northern Natural Gas was unique in that both its chairman and its president appeared on the list in 1966. Union Pacific might be considered a ninth member of the group. Its president did not appear on the 1952 list, but, given the size and importance of his corporation, he undoubtedly had considerable influence. The Union Pacific president did appear on the 1966 and 1980 lists, however.

The 1966 list represented the apparent coming of age of four companies: Peter Kiewit Sons', Leo A. Daly Company, J. L. Brandeis and Sons, and Woodmen of the World. Kiewit and Daly probably reached the top ranks of influence before 1966. One indication of having made it was election to the honorary title King of Quivera. Each autumn, Omaha's major civic organization, Ak-Sar-Ben, chose a man known for business or civic leadership and the daughter of a prominent family to reign as king and queen of the social season. The pomp and circumstance was perhaps a bit much, but the honor was real. Kiewit was elected king in 1959, Daly in 1961. The J. L. Brandeis executive charged with community service, John Diesing, reached the top by 1966 (his predecessor, E. F. Pettis, probably exercised much influence, too, as he was elected king in 1950). Nick Newberry of Woodmen of the World was a definite up-and-comer. He came from a very prominent family long associated with Woodmen of the World (his father, Farrar Newberry, was quite influential in his day). Nick appeared on the 1981 leadership list, so only he really arrived in 1966; the others attained their positions somewhat earlier. Most important, once these men made the list, they remained on it, each holding top spots well into the 1970s.[39]

By the mid-1970s, three more corporations found representation in the top leadership ranks: Paxton-Vierling Steel, Nebraska Consolidated Mills (ConAgra), and Commercial Federal Savings and Loan. That brought Ed Owen, J. Allan Mactier, and William Fitzgerald to the fore. Exactly when they reached the top is hard to pinpoint; all appeared on the 1981 list, and journalist Paul Williams's article indicated they had occupied their positions of power for quite some time.[40]

The lists do not include the names of individuals on somewhat lower levels of influence. Many men and women were influential in certain limited areas. Rachael Gallagher, for example, exerted much pressure on behalf of city parks. John Latenser, architect and longtime chairman of the Omaha City Planning Commission, helped shape early city planning policy. Ironically, Eugene Eppley, a wealthy hotelier, proved most influential after his death. The Eugene Eppley Foundation, an early and large source of capital, provided seed money for several important projects. Many officers of the Chamber of Commerce, some city officials, and a number of prominent Omaha families also fell into that category, so Williams's lists do not exhaust the sources of potential civic leadership. Most of the major decision making in the private sector, however, occurred at the top of the leadership structure, not the lower level.

Changes in the corporations providing leadership were significant. They brought a number of new businesses to the forefront and pushed others into the background. Perhaps most important were the changes in personnel. Only V. J. Skutt remained a top leader during the entire period. Despite his longevity, in no way did he dominate the power structure. Several individuals shared the very top leadership. Further, new men rose to the top throughout the period. The changing personnel helped make the leadership open to new ideas. These did not take hold overnight, but new leaders often brought fresh perspectives. Fundamental ideas were slow to change, but the fluidity that did exist in the power structure let new ideas filter in and gradually take hold.

A characteristic of the top leadership that did not change was strong adherence to privatism. The private sector believed not only that it should take action, but that it was the proper source for nearly all civic activity. Its leaders participated vigorously in a wide range of civic activities and felt quite comfortable setting community priorities, partly because of local government's inability to act. Very often the private sector had to seize the initiative. This changed with the rise of competency at city hall by the early 1970s, but the private leadership still expected city hall to follow its lead in most matters. Thus most of Omaha's planning activity—initiating plans, promoting programs, pushing for funds—was centered almost exclusively in the private sector until the early 1970s.

Toward the Livable City

The journey from old Omaha to the new one was long, labyrinthine, and not immediately understood by those involved. In the late 1940s there was no map to point the way. Models that sought to explain how the city worked were based on a perception of conditions that became inadequate in the face of rapid changes. New models were not developed until long after the changes had already transformed the city. Omaha had begun its movement toward growth, toward social and political change, and toward service-sector dominance by the 1950s, but understanding of the road traveled did not come, nor was it articulated, until the late 1960s and early 1970s. Studies to provide information about the economy continued to concentrate almost exclusively on manufacturing, ignoring or discounting growth in the service sector. Not until the early 1970s did a study of the Omaha SMSA economy acknowledge that the service sector was and had been the vital element.[41] There was a lag between change, perception of change, and action based on a new understanding of the city. Those involved in the city planning process in the public and private sectors seemed no more perceptive. They did not fully grasp and act on what was happening to Omaha until the late 1960s. City planning, therefore, very often proved to be a response to change rather than anticipation of change. Planning and development ideas shifted slowly as understanding of the transformations at work in the city gradually emerged. The old emphasis on the city efficient gave way only slowly, and sometimes reluctantly, to emphasis on the livable city.

Much attention in postwar Omaha, as elsewhere, focused on the downtown and the riverfront. As early as the 1920s the downtown became the symbol of the city and its vital core. A healthy city was equated with a healthy downtown. The changes of the postwar period altered the role of downtown. It still existed as a symbol of the city, but the decentralization of retailing, warehousing, and offices diminished its traditional position. In the face of these changes, the downtown did not age gracefully. The riverfront section deteriorated even faster than the rest. It was the oldest part of Omaha and it showed signs of age and neglect. Ignored by many, its waters fouled by pollution, the riverfront ceased to play much of a part in the life of the city. The only roles conceived for it were those of a highway for goods and a sewer of least resistance. Gradually, however, both the downtown and the riverfront took on new life as they became focal points for expressing Omaha's new image.

Changes occurred at varying rates during nearly three decades and evoked a complex series of reactions. After all, the older Omaha did not disappear overnight, nor did the newer Omaha suddenly appear one bright and shining morning. Rather, it was a long process that produced both positive and negative reactions. The meaning a city has for its people is largely intangible. Steel City, the Big Apple, Second City, Motor City are all catch words that evoke a complex of images, symbols, and emotions. The full range of their meaning may never be fully articulated, yet, like any other set of symbols and ideas, they can take hold of the imagination, and once in place they are difficult to dislodge. When the conditions that established some vision of a city are changed, it is not easy to develop a new set of images, symbols, and ideas to redefine the city. Changes in the vision of what a city is and what it should become evolve slowly and come only after large-scale transformations have taken hold, rendering the old vision invalid.

As a group, business and civic leaders probably directed the most energy toward articulating what the city was, how it worked, and what made it worthy of notice. Only slowly did they realize and comprehend exactly what was happening. They learned they were no more adept than anyone else at shifting from one vision and course of action to another very different view and agenda. Plans, hopes, and dreams based on an earlier definition were not dismissed easily, even in light of changes that increasingly made them unfeasible. During a period of transition, older ideas stubbornly hung on; only time and a series of crises forced a rethinking of the situation and finally pushed them into the background in favor of newer ideas and action strategies. Remaining constant, however, was a desire to boost the city and promote its growth and development through planning initiatives.

As an important component of boosting, city planning remained prominent. However, strategies and priorities gradually shifted in response to long-term changes. The more educated white-collar population stimulated the demand for more and different urban amenities. In a pioneering article in 1954, Edward L. Ulman identified amenities as an important factor in promoting growth.[42] At that time the definition of amenities was narrow, focusing primarily on climate. Over time, it broadened to include far more than annual mean temperature and rainfall. The definition of amenities in general expanded to include cultural and recreational factors: parks and open spaces, cultural and entertainment facilities, outlets for leisure-time recreational pursuits. Environmental amenities gradually went beyond climate to include air and water quality. This reflected changing consumption patterns and consumer preferences generally associated with demands for a higher quality of life.

The opportunity for living well became an important factor in location decisions for both companies and individuals. In a 1970 interview Thomas Nurnberger, president of Northwestern Bell Telephone, "mentioned the importance of such amenities as cultural attractions, symphonies, theater, art, zoos, 'and without a doubt, recreational areas'" in influencing a company's decision to locate in a particular city. He did not discount the continued importance of such factors as labor supply, efficient transportation, tax policies, and market potential. He did state, however, that after all those factors were taken into account, "quite often the top man starts rationalizing and his recreational interests have a way of getting into the picture."[43] A 1977 *Fortune* magazine study of facility location decisions over a ten- to fifteen-year period supported Nurnberger's observations. It concluded that while traditional factors remained part of the picture, "personal preferences of company executives" and "style of living for employees" were vital elements, at least in decisions concerning the location of corporate headquarters.[44] The shift in what attracted people—including business leaders and their companies—to a city promoted a transformation in business development strategies, including planning schemes. While previously the emphasis had been on promotion of city planning to improve physical infrastructure, it now shifted toward promotion of ways to improve the living environment. The emphasis was no longer on the city efficient, but on the livable city.

THREE

Setting the Agenda: Planning, 1933–1945

During the 1930s, those seeking to establish a planned program of infrastructure construction, to promote civic improvements, to clean out slums, and to boost their city's economic development saw a number of federal government departments, agencies and bureaus as fresh sources of funds. Thus, while programs created in response to the Great Depression, such as the PWA (Public Works Administration), the CCC (Civilian Conservation Corps), and the WPA (Work Progress Administration), provided an opportunity for employment, in practice they also gave civic and business leaders the opportunity to construct public works. At the close of the decade as national spending priorities shifted toward defense, cities followed, adjusting their efforts from attempting to obtain public-works funds to scrambling for defense projects (bases, plants, airfields) that would increase municipal income and promote development. Omaha followed that general pattern. During the 1930s a small but determined number of individuals and groups leapt at the opportunities national programs gave them to advance their favorite projects. Civic leaders quickly jumped on the defense-contract bandwagon as early as 1935 and especially so as the decade came to a close and the nation geared up for war.

The downtown and riverfront figured prominently in the planning and development thought. The downtown, its shopping streets, institutions, and skyline, physically symbolized the city. Its role as the city center remained largely unchallenged. The assumption that it would continue to

77

play that role, moreover, was firmly established and underlay most of the planning. The Missouri River also acquired clear roles in Omaha life during the 1930s and early 1940s. Channelization of the river and promises of flood control strengthened its role as a highway for goods. And it continued in its longtime role as a convenient sewer.

Setting the Agenda: The National Context

Two national public-works programs were the most important sources of funds for cities. The National Industrial Recovery Act of 1933 (NIRA) established the first, known as the Public Works Administration. Except for its housing projects, the PWA constructed no public works; rather, it coordinated spending on public works, both for federal projects and newly authorized nonfederal projects. The federal government had long been in the business of constructing public works. Projects dated back to 1791 and included lighthouses, public buildings, river and harbor improvements, roads, canals, railroads, reclamation projects, and the Panama Canal. Under the NIRA, however, the federal government established an aid program to help finance public works that were planned and constructed at the state and municipal levels. With grants or loans and technical assistance, the PWA supervised allocation of funds for a wide variety of locally initiated projects.[1]

From 1935 to 1938, legislation linked the PWA to the Works Progress Administration, the second national program that influenced city building in the 1930s. Under the terms of the Emergency Relief Appropriations Act of 1935, public works and work relief were linked as the law required PWA-financed projects to draw their labor, as much as possible, from WPA relief rolls. (Subsequent legislation severed this connection. Under the Public Works Administration Appropriation Act of 1938, the PWA once again received financing independent of direct relief employment requirements.) In addition, the WPA financed and provided manpower for many types of projects, including highways, roads and streets, public buildings, parks and other recreational facilities, conservation efforts, sewer systems and other utilities, airport and airways construction and extension, sewing centers, sanitation programs, and professional and service projects.[2] Together, the

PWA and WPA provided both jobs and, for those anxious to reshape the city, an opportunity to act.

In 1939 the PWA published an appraisal of the architectural quality of construction projects completed under the program, citing examples of the best of the various types. Because of its comprehensive nature, the appraisal provided a convenient list that indicated clearly the wide range of municipal projects. The list included local-government buildings (city halls, court-houses, police and fire stations), auditoriums, memorials, libraries, school buildings (elementary through postsecondary), social and recreational buildings, waterworks, and airfields.[3] Hence the PWA afforded cities the opportunity to construct any number of desired projects.

The PWA's role in creating jobs (in general, if not specifically for relief purposes) and stimulating the economy remained prominent in government documents published in its support.[4] Official publications also hinted at another role: giving interested parties a chance to act on ideas for civic improvements. In addition, the PWA public-housing program not only constructed housing for the needy but assisted with slum clearance, a long-standing priority of many involved in the city-building process.

In 1939 the Division of Information in the Public Works Administration published *America Builds*, an official record of PWA accomplishments.[5] It reiterated the variety and far-reaching nature of its programs, described local PWA projects, and indicated that the agency saw itself as having more responsibility than creating jobs and stimulating the economy. A section on grants and loans for public and semipublic buildings emphasized the PWA's role in facilitating the expansion and improving the quality of municipal services. Further, it specifically credited the public-housing program with housing construction and with eliminating slums and reforming the character of urban areas.

The section on PWA allocations to local governments began with the assertion that citizen demand for services burdened local governments and required construction of more up-to-date facilities to provide them. For that reason, the PWA was in the business of assisting the construction of public buildings. The list of those constructed indicated the level and quality of municipal services in demand. New courthouses, city halls, police and fire stations, jails, auditoriums, civic centers, convention and music

79

halls, memorials, public market facilities, and warehouses highlighted the roster. These were not necessarily new municipal services, but modern and efficient facilities to provide such services were important, especially in the eyes of city boosters. The host of reasons for constructing the facilities revealed motivations beyond job creation and economic stimulation.[6]

Civic pride and the desire to have a courthouse—a symbol that clearly reflected the stature of a community—evidently were important factors in the decision of Alameda County, California, to seek PWA funds to build a new Hall of Records in Oakland. The paragraphs describing that project indicated a genuine need for new facilities and more than hinted at acknowledgment of civic booster motivation:

> Alameda County, California, decided that the Hall of Records (the county courthouse) in Oakland, which had been built in the 1870s, had outlasted its usefulness. The citizens found in their Hall of Records no source of civic pride.
>
> It was such a little courthouse for such a big and wealthy county. It was so little that the citizens had to pay $25,000 a year extra to rent space for essential functions in buildings scattered around Oakland. Sixty years of records bowed the floors. Since the structure preceded modern plumbing and electric lighting, the building was unsanitary and uncomfortable. Although it was red brick outside, the inside was a wooden shell—a fire hazard that may have burned, destroying all the valuable records with it.
>
> A Federal grant of $452,000 started a new $1,988,000 eleven-story building soaring skyward in 1934. Into this new structure were gathered all the scattered administrative activities of Alameda County government.[7]

PWA funds also gave cities and their suburbs more police and fire protection in the form of grants for modern police headquarters, new police and fire stations, and improved fire-alarm and police-communication systems.[8] Aside from the obvious safety benefit, provision of these services answered demands by civic boosters and insurers alike for lower insurance rates. A lower theft and fire rate meant a more attractive business environment (lower insurance costs to businesses and industries) and a more attractive home-building environment (the lower rates also applied to residences). This statement clearly demonstrated the motive:

> It is hard to calculate the dollar return from these improved protective facilities. But in many cases cities have been able to obtain substantial reduc-

tions in their theft and fire insurance rates paid by the citizens after the new equipment was installed. Charlotte, N.C., with $41,000,000 invested in 200 cotton mills, cotton oil plants, knitting mills, refining plants and other industries had much at stake. Yet the application to PWA stated that some sections of the city were a mile and a half from the nearest fire-alarm box. An allotment provided 126 new alarm boxes, which have resulted in reductions in the insurance rates.[9]

A number of projects described under the heading "Miscellaneous" demonstrated the PWA's role in promoting local enterprise. For example, Port Lavaca, Texas, built a cannery "so that its citizens could obtain their share of the Gulf Coast oyster and shrimp canning business." Stockton, California, built a cotton warehouse "to afford adequate facilities for handling, warehousing, baling and shipping of California's long staple cotton." It is reasonable to assume that those projects helped bolster those communities' claims to their fair share of the business that was generated. The boardwalks constructed at Long Beach, New York, and Cape May, New Jersey, which were intended to foster the tourist trade, more clearly fell into the civic-booster category.[10]

The description of an Oklahoma City project and the section on public housing made clear the PWA's role in city planning. In Oklahoma City, the PWA helped bring to fruition a project planned in the 1920s, a decade during which planners wanted to rid the city of railroad tracks cutting through the center of town. An exchange gave the city railroad right-of-way in a four-block area. On that site, planners envisioned a civic center consisting of a city hall, a municipal auditorium, a courthouse, and a jail. A PWA grant helped Oklahoma City begin construction.[11]

Finally, the section on public housing emphasized the PWA's role in realizing a long-standing goal: slum clearance. The introduction to that section told a story illustrating the civic-booster aspect of the PWA public-housing program. It spoke of the "discouraging aspect" of a trip downtown for "the young ladies of Peachtree Street, Atlanta." In order for them to reach the shopping district, they had to pass a "notorious" slum, an area the Chamber of Commerce in 1933 labeled "Atlanta's Problem Area No. 1." It was "adjacent to the campus of the Georgia Institute of Technology" and "at the doorway of downtown Atlanta." By 1936, thanks to the PWA-constructed Techwood housing project, the slum had disappeared, "giving way to trim brick apartment buildings and group houses with clean-cut lines, set amid pleasant green lawns."[12] Not only did the PWA project provide construction jobs and needed low-cost housing, it also improved the neighborhood of an important educational institution, made more pleasant an access route to the downtown shopping district, and rid Atlanta of a recognized "problem area."

Unlike the purpose of the PWA, creation of jobs was the central goal of the WPA. Its laborers worked on PWA projects and public works projects sponsored by other agencies, yet the work undertaken, like that under the PWA, aided those seeking to reshape the city. Moreover, the WPA financed smaller, labor-intensive civic projects: laying storm and sanitary sewers; making improvements at schools and hospitals; constructing stadiums, bleachers, grandstands, and other recreational facilities; and building streets.[13] Perhaps most important, WPA white-collar professionals in service projects conducted studies and surveys that provided a key to planning action: information.

In a 1939 report the WPA described some of its nonconstruction activities. Besides working in libraries, sewing rooms, school lunchrooms, and art, music, theater, and writing projects, WPA professionals conducted planning surveys and research and statistical studies and drew maps. As of 1938, workers had completed 757 planning surveys, 1,282 research and statistical studies (although only a small number concerned cities), and 116,000 maps (delineating corporate limits, identifying taxable properties, marking streets).[14]

The WPA's final report, issued three years after its demise in 1943, expanded on its contributions and discussed its relationship to planning activities. Recreation, for example, received a great deal of WPA attention. The WPA staffed local recreational facilities and organized local advisory committees that conducted studies and made plans to provide for urban recreational needs. The studies were valuable in putting together city park and recreation plans. The social and economic surveys and studies were another important source of information. The most notable was an extensive land-use survey conducted in Chicago and sponsored by the Chicago Plan Commission. Inventories of housing facilities and business enterprises, health surveys, and tax studies also swelled the amount of information made available to local officials through the WPA.[15]

When spending tied to the PWA, WPA, and other New Deal programs tapered off in the late 1930s and priorities shifted toward defense spending, cities followed the outlet of federal largess. The role of defense spending in the growth and development of regions, especially the South and the West, and the cities within them has been well documented.[16] Cities and their business leaders aggressively lobbied for war-matériel plants, military bases, and other defense-related activities. With nearly a decade of experience in dealing with federal governmental agencies behind them, cities quickly shifted their efforts away from attempting to gain PWA- and WPA-type projects toward campaigns to ensure that their cities would benefit from the defense-related economic activities gearing up in the late 1930s. Even more clearly than programs of action pursued in the early and middle 1930s, campaigns initiated in the late 1930s and continuing into the war years concentrated on yet another crucial aspect of the whole planning picture: promoting economic development. Thus, rather than strengthening the physical infrastructure, the goal was to strengthen and expand the economic base. As the end of the war and its related spending approached, civic leaders reacted by planning for the postwar years.

The federal spending programs of the 1930s and early 1940s especially PWA, WPA, and defense, played roles that varied from those traditionally assigned them. While economic stimulation, job creation, and preparedness were indeed policy goals, at the local level these programs promoted other goals as well. They gave groups and individuals interested in city building, planning, and promotion a chance to act. The general pattern—seizing opportunities and following the flow of federal monies—marked the response of many cities, including Omaha.

Setting the Agenda: The Local Context, 1933–1940

Throughout the 1930s, Omaha's civic leaders, generally sharing the common bond of Chamber of Commerce membership or affiliation, pushed for participation in federal public-works programs. Despite a usually conservative image, civic and business leaders eagerly seized opportunities provided by the availability of federal funds. The enthusiasm slackened in the late 1930s but never disappeared, especially in relation to a number of highly favored projects. The drawing up of an informal and vaguely organized wish list of civic improvements resulted from all that planning activity. The list represented civic and business leaders' thinking about the planning needs of a modern Omaha. Further, the motivation behind support of such projects went beyond relief and recovery to include a healthy dose of civic boosterism.

The law that created the PWA was barely two months old when Omaha's congressman, Edward R. Burke, returned home to announce his support of eight local public-works projects. They included "the model housing plan, home renovizing [sic], utilities district extensions and improvements, Municipal university new buildings, the Farnam Street bridge, the South Omaha Bridge, Missouri River navigation and the Dodge Street widening project." Burke's statement emphasized the jobs that would be created, and the following month a petition endorsing the projects, signed by many business leaders, stressed unemployment relief.[17] As time passed, however, the emphasis on creation of jobs proved to be secondary to other long-term benefits.

An October 1933 editorial in the largest Omaha newspaper, the *World-Herald*, quite early suggested a multifaceted role for and perception of the public-works program of the NIRA:

> The public work act is, of course, primarily a recovery act. If there had been no economic emergency the act could not have been passed and the vast program of public works could not have been undertaken. Yet the physical results of the act may be far more important than the economic results. If projects now pending are carried to completion the midwest centering about Omaha, for example, may receive these permanent improvements:
>
> A canalized Missouri River, insuring a perpetual cheap freeway to the sea.
>
> Permanent cauterization of dangerous slum areas, and construction of long-wearing, low-cost residence areas.
>
> Wide, safe master highways leading into principal cities.
>
> Needed utilities extensions.
>
> Important new bridges and public conveniences of all sorts.
>
> These projects will furnish employment to thousands of wage earners during the coming winter, and that is important. But it is also highly important that they will afford economic relief, pleasure and security to the people for generations to come. The NRA [National Recovery Administration]

conceivably might fall, the depression persist and the entire economic system collapse, but the concrete highways, the steel bridges, the enslaved river, the new water power, would remain.[18]

Although perhaps guilty of hyperbole, the editorialist nonetheless recognized the broader opportunities afforded by federal public-works programs. Such acknowledgment of broader reasons for pursuing works funds became clearer and stronger over time.

As the timing of Burke's visit indicates, Omaha's civic and business leaders jumped on the public-works bandwagon early. Over the next few years through the Chamber of Commerce, its committees and affiliated groups, other civic forums, and individually, Omaha's leaders championed a large number of public-works projects. Gradually, a loose agenda emerged. Among the more important items were slum clearance (initially through public-housing construction), development of Carter Lake, highway and boulevard extensions and improvements, a new physical plant for the municipal university, sewer construction, park and recreation development, construction of civic buildings (auditorium, city hall, stadium, civic center), general beautification efforts, and provision of river terminal facilities.

Slum clearance appeared quite early on the civic agenda. Mayor Roy N. Towl announced housing projects as early as September 1933. An engineer by training, Towl was a Progressive Republican and entered city government as a member of Edward Smith's reformist administration (1918–21). It is not entirely clear why Towl championed slum clearance and public housing, but perhaps his engineering training made him amenable to city planning in general. Whatever the reasons behind his support, the housing proposals were known as "Mayor Towl's pet projects."[19]

Two statements Towl made in 1933 suggest that he was attracted to the public-housing program not only by possible humanitarian motives, but also by its inherent potential for furthering city planning in Omaha. In a September newspaper article announcing an invitation to federal officials to come to Omaha to study the housing problem, the mayor said, "I believe this may prove to be the beginning of interior city planning. . . . If details can be worked out, we hope to develop projects which will wipe out the near-in blighted areas and substitute model residential districts. I believe this movement will continue long after the NRA is over." The following month he addressed the Public Works Committee of the Chamber of Commerce, emphasizing that "his primary purpose was solving the problem of blighted areas." He suggested that the program would "help property values." It was not surprising for the mayor to make such statements to the chamber. Taken together, however, they suggested his desire to use the opportunity provided by the PWA to advance city planning.[20]

Two projects eventually were planned and constructed: Logan Fontenelle Homes in North Omaha (just a few blocks beyond the fringe of the downtown area) and Southside Terrace Homes in South Omaha (adjacent to the packinghouse district). The PWA's housing division allotted the money for the north-side project in 1935 and construction began in 1936; construction on the south-side project began two years later. In 1933, reportedly, even the Omaha Real Estate Board, traditionally a source of strong opposition, offered at least some support to the housing project.[21] By 1938, however, as the second project was under way, public housing rapidly lost any friends it may have had in the business community. In 1938 and again in 1939, the Chamber of Commerce, the primary organized voice of the business community, announced its opposition to public housing.

At least publicly, the chamber based its opposition on the costs the city would have to shoulder. In February 1938 its board of directors condemned the financing plan of the South Omaha housing project on the grounds that "the city of Omaha [was] required to pay ten per cent of the operating losses" and that it would result in the loss of tax revenue. Later that year the chamber's Municipal Affairs Committee voted not to support the project. By 1939 the chamber had accepted the projects as a *fait accompli* but strongly opposed further construction. It may have been more than coincidence that opposition coincided with announcement of "the largest individual residential building program ever attempted in Omaha," a $250,000 venture by the H. A. Wolf Company, to construct forty moderately priced homes ($5,250 to $7,000). Such an announcement also might have indicated recovery in home building, which, in the perception of the business community, might have been threatened by additional public-housing construction.[22]

Opposition to public housing was not necessarily opposition to slum clearance. That remained on the civic agenda, albeit divorced of its connection to public housing. The opposition to public housing that emerged in the late 1930s, however, did mark an early expression of a persistent hostility to that particular government program. In contrast, the civic leadership embraced more fervently a well-organized drive to take advantage of federal programs to develop Carter Lake Park as a recreational area.

The Carter Lake development experience was important on several levels. It was a primary example of the intensely private nature of city planning, a quality prominent in Omaha not only in the 1930s but generally throughout most of the period under study. Further, it provided an important example for private-sector action: the creation of a special legal entity to coordinate efforts and act on behalf of favored projects. And it provided experience in dealing with different governmental agencies at the local, state, and national levels.

In 1877 the Missouri River flooded and changed its channel. An oxbow lake was left behind, and a small piece of Iowa found itself on the Nebraska side of the river. The lake, a few miles northeast of downtown Omaha, became the site of various recreational activities, primarily boating and fishing, and Swift and Armour built ice plants on its shore.

In 1908 the lake and several hundred adjacent acres became part of Omaha's parks and recreation system. Mrs. Selena Carter Cornish donated funds that made possible the initial purchase of land. The park area was named Carter Lake in honor of Mrs. Cornish's deceased first husband, Levi Carter, owner of Carter White Lead Works in East Omaha. The Cornish family, although it had relocated in New York City, remained vitally interested in the development of the park well into the 1930s.[23]

During the late 1920s the Cornish family commissioned a landscape architect to draw up plans for the general improvement of the park. Nothing was done until 1934, when local supporters of the Cornish family's plans hit on the idea of taking advantage of a federal work-project program to transform the vision into reality. In that case it was not the PWA or the WPA that provided the opportunity, but the Civilian Conservation Corps. Created in 1933 and placed under the jurisdiction of the National Park Service, the CCC offered young men employment in soil conservation, reforestation, national-park development, and other less extensive conservation works. Organized into camps, CCC workers completed hundreds of projects, large and small, all over the country. In 1935, under the general sponsorship of the City Appearance Committee of the Chamber of Commerce, civic leaders banded together to form the Carter Lake Development Society, a nonprofit corporation to act as a clearinghouse and negotiator for those interested in developing the park.[24]

The Carter Lake Development Society was an invention born of necessity. In 1934 the City Appearance Committee discovered that because most of the park area was in Iowa, Nebraska relief workers could not make the improvements. This proved to be only the beginning of the jurisdictional complications. As it turned out, the project involved the city of Omaha, Nebraska, the village of Carter Lake, Iowa (developed on the small wedge of that state's territory left behind by the 1877 flood), several counties, and the states of Nebraska and Iowa. The nonprofit corporation's task was to cut through that jurisdictional maze and complete negotiations for the CCC camp with the National Park Service's Iowa district office. It had authority to act on behalf of all the jurisdictions involved in the improvement project.[25]

Because of lobbying by the Carter Lake Development Society, the CCC established a camp at the lake in 1935. It stationed two hundred men there and spent nearly one million dollars. WPA laborers also participated. The workers dredged the lake, removed a railroad trestle that crossed one end of it, constructed beaches and boat landings, and planted trees. The society's activities continued into the early 1940s, after which reports of its actions gradually disappeared from Chamber of Commerce records and publications.[26]

It is important to note that the private sector, through the Carter Lake Development Society, initiated and carried out the entire project. Mayor Towl did serve as a member of the society, but apparently that was the extent of the city's involvement.[27] The society was the first of a long line of private organizations formed, usually under sponsorship of the Chamber of Commerce, to promote civic projects in the absence or improbability of governmental action. For the business community it provided an important lesson, one of many during the 1930s, in negotiating with the different levels of government and with federal agencies.

Besides Carter Lake, the civic leadership eagerly embraced another early program: construction of a new physical plant for the Municipal University of Omaha. Negotiations were under way as early as 1933 and plans reached the final stage in 1936. One issue concerned whether the new buildings should be constructed on a downtown site or on the outskirts of the city. For reasons not recorded and evidently with little debate, the leadership decided in favor of a suburban location. The project had the one result of removing an important institution from the central city. More important, though, it was an early example of civic support for the expansion and improvement of higher education, support that grew over time.[28]

On a more practical and less glamorous note, the civic leadership also turned to federal works programs to make basic infrastructure improvements. In this general category were storm and sanitary sewer construction, and highway and boulevard extensions and improvements. Before the 1930s, such projects were strictly local matters, but when money from the federal government became available, the local government wasted no time in taking advantage of it. In this it generally enjoyed the support of the business community.

Street improvement appeared on lists of potential public works projects when those lists were drawn up. Although interest first centered narrowly on the widening of Dodge Street, Omaha's main thoroughfare, it rapidly broadened to encompass the general improvement of streets and boulevards throughout the city. The original lists did not include the construction of storm and sanitary sewers, but by 1935 such projects were on the civic agenda. Also narrowly focused at first—concentration being on the construction of the major Burt–Izard Street sewer—attention and support broadened quickly to include general extensions and repairs.[29] Neither street nor sewer construction created much public enthusiasm. Nonetheless, they enjoyed a fair measure of support. Moreover, not only did the projects mark the forging of a local-federal government partnership in an area previously strictly local, they were important for other reasons as well. They demonstrated the acknowledged infrastructure needs of the city and composed an important episode in the long campaign to improve the quality of streets and sewers. And the support for the projects hinted at boosterism.

The projects' importance to Omaha can be seen in municipal spending. Financial records from the era are scarce, but a newspaper account of how revenue from a special tax levy was divided among various projects clearly demonstrated the preeminence of basic street and sewer work. In 1938 the city enacted a one-mill tax levy to match funds provided by the WPA. Of the $216,000 collected, $150,000 was earmarked for streets and sewers. An earlier newspaper article suggested that a sewer project (a West Omaha intercepting sewer) was the chief reason for the the special levy. Although the work completed during the 1930s was significant, in no way did it satisfy the full needs of the city. The push for more and better streets and sewers continued into the postwar years.[30]

Civic boosterism gained from the street and sewer improvements. While perhaps not as glamorous as the Carter Lake Park or Municipal University of Omaha projects, the infrastructure improvements firmly supported the desire for further growth and development of the city. Reconstruction of the popular boulevard system, for example, figured high on the list of projects. Much of the work focused on major thoroughfares, thereby improving traffic circulation. Finally, one of the major sewer projects, because of its location, clearly aimed to increase outward growth from the city's older sections.

Omaha's parks and recreation system was as a source of civic pride from the 1890s, when the city, using a plan drawn up by noted landscape architect H. W. S. Cleveland, began construction. Although never totally completed, the plan linked a number of parks with boulevards and extended from the southwest to the northwest sections of the city. According to a report issued in 1942, the project to reconstruct the boulevard system garnered 40 percent of the revenue Omaha received from its wheel tax, a general levy on all motorized vehicles. The money helped finance WPA work that added thirty miles to the existing sixty-five and the resurfacing and beautification of the entire system. The report may have exaggerated the accomplishments, but it nonetheless suggested that such a beautification project, a staple of civic boosters, ranked relatively high on their list of priorities.[31]

More to the point, much of the street work focused on important thoroughfares. Major east-west streets (Dodge and Farnam) and several north-south routes (Tenth, Thirteenth, Twenty-second, and Twenty-fourth streets), all of which ran through or connected with the downtown, received special attention. In addition, Omaha looked beyond its own boundaries as the Chamber of Commerce supported street and highway projects to improve access to outlying areas of the city and to neighboring communities. One of the most extensive projects on the agenda was the proposed construction of a north-south superhighway through the city. All of these projects were intended to improve the traffic system. In the minds of civic boosters, improved access resulted in improved business.[32]

The construction of the West Omaha intercepting sewer was obviously intended to facilitate the outward growth of the city rather than meeting current needs. That motivation came to light in 1937 discussions of the plant. In the 1930s most of Omaha—its population and its built-up districts—lay east of Sixtieth Street. The West Omaha sewer, which ran along Seventy-Eighth Street, was designed to serve the less developed western area. In a city council meeting to discuss the project, one member rejected as impractical the idea of building a larger plant to serve the eastern half of the city instead of the West Omaha sewer despite his admission that, "[e]ventually, we will be forced to build a plant for the east half of Omaha."[33] The West Omaha sewer received priority while in all probability the need was greater in the older southeastern section of the city, where open sewers existed and packinghouses spewed untreated waste into the Missouri River.

Parks and recreation also received federal aid and plans for them were infused with a healthy component of civic boosterism. The program benefited from both a National Recreation Association study and WPA labor. The City Improvement Council, which grew out of the City Appearance Committee of the Chamber of Commerce, led the effort. Financed entirely by private-sector contributions, the council sponsored a National Recreation Association study of Omaha's parks and recreation system. The press favorably received the survey, published in August 1936. A *World-Herald* editorial suggested that it "might serve as the basis for an expanding life in Omaha, a happier, friendly, more useful life in the future." The detailed report may not have fulfilled that lofty goal, but it did give parks and recreation supporters a tremendous amount of information. It not only provided a useful description of existing facilities but also made suggestions for possible improvements. The information and suggestions guided the activities of parks and recreation supporters and provided a strong base for planning.[34]

Through the City Improvement Council, supporters lobbied for WPA recreation projects in the parks. Throughout the 1930s the city's recreation program depended completely on support from the WPA. Despite the lack of city financing, recreation ranked high as a civic interest. Through the City Improvement Council, Omaha created a recreation department in 1938. Thus both parks and recreation ranked high on the list of services civic leaders thought a modern city must provide.[35]

In the long run, however, perhaps the most significant outcome of the parks and recreation effort was the emergence of a persistent park lobby, which surfaced in many organizational forms over the years and persevered over several decades under the leadership of Mrs. Paul (Rachael) Gallagher, wife of an influential businessman. She began her campaign in the 1930s as a member of the City Improvement Council and remained a prominent and often powerful spokesperson for parks until her death in 1970.[36] Her work kept parks high on the planning agenda.

The examples of sewer construction, street and boulevard extension and improvement, and expansion of the parks and recreation system together suggest that basic infrastructure improvement commanded a prominent position on Omaha's general civic agenda. That was not necessarily a departure from past practices. Cities long provided for sewers, streets, and parks. However, the work did represent a demand for higher quality in the provision of those services. That heavy focus on infrastructure improvement, moreover, continued into the postwar period and helped shape much of Omaha's planning activity.

The projects discussed thus far largely have concerned Omaha in general. Three additional project categories focused more narrowly on the downtown and the riverfront. These included proposals for the construction of a civic buildings, a beautification program, and development of river terminal facilities. They shared with the others already described a characteristic city booster appeal. Further, they represented the thrust of the civic leaders' planning for the downtown and the riverfront, their perceptions of those areas and the solutions they accepted. To a great extent, the ideas for downtown and riverfront planning were formulated during the 1930s and continued to influence the agenda into the postwar years.

With the exception of a municipal stadium, downtown proved the location of choice for various public buildings proposed during the 1930s. A civic center, a new city hall, a new city auditorium, and a municipal stadium all found advocates. Though none was constructed in the 1930s, the lack of positive results did not mean the end of lobbying for them. Rather, such efforts persisted into the postwar years.

The advent of the PWA and WPA evidently inspired a number of individuals and groups to consider what type of large-scale public-building projects might be undertaken downtown. A civic center, city hall, and auditorium were the three most frequently mentioned possibilities. In fact, they could almost be thought of as a single project since one version of the envisioned civic-center complex contained both a city hall and an auditorium. Each project moved forward with individual momentum, however, and very quickly it became apparent that the auditorium had the most immediate support. In 1935 the Chamber of Commerce sponsored a city auditorium committee charged with bringing that project to fruition, and prominent Omahan W. O. Swanson launched a personal campaign on its behalf, declaring in a 1937 radio address that an auditorium was "one of the most urgent needs of Omaha." An adequate facility could provide space for—among other things—conventions. Conventions not only introduced out-of-town and out-of-state businessmen to the city but also brought additional customers into the downtown.[37]

While the auditorium project moved forward on its own, the idea of making it part of a larger civic center complex was not forgotten. Plans for the civic center remained alive and well and by 1940 had been expanded to include not only an auditorium and city hall but also, by virtue of the favored location for it, Joslyn Memorial Art Museum, the Knights of Columbus Club, and the Jewish Community Center. The Engineers Club, another group of Omahans with a professional interest in city planning, presented a proposal for a more extensive—almost ecumenical—civic center to the Chamber of Commerce and the City Improvement Council.[38]

Plans for a municipal stadium also enjoyed organized support. Advocates organized the Omaha Stadium Association to promote it, hoping that with the city providing the material WPA laborers could construct it. The effort managed to add a stadium to the civic agenda, but successful action had to wait. Only the plans for a new city hall seemed to reach a dead end in the 1930s. Statements made in 1938 by Dan Butler, Omaha's other Great Depression-era mayor, appeared to close the door on the possibility of building a new city hall. He renewed the city's application to the PWA for such a project but said he had no intention of advocating a bond issue, the only way Omaha could raise its share of the project's cost. Perhaps more telling, the chamber organized no group to promote a new city hall.[39]

With the exception of the stadium, the proposed civic buildings shared downtown locations and strong connections with a well-organized drive to beautify the downtown. The old City Beautiful movement (the name given to the turn-of-the-century civic improvement drive) may have been dead long before the 1930s, but old city beautifiers lived on. In Omaha, they enjoyed organizational life through the City Appearance Committee of the Chamber of Commerce and, to a certain extent, the City Improvement Council. Their activities suggested many of their ideas for the planning and improvement of downtown Omaha. Its center-place role was never questioned and none of the proposals suggested its diminishment. The primary need, according to the beautifiers, was a face-lift. Seemingly, they thought the downtown needed some cleaning up and clearing out, especially around its edges. Moreover, their activities reinforced certain negative public perceptions that were just beginning to be expressed in the 1930s. The downtown, probably with some justification by then, was seen as dirty, run down, and developing a heavily blighted fringe.

As organized, the City Appearance Committee dealt with four issues: improvements to main highways, park improvements, boulevard improvements, and the elimination of trash dumps along city streets and main roads. The following year, however, a subcommittee emerged to deal specifically with improving the downtown, and very soon thereafter it proposed a number of projects, including improvements in two small downtown parks (later dropped) and the landscaping of the courthouse lawn. The subcommittee also came out in favor of the proposed civic center. It hoped to find a way to use WPA labor on these projects.[40]

A subcommittee letter to the mayor in August 1935 outlined a more detailed program that included six projects. Once again, although all were possibilities for WPA labor, civic-boosting results, not the jobs they would create, seemed to be the primary reason behind them. The program suggested that unsightly downtown vacant lots be fenced and proposed construction of a scenic river drive. Then, to give visitors passing through the city a more pleasant view (hence a better image) of the city, the subcommittee advocated clearing out junkyards and tearing down dilapidated buildings. Interestingly, it largely abandoned downtown's Jefferson Square to the park's less-than-desirable clientele. It also backed away from elaborate plans for the improvement of Turner Park on the western fringe of the downtown. Thus, although some members of the original City Appearance Committee went on to be strong park advocates, others apparently considered downtown Omaha's two parks not worth saving. Finally, the program reiterated a desire to rid the downtown of buildings that had become eyesores.[41]

Those concerned with improving the downtown obviously saw it as run-down and needing a face-lift. A study prepared by the Bureau of Social Research at the Municipal University of Omaha in 1938 reinforced that image. With assistance from the WPA, T. Earl Sullenger produced "An Ecological Study of Omaha" that provided information on every district of the city for those interested in planning. If those arguing that downtown needed cleaning up wanted hard evidence to back up their claims, the report provided it. The adjectives "old," "dirty," "crowded," "run down," and "cluttered" permeated the pages describing downtown and its fringe. More evidence appeared in the minutes of a chamber board of directors meeting held in late 1938. During the session, held to discuss possible revision of the city's zoning ordinance, a letter from the Municipal Affairs Committee was read. It mentioned a "distinct twilight zone around the business district."[42]

In all of these discussions of the downtown there was as yet no sense of urgency. No one rose up to declare that the downtown was dying or in danger of imminent collapse. While not surprising, it shows that the effects of the automobile and decentralization on downtown Omaha had not yet been grasped fully. Planners and boosters still perceived the downtown as occupying center place, and apparently they assumed that it would continue to do so. All they really needed to do, therefore, was to clean it up, make it more attractive, and perhaps help meet both ends by adding a few public buildings. Combine that with improved access routes, and the downtown would be fine. Such lack of urgency and the assumption of a continued center-place role influenced downtown planning into the postwar years and retarded extensive action until the decline was well advanced.

The civic leadership did exhibit a sense of urgency, however, about the river, created not by crisis but by opportunity. During the 1930s the U.S. Army Corps of Engineers devised an extensive program to channelize the Missouri River, opening it to navigation. Almost immediately after the announcement of that project, Omaha business leaders began to promote a plan to take advantage of the opportunity. As early as 1933, through the Chamber of Commerce, a number of business leaders came out in favor of constructing river terminal facilities.[43] If barge traffic was going to be a significant economic activity on the Missouri River, Omaha was going to be a part of it.

Plans for the facilities moved forward and by early 1937 supporters were ready to take firm action. The first step recalled the Carter Lake Development Society precedent. In order to expedite the matter, the Chamber of Commerce, through its Waterways Committee, encouraged introduction in the state legislature of a bill to create a dock board. According to the bill, the three-member board was to serve without compensation, had no taxing power, but could petition for the issuance of revenue bonds. Most important, it would have authority to accept PWA funds to build terminal facilities. The reasons were clear. The chamber and the Waterways Committee wanted Omaha to "capitalize on the Missouri River improvement." Supporters believed "that a water route to the world's markets [would] reduce transportation costs for Omaha manufactured projects and for the agricultural products of the entire Midwest." Furthermore, Omaha's hometown railroad, the Union Pacific, supported the effort, thinking the facilities would enhance rail traffic as well (the grain and produce had to get to the river first).[44]

The legislation was passed and in 1938 the Dock Board requested three million dollars from the PWA to build "one of the finest river terminals in the country." The Omaha architectural firm of John Latenser and Sons drew up the plans (Latenser, coincidentally, also happened to be Nebraska's PWA director). The request was denied. Consequently, barge traffic opened on the river during the summer of 1939 without new dock facilities. Supporters were persistent, however, and in 1940 turned to the Reconstruction Finance Corporation (RFC) for a loan. That failing, they next turned to the WPA for assistance in building "a small initial Missouri River dock." Despite all their efforts, no dock was built, but their repeated attempts to find some way to accomplish their goal demonstrated that they were not about to give up. With channelization, the Missouri River was a highway and Omaha was going to have full access to it. River terminal facilities thus remained a priority on the civic agenda.[45]

Apparently, not everyone thought of the river merely as a highway. The announced channelization inspired thoughts of its use as a recreational resource. However, these ideas were not translated into extensive action, yet neither did they fade. Rather, they remained as an alternate view of the river that gradually became more popular. Two early ideas were the most prominent: boating and the construction of a scenic river drive. Boaters took to the river in the late 1930s with little fanfare. A 1939 newspaper article described pleasure boaters and suggested the growing popularity of such activity.[46]

Pleasure boating did not attract anywhere near the attention given the construction of a scenic river drive. The idea was not only an old one, it threatened the proposed river terminal. Citizens' groups proposed one in 1915 and the 1919 city planning report called for its construction along the entire length of Omaha's riverfront. Two sections of the proposed route, one in the southern part of the city and the other in the north, were completed in the 1920s. By 1935 the chamber's City Appearance Committee suggested that the two sections be joined by a road running along the eastern edge of the downtown. John Latenser immediately opposed the idea, feeling it would interfere with the proposed dock facilities (he drafted plans for terminal facilities three years later). And although a 1938 article in one of the smaller local papers rhapsodized about Omaha's reclaiming the river and its beautiful views, the idea of the river as a commercial highway remained dominant. Further, the lack of sewer expansion and modernization in the eastern and southern sections of Omaha suggested willingness to continue using the river as a sewer, which may help to explain its apparently limited use for recreation.[47]

Setting the Agenda: The Local Context, 1940–1945

All of the energy expended on behalf of public-works projects found an alternate outlet in the late 1930s as national spending priorities shifted from public works and job creation to defense. In tandem, local promotional priorities shifted from a concentration on PWA and WPA projects to garnering defense plums: bases, plants, and airfields. The Omaha area had two relatively small military bases, Fort Omaha in the northern part of the city and Fort Crook just south of the city near the small community of Bellevue. The chamber's Military Affairs Committee lobbied on behalf of PWA-defense projects at the bases in 1935,[48] but the idea of developing them did not receive intense support until 1939–40. After that, in rhythm with national policy, civic energies focused on defense. Even more clearly than in the case of public works, city boosterism underlay much of the effort. The public-works projects proposed in the 1930s were not forgotten; like everything else, they simply took a backseat to the all-out war effort. What remained was a determination that Omaha would gain from federal spending.

In August 1940, the Chamber of Commerce outlined its defense program for the state. It included plans to bring an aeronautical research laboratory to Omaha along with munitions plants, warehouses, and general war contracts; it called for airport improvements, an airplane plant, and a pilot training center; it sought expansion of Fort Crook, a new armory, officer and vocational training program centers, and help in the construction of housing for all of the people who undoubtedly would be drawn to Omaha as a consequence.[49]

Material published the following month made even more obvious the potential for growth and development through defense spending. In the September 1940 issue of the chamber's *Journal* was an advertisement promoting Omaha as the ideal location for defense industries. A map of the United States highlighted Omaha's location 1,130 miles from the East Coast and 1,460 miles from the West Coast. Nestled in the nation's heartland, Omaha was "safe for national defense industries." The same issue contained a lengthy article, "How to Get Defense Orders," and announced that the chamber was raising ten thousand dollars to support a lobbyist in Washington, D.C., John Latenser. He was in Washington to make sure that Omaha and Nebraska received their fair share of defense projects.[50]

Omaha got at least one giant defense plum: the ten-million-dollar Glenn L. Martin bomber plant at Fort Crook, construction of which was announced in December 1940. The plant required "between two and three hundred acres and . . . a main building three blocks long and two blocks wide" and promised employment to thousands. Its construction raised the issue of how to install roads and build housing for its employees. In its determination to solve that problem, the city of Omaha clearly demonstrated its desire to expand and benefit from the national defense program.

Frequently in the 1940s, as today, Omaha was cited as the site of both the Martin bomber plant and Fort Crook, as well as Offutt Air Force Base and the Strategic Air Command headquarters, located there in the late 1940s. The fact is, all of these were, and are, not in Omaha or Douglas County, but near Bellevue in neighboring Sarpy County. However, Omaha, by far the more dominant of the two communities, considered the defense installations and military outposts as very much within its sphere of influence if not its corporate limits. Consequently, when the question arose over which governmental agency—Omaha, Bellevue, or Sarpy County—would zone and hence have a measure of control over the plant location and the area that would contain all of the new housing, Omaha asserted its territorial rights. The jurisdictional disputes between Omaha and Sarpy County involved even the most trivial matters to include such things as which vice squad would "clean up" the area. More to the point, the Omaha Planning Commission announced its intention to lobby for expanded authority. Under state law, the city's zoning authority extended three miles beyond its corporate limits. The commission proposed legislative bills extending the radius to five miles. The fact that Omaha would be reaching beyond its city limits and across county lines complicated the matter. Both Bellevue and Sarpy County vigorously opposed such expansion. In the end the state assumed authority for zoning the defense plant site.[52] Omaha may have lost that round, but it clearly demonstrated a keen desire to take advantage of an opportunity to extend its boundaries and influence.

A Common Theme: The Drive for City Planning

A very crucial thread connected the campaigns to garner public-works projects during the 1930s and defense-related activities in the early 1940s. Running as a slow but steady current through both was the desire to integrate the various projects into a cohesive city planning program. The call for planning was issued in 1937 and repeated several times during the next six years. It culminated when, only three years after it began to concentrate on defense spending, the Chamber of Commerce began to worry about what would happen when the spending stopped. Subsequent discussions revealed many Omaha planning characteristics. The private sector independently did most of the work through the chamber, leaving the city and its official planning commission a minimal role at best. Nor did the civic leaders call in outside experts; they preferred to do any planning themselves at less cost. City planning was intimately linked with civic boosterism. The civic leadership viewed the end result of planning not only as the completed projects but also as the promotion of Omaha to the rest of the country. Planning issues often came down to a struggle between those who felt the city could and should risk going into debt to finance projects and those who preferred a pay-as-you-go method of financing. (The pay-as-you-go proponents won in the late 1930s, and frequently thereafter, explaining why more public works were not constructed.) Although the role of the city and the planners in its employ expanded over time, in general the characteristics mentioned above described most planning activity in the postwar years and well into the early 1970s.

In 1937 Mayor Dan Butler, somewhat out of character and probably much to his regret, made the "rather casual suggestion that Omaha public officials and civic leaders ought to get together and decide what should be done in the city in the next few years."[53] After that initial proposal by a public official, the initiative shifted completely to the private sector. A flurry of activity followed, directed by the Chamber of Commerce. The chamber first asked its members to suggest Omaha's most pressing needs. The letters received in reply produced a rather eclectic collection of proposals ranging from modest schemes to clean up the city and plans for sponsoring rodeos to a major effort to bring in factories.[54]

The chamber issued a full-scale development scheme in October 1937. Announced in a speech by President W. D. Lane, it contained fourteen major points, including these: new industries and payrolls, more conventions, "a more extensive publicity and advertising campaign for Omaha, both at home and abroad," a "good will" campaign aimed at neighboring communities, completion of the toll-free bridge over the Missouri River at Dodge Street, "aggressive promotion of meritorious public works, including particularly the Missouri River channel, Carter Lake development, airport improvement, good roads, post-office and streets," further development of the state's agricultural industry, city beautification, public health and safety, rate equality for Omaha's shippers, wholesale and retail trade extension, "clean, economical government and legislation favorable to business development," encouragement of civic leadership, individual enterprise, and the city's educational and cultural institutions.[55] Clearly, in the mind, chamber's planning and promotion went hand in hand.

The beginning of agitation for planning was also the beginning of debate on whether the city should increase its bonded indebtedness or adopt a pay-as-you-go finance plan. Once the mayor's statement set the planning wheels in motion, supporters of planning in general divided into two camps. One advocated more city spending, believing the city should issue bonds to match WPA and PWA funds and undertake many of the proposed projects. The other felt the city should be cautious and dovetail its public-works program with a scheme to pay off city debt; it opposed bond issues. Beneath the financing debate was the issue of whether Omaha should promote itself through infrastructure improvements—better streets, sewers, public buildings—or as a debt-free city. During the 1930s the state of Nebraska promoted itself as "the White Spot of the Nation," clean of any taint of sales tax or a state debt. In resolving the financing issue, the civic leadership apparently followed the state's lead. Again and again in the newspapers and in Chamber of Commerce publications, the promotion of Omaha as "a debt-free city in the debt-free state" was favored. Thus a special relief tax was levied in 1938, but no bonds were issued for PWA or WPA projects. Such fiscal conservatism remained characteristic of both public officials and the civic leadership.[56]

The chamber did take one step toward transforming the developmental scheme outlined by its president into a comprehensive city plan. In mid-1938 it invited planning expert Harland Bartholomew to visit. Bartholomew served as the city's planning consultant in 1918–19 and directed the publication of "City Planning Needs of Omaha," a report issued in late 1919. He was consulted periodically thereafter. Several months after his Omaha speech in 1938 and after consultation with the chamber, Bartholomew offered to conduct a planning survey and from it develop a revised zoning ordinance and a master plan. His asking price was thirty thousand dollars. The chamber's board of directors endorsed his hiring and especially the proposed revision of the zoning ordinance. The city, however, was willing to spend only twenty-five hundred dollars and used the money to hire Rodney Gibson, an engineer, to work with the Omaha Planning Board in January 1940. The chamber and the Planning Board (composed of the city building inspector and four citizens holding Chamber of Commerce memberships: Edwin W. Bedford, L. J. TePoel, George T. Morton, and the ubiquitous John Latenser), seemingly accepted the decision not to hire Bartholomew. In fact, Latenser said "that in his judgement Omaha was not ready for an expert planner to be brought in." From the time of that initial decision not to bring in an outside expert until well into the 1960s, civic leaders preferred to do all planning themselves, with only minimal outside technical assistance.[57]

The advent of World War II pushed planning initiatives into the background, but only temporarily. The city took its one and only planning initiative when it published *1942: Manual of Civic Improvements Sponsored by the Mayor and City Council of Omaha*. That thin document was not a plan, but a series of reports on the progress Omaha had made during the past decade in recreation, parks, boulevards, airport improvements, general public improvements, police and safety, and the Fire Department. Again the private sector put the planning wheels into motion. In January 1943 the Chamber of Commerce launched "a post-war problem offensive" to study reconversion and outline "a broad public works improvement program for after the war years." The two efforts were conducted under the sponsorship of an umbrella postwar planning committee, yet they moved forward separately.[58]

The members of the Postwar Planning Committee concerned with reconversion and promoting the future industrial development of Omaha began work immediately after the committee's first meeting in July 1943. The committee raised money to determine the best way to promote industrial development, and the Chamber of Commerce hired William J. Moll, a national expert on reconversion, to conduct a study. It also contracted with William D. Weidlein, a Minneapolis consulting engineer whose research concentrated specifically on industrial expansion. The chamber then commissioned a report by Leo M. Christiansen, a chemurgic researcher at the University of Nebraska. The three men came up with all kinds of ideas for new industries: linseed oil, corn byproducts, soybeans, leather, coal processing, plastics, synthetic fuels, alcohol. Little positive action followed, however, and the reasons are not clear. The chamber did show tremendous interest in one developmental area, the Army Corps of Engineers plan for Missouri River improvement. In September 1943 chamber representatives attended a conference at which they heard Colonel Lewis Andrew Pick outline his visionary scheme for flood control in the Missouri River Basin. The chamber formally endorsed the plan in March 1944.[59]

Efforts to develop a plan for postwar public-works improvements began in July 1943. As it had done in 1938, the chamber used a statement by Mayor Dan Butler as a springboard for action. A report by the chamber's general manager that Omaha was behind the West Coast in postwar planning provided more push. In response, the Postwar Planning Committee conducted "a survey of potential post-war public works" and issued its initial report in October, declaring that no progress had been made, no plans were in the works, and no method of financing projects had been developed. It further suggested that Omaha act immediately to prepare a city plan.[60]

Following up on that suggestion, the chamber announced a fund-raising campaign under the leadership of Russell J. Hopley, president of Northwestern Bell Telephone Company, in November 1943. The goal was to raise fifty thousand dollars over the next two years to support planning activity. Concurrently, the chamber sponsored a joint chamber–Omaha Planning Commission–City Improvement Council–civic group effort to develop a master plan. One member group, the City Improvement Council, briefly discussed bringing in an outside expert, but the idea was rejected as it decided to move forward without expert assistance. However, the chamber did receive an offer of free technical advice from the Omaha Engineers Club.[61]

During 1944 the chamber and Creighton University cosponsored a series of seminars on postwar planning. Creighton, a private Jesuit university, was on the northwest fringe of downtown Omaha. Because of its location and its desire to grow, Creighton became intensely interested in plans for the downtown and its fringe. The seminars were the beginning of the university's involvement with city planning and covered a broad range of topics, offering yet another opportunity for study and discussion.[62]

The reports, meetings, conferences, and resolutions of 1943 and 1944 served to fix the idea of planning firmly in the public mind. They were the preliminaries to appointment of the Mayor's City-Wide Planning Committee in 1945. It was the beginning of Omaha's initial large-scale postwar planning campaign.

Conclusion

The activities carried out between 1933 and 1945 taught civic and business leaders many important lessons. They gained valuable experience in dealing with governmental agencies and forged the first tentative links with a new partner, the federal government. They found innovative methods through which to advance their goals in the Carter Lake Development Society and the Dock Board. They were inspired to give considerable thought to deciding what it was their city needed in order to be modern and up to date, what it needed to continue to compete effectively with other cities. And they formulated ideas about their city that, while not fully integrated, were sufficiently developed to begin implementation when the opportunity presented itself.

In many ways, therefore, the planning committee appointed in 1945 had at least a twelve-year history. It was the result of planning efforts dating back to 1933 rather than the beginning of a fresh venture. Because it was the product of what had come before, it was shaped by the characteristics of that which had preceded it. In its composition, its links to civic boosterism, its proposals, and its perceptions of Omaha's needs, it was very much a product of its past. Omaha thus entered the postwar phase of its planning activity with perceptions of its needs generally and those of the downtown and riverfront specifically, which were formulated in an earlier time under different circumstances. The general emphasis fell on basic infrastructure improvements. The downtown was the center of the city and, with a face-lift to help it, would remain so. The river was Omaha's highway to the world and its sewer of last resort. These perceptions were set firmly in the public mind. Even though Omaha entered a period of relatively rapid change after 1945, these perceptions remained dominant for many years.

FOUR

Traditional Planning for
a Traditional City,
1945–1958

The first postwar planning period, 1945 to 1958, witnessed the development and promotion of two major city plans. In 1946 a mayor's committee issued a voluminous planning document known generally as the Blue Book. A second plan, known as the Omaha Plan, appeared in 1957. The relatively low-cost Blue Book ideas won voter approval, while the more controversial and expensive Omaha Plan proposals went down to defeat. Despite the quite different responses from voters, the two shared many basic similarities. The projects proposed in both reflected the standing informal planning agenda and a strong emphasis on basic infrastructure improvements. Both were the product of private-sector planning initiatives and were part and parcel of a persistent booster mind-set.

Closely related to the planning activity were several campaigns to modify and modernize Omaha's system of municipal government. The Blue Book plan proposed several special commissions, and an effort to install the city-manager form of government followed it closely. The Omaha Plan was developed concurrently with the adoption of a new city charter, which provided for a strong-mayor form of government and the professionalization of much of Omaha's administrative structure, including the hiring of a professionally trained planner. The charter changed the form of city government, yet it did not immediately increase city hall's influence. It did, however, provide a framework within which city government could grow in expertise.

There were other important developments in the postwar period. After a devastating flood in 1952, some businessmen who were concerned about the city's future established the Omaha Industrial Foundation, a nonprofit organization chartered to buy, develop, and sell potential industrial sites in the southwest suburbs. The suburbanization of industry and population helped to foster a metropolitan vision of the city. The early 1950s also brought the first expression of concern for the downtown. Several civic organizations declared their determination that the downtown would maintain its position as the center of the city. Similarly, others were concerned that the river also maintain its traditional role. Perhaps most important, however, the 1950s marked the emergence of the service sector as an important component of the Omaha economy. Yet the traditional image of the city remained in place.

During the 1950s as well, older Omaha, particularly the southeastern section of the city, felt the challenge of suburbanization and of the dreams of urban renewers and highway engineers. Already losing population, blue-collar neighborhoods then faced urban renewers who wanted to remake and highway engineers who wanted to tear down their part of Omaha. Those who were threatened formed the core of resistance that defeated the Omaha Plan in 1958. Thereafter they fought many of the initiatives of those who represented the new Omaha that was emerging by the end of the 1950s. The conflict between old Omaha and new continued to influence city politics into the early 1960s.

Step One: The Blue Book Plan

Omaha entered the postwar period with more than a decade of rather intense planning activity behind it. The 1930s and the early 1940s produced an informal agenda that, for a variety of reasons, failed to come to fruition. The city, especially its business leaders, was anxious to move forward after the stagnation of the Great Depression years. Even while the war still raged, civic and business leaders made plans for an improved peacetime Omaha. During the last summer of the war, Mayor Charles Leeman announced appointment of the Mayor's City-Wide Planning Committee, charged with developing a city plan. Work began in earnest in

August 1945. The city received its first look at the results in March 1946 when the committee released its thick collection of recommendations. The report's cover gave it its popular nickname, the Blue Book.

The Chamber of Commerce had launched a "post-war problem offensive" in January 1943. The drive tackled the issues of reconversion and civic improvements. The economic-development planning failed to attract sustained enthusiasm. In fact, the only program for which the chamber showed much support was the ambitious U.S. Army Corp of Engineers Pick-Sloan Plan for Missouri River Basin flood control and development. Spring flooding was a perennial headache that significantly diminished the industrial-use value of riverfront property, so any plan promising a flood-controlled Missouri was welcomed. The civic-improvement side of the offensive received the most sustained and enthusiastic attention. Committees were formed, seminars held, and money raised on behalf of the project. These activities created a very favorable climate for extensive civic improvement planning.[1]

In late 1943 the chamber's postwar Public Works Committee, the City Improvement Council (an affiliated group), and the Omaha Planning Commission began laying the groundwork for a master improvement plan. The Omaha Planning Commission enjoyed influence at that time. During most of its existence the appointed citizen commission worked without much of a professional staff. Briefly during the early 1940s, however, Rodney Gibson, a trained engineer-planner, worked for it. In a familiar pattern, he worked very closely with the chamber group, reporting to it as well as to his official employers. In November 1943 he appeared before the chamber's Postwar Planning Committee and announced that the Planning Commission had approved the idea of developing a master plan. He further stated that the plan should be worked out in cooperation with the chamber and the City Improvement Council. The next month, the Planning Commission authorized Gibson to begin a "Population Survey," designed to serve as "Part One" of a master plan.[2]

The Planning Commission's annual report, issued in January 1944, indicated the low level of planning activity. The commission held only thirteen formal meetings in 1943 during which only ten acts of official business were conducted: five rezoning proposals, three subdivision-plat proposals, and two street-vacation proposals. The report emphasized the close relationship among the city, the chamber, universities, and public utilities in making Omaha bigger and better. Discussing progress of the population survey, it noted that the "Chamber of Commerce, Creighton University, Omaha University, Northwestern Bell Telephone Company, Metropolitan Utilities District, and the Nebraska Power Company [were] cooperating in this study." All of these entities naturally were interested in promoting the growth of Omaha because in large measure their own growth depended on the growth of the metropolitan area, so their interest in planning continued throughout the postwar period. And the report suggested, not surprisingly, a link with the Real Estate Board. The board's interests at that time were somewhat more limited than the chamber's. A proposed revision of Omaha's zoning ordinance captured most of the attention.[3]

The report concluded with a tentative outline of a master plan in sections: "Population," "Economic Base of Omaha," "Land Use Plan," "Traffic, Transit and Transportation," "Parks, Recreation and School Plan," "Public Buildings and Properties," and "Comprehensive Master Plan for Omaha and Adjoining Territory." The outline was fairly standard, although it had one interesting aspect: it listed under "Parks, Recreation and School Plan" an item on riverfront development. That represented one of the few quiet urgings during the early postwar years for a use of Omaha's riverfront for something besides strictly utilitarian transportation and waste-disposal purposes. The evidence suggested that work on the plan proceeded only with difficulty. Eight months after the outline was announced, John Latenser, still a very active member of the Planning Commission, told the City Improvement Council that because of a very limited staff the work on the various studies was proceeding quite slowly.[4]

A plan based on the outline did come out in 1945. The evidence suggested, however, that it was never formally adopted. At least it never received the public recognition afforded the private-sector planning that also began in 1945. Moreover, even though the planning seminars cosponsored by the chamber and Creighton University covered many of the topics in the master-plan outline, limited projects, rather than comprehensive planning, clearly aroused the most enthusiasm.[5]

Capturing most of the attention was an improvement scheme for the northwest section of the downtown: Fifteenth Street to Twenty-Fourth Street and Farnam Street to Burt Street. The area already contained or bordered on Joslyn Museum, Central High School and Creighton University. In September 1944, Gibson proposed to turn that area, considered "one of the worst blighted districts" in Omaha, into a civic center.[6] The plan called for public buildings (post office, auditorium) and apartments in the area, plus a mall or parkway along Twenty-Fourth Street (first proposed by the City Improvement Council in 1936). The area was more or less the same one suggested as a possible site for a civic center in the 1930s. Gibson's proposal appealed to friends of Omaha's most prominent cultural institution and to Creighton University, whose administration had ambitious plans for postwar expansion. Rather than any master plan, the civic center idea seemed to capture the most attention.

To transform the area, however, the city needed authority to take advantage of federal funds for slum clearance. The Omaha Housing Authority did not have sufficient powers to act on such a scale, and there was strong aversion to any project that might involve public housing. In 1945 the Chamber of Commerce encouraged introduction of a legislative bill enabling the Housing Authority to act, but its connection with public housing raised the hackles of the real-estate lobby and caused the bill's withdrawal.[7] The project remained alive despite the legislative defeat; supporters simply had to find an alternate method of financing.

Construction of a municipal stadium was also part of the city's informal agenda. Unlike the civic center backers, stadium supporters succeeded in achieving their goal in 1945. The private Municipal Sports Stadium Committee managed to get a bond issue on the April 1945 ballot providing for $480,000 to construct a stadium at Thirteenth Street and Deer Park Boulevard in southeast Omaha. The bond issue won overwhelming support, more than three to one,[8] and catapulted John Rosenblatt, the committee's chairman, into prominence. It was his debut as a popular political leader.

The overwhelming success of the stadium bond issue encouraged those who wanted extensive and expensive civic improvements. Perhaps the traditionally fiscally conservative city was ready to loosen its purse strings; certainly those involved in planning and boosting activities were eager to see some positive results. Cities all over the country were planning improvements, yet the Omaha's Planning Commission had once again demonstrated it was not up to the task. In the summer of 1945, *World-Herald* Publisher Henry Doorly mounted a successful campaign to create the Mayor's City-Wide Planning Committee. Mayor Charles Leeman followed Doorly's lead and in July agreed to such a committee under the chairmanship of Russell J. Hopley, president of Northwestern Bell Telephone Company. Within a month the Mayor's Committee, as it came to be called, was ready to act.[9]

Mayor's Committee was a misnomer. Neither the mayor nor the city council had much to do with it. Similar to Pittsburgh's Allegheny Conference, although on a vastly different scale, the City-Wide Planning Committee was a private-sector group; the Chamber of Commerce provided most of its funds. The committee's membership list read like a who's who of Omaha civic and business leaders. Nearly every significant local business, industry, and institution was represented. The 168-member committee was drawn from and clearly reflected the interests of that sector of the population most interested in promoting the growth and development of the city. Unlike the Pittsburgh example, Omaha had no David Lawrence in the mayor's office to match the leadership provided by the private sector. Leeman's election was a complete surprise, and he was never able to develop a popular following. Also unlike the Pittsburgh group, the committee was scheduled to disband once it had completed its task.[10]

The general committee divided into seventeen project committees, each charged with investigating and reporting on specific parts of the overall scheme. The tasks undertaken by the smaller groups clearly reflected the plan's connection with the preceding decade or so of planning activity. Many of the subcommittees took up items on the informal city planning agenda; in that way, the planning of 1945–46 grew out of a sequence of planning actions reaching back to at least 1933. Projects received attention from these committees: Auditorium; Civic Center and City Hall; Library; Municipal Garage–Police and Fire Stations; Public Market Facilities; Grade-Crossing Elimination and Viaduct; Parking (Downtown and Suburban); Sanitation; Streets, Boulevards and Traffic Control Signals; Street

Lighting; Airports and Air Transportation; Bus Transportation Facilities and Armory; Housing and Slum Elimination; Parks, Playgrounds and Recreation; River-Rail Terminal and River Transportation. The Correlating and Finance Committee and the two-man Labor Advisory Committee rounded out the list.[11]

Very few of the projects were new. Parking had not been much of an issue before 1945, and the armory question arose only after discussions on what to do with the old auditorium once the new one was built. Many projects had specific plans drawn up long before the committee was born. The parks and recreation committee drew on the 1936 National Recreation Association study and a 1945 update of it by City Planning Director Gibson.[12] The civic center and city hall committee had the 1945 plans with which to work. Latenser's plan for a dock facility, drawn in the late 1930s, was still around, and the auditorium, airports, and streets and boulevards committees could all look at plans developed during the 1930s. Nearly all of the projects had had at least some measure of public notice before their inclusion on the Mayor's Committee's list.

The fact that there were plans or at least well-developed ideas for the projects before the committees were appointed could explain two aspects of the process. First, it could explain how a collection of businessmen and businesswomen with minimal staff support could produce a two-hundred-page plan in approximately four and one-half months (the project committees met, investigated and completed their reports between August 21, 1945, and January 1, 1946).[13] Second, it could explain why the projects, or at least most of them, were so readily popular. Most of them had been promoted, often vigorously, for the better part of a decade. The public was familiar with them and long had heard arguments in their favor.

Financing stood as the major obstacle between the planning process and concrete results. The vote on the stadium demonstrated that the people of Omaha were willing to incur more bonded indebtedness to enjoy a civic improvement. Members of the Mayor's Committee realized that the public's generosity had limits, though. They needed to find a way to finance the projects with bonds without significantly increasing city debt and, most important, without raising taxes. In doing so they were thinking not just of the general public; boosters frequently used low taxes to attract business and industry. Remarkably, the Correlating and Finance Committee, working from January 2 to March 1, 1946, achieved both goals.

The committee accomplished the feat in two ways. First, it asked the various project committees to divide their plans into three categories: urgent, necessary, and desirable. The total recommended expenditure for all three categories of projects was $43,847,983. The Finance Committee concentrated on the urgent projects, discarded the desirable and necessary from consideration, and came up with a total necessary sum of $14,638,723. By spacing out the bonds and their retirement over a fifteen-year period (the last scheduled to be retired in 1961), the committee calculated that the urgent projects could be completed and the city remain financially sound without new taxes. The report assumed several improbable facts, including the notion that the city would issue few other bonds throughout the entire period.[14] Nonetheless, it proved quite attractive to fiscally conservative Omaha.

The full Blue Book was then trimmed back to include only those projects considered urgent. The urgency reflected the priorities of the civic and business community and the fact that Omaha needed some basic infrastructure improvements. In fact, most of the urgent projects involved work on the infrastructure: streets, fire stations, parks, and sanitation. Obviously, when civic and business leaders thought about planning for a better city, they focused on infrastructure matters, on projects that would make the city more efficient. Two of the three largest categories of spending, each commanding more than three million dollars, were (1) streets, boulevards, and traffic-control signals and (2) sanitation. The boosting element was even clearer in the third, the auditorium, which required three million dollars.[15] Auditoriums may not make a city more efficient, but they do attract the all-important convention trade.

The lack of spending on another of the Blue Book projects also spoke much of the thinking of those involved. The Housing and Slum Elimination Committee conducted surveys of two areas considered blighted: the northside district (Sixteenth Street to Thirtieth Street and Cuming Street to Bedford Avenue), which contained the Logan Fonentelle Homes public-housing project, and an area in South Omaha (between M and Q streets and

Twenty-Fifth Street "to the railroad tracks," roughly Twenty-Seventh and Twenty-Eighth streets), a wedge of housing between the South Omaha business district and Union Stockyards. It found these areas in very poor physical condition—old, overcrowded buildings, lack of services—and urged the use of condemnation, tax foreclosures, revised zoning and perhaps a new building code to clean up and rehabilitate the areas. It did not call for slum clearance. Slum clearance meant public housing, and the opposition to public housing in Omaha, especially in the real-estate community, was clear by the late 1930s. Real estate men, builders, architects, and mortgage lenders dominated the committee. Significantly, among its members was the influential Theodore H. Maenner, a real-estate developer and strong vocal critic of public housing. Unlike other cities, time and time again Omaha rejected any use of either urban-renewal or urban-redevelopment money, largely because of the link, real or imagined, to public housing.[16]

The Blue Book plan obviously differed greatly from the master plan developed by the Omaha Planning Commission. The Blue Book was a collection of discrete plans for specific projects that had very concrete and tangible results: sewers, streets, buildings. The committee argued that the plan was citywide in scope and each part was dependent on the other. In reality, many, if not most, of the projects could be undertaken independently. The auditorium could be built without new sewers, even, conceivably, without a new civic center. Streets could be well lighted without eliminating grade crossings. And a river port could be built while adding no parks. The earlier Planning Commission plan had a number of concrete proposals within it, specifically for streets, parks, and public buildings. On the other hand, it also dealt with somewhat more abstract and intangible subjects, such as population characteristics, land-use patterns, the economic base, and growth patterns. One could point to a new park or a new building and demonstrate a result of planning activity. It was a bit more difficult to put one's finger on a population characteristic or a land-use pattern. Also, the commission plan included items dealing with the Omaha metropolitan area, not just the incorporated city. All of the Blue Book plans, with the possible exception of the sanitation proposals, dealt with projects within the corporate limits of the city. The Planning Commission thus exhibited a wider view of Omaha than that of the Mayor's Committee.

More than a decade passed before the private sector became truly comfortable with a metropolitan view of Omaha. The differences between the plans also suggested a difference in definition. When the civic and business community thought "plan," it thought in terms of projects with concrete, verifiable results. Professional planners saw their work in a more abstract light.

Both visions of the nature of the planning process held in common a booster theme: a desire to promote growth and development of the city. The booster element was readily apparent in both the text of the widely distributed Blue Book and in the series of newspaper articles published between March 23 and April 8, 1946, on its behalf. The articles highlighted the advantages of all proposals, not just the urgent ones on which the Finance Committee decided to concentrate. (Perhaps in publicizing all the plans, supporters hoped to lay the groundwork for support of action on those proposals put aside in the initial go-round.) Over and over again the need for the projects to push Omaha forward received emphasis.

The booster theme was the most explicit in discussions of the auditorium and civic center. Two arguments ran through the report on the auditorium: the need to build it to promote growth and the need to keep up with developments in other cities. The Auditorium Committee stated plainly that "if Omaha is to progress and grow as a metropolitan city, proper facilities must be made available." It repeated that general sentiment several times, such as when it argued that "the City as a whole will benefit as a result of the sums of money spent by the people who are attracted to Omaha to see the various events." The report's concluding paragraph stated it even more clearly: "Without a new auditorium and proper facilities, Omaha will continue to slip from its proper place with cities of this type as a meeting place for conventions, and as a place where exhibitions and cultural gatherings can be held." The committee further urged action because the "[m]any other cities, during the past few years, have built new auditoriums while Omaha sat on the sidelines and did nothing." It then listed some of the cities that had built or were building auditoriums.[17]

The Civic Center and City Hall Committee echoed the sentiments of the auditorium supporters. In reply to the question "Should Omaha have a civic center?" the committee stated that "if Omaha is to progress, and become a city that will attract more people and more business, and also be a better place in which the present citizens are to live, ... we should plan such a center as an 'urgent' project." The project also offered a general face-lift to an area of the downtown long considered blighted. The committee admitted that goal when it stated: "In this area are many old homes, apartment houses and business buildings and there is also quite some vacant property and in our opinion, there is no section of the City which needs a complete cleaning up more than this area." The need for the general clearance of a large area was perhaps the project's downfall. Omaha's voters seemed particularly reluctant to approve any project that would tear down built-up areas. The civic center plan in no way called for participation in national slum-clearance and housing programs. In the popular mind, however, clearance and public housing oftentimes were linked.[18]

The Airport Committee echoed the "keeping up with the Joneses" side of the booster argument. The newspaper article written on behalf of the proposal declared: "From Podunk to New York communities are trying to provide themselves with adequate facilities for aerial transportation."[19] Omaha could not match New York, but at the very least it had to keep up with Podunk. Also, as more businessmen flew, an adequate airport emerged as a business necessity.

As for a new library, it was considered necessary, not urgent. Almost the entire argument on its behalf, however, was framed in terms of the need for Omaha to increase its level of library services to match those offered by other cities. The committee did recommend that the city increase the library budget.[20]

The Parks, Playgrounds and Recreation Committee had perhaps the most impassioned argument. In fact, it all but declared that the future of the city depended on adequate parks and recreational facilities. Led by long-time park champion Rachael Gallagher, the committee said: "We have no way of measuring the cost of mental and moral disintegration in our City because of our complacency in letting our parks, playgrounds and recreational programs deteriorate. It is probably best that we can't. Let's not continue down the road of self-destruction further. Let's resolve to discharge our proper moral obligation from this point on."[21] How could a city possibly grow while mentally and morally disintegrating and acting self-destructively? More to the point, the park and boulevard system long had been a source of civic pride and received frequent mention in booster material.

Somewhat more practical were the arguments for sewer improvements. The Sanitation Committee recommended eighty-seven projects at an estimated cost of $14,783,400—by far the largest spending recommendation turned in by any of the committees. The Finance Committee trimmed the recommendations down to the thirty-six it considered most urgent, costing an estimated $3,053,600. Eliminating the open sewer in the South Omaha stockyards district ranked as the most urgent project. Interestingly, the committee called the open sewer first an eyesore, then a menace to public health. The sewer was also seen as a hindrance to industrial development. Quoting Harry B. Coffee, president of Union Stockyards Company, the committee reported: "If this open sewer can be eliminated soon, I [Coffee] know of two industrial plants that could be located in this area because of proximity to the stockyards and railroad connections."[22]

The Missouri River and riverfront received attention from both the Sanitation and the River-Rail Terminal and River Transportation committees. The Sanitation Committee report acknowledged that untreated sewage was being dumped into the Missouri River. Correction of that problem was listed only as "desirable." The report further admitted that only congressional action outlawing such dumping would bring local action. A more commercial frame of mind shaped the committee's other recommendations. It reported that cities along the Missouri were preparing to take advantage of the increased barge traffic soon to flow after river basin improvement. Omaha must take advantage of the burgeoning river trade as well.[23]

Clearly, boosterism underpinned the arguments for the Blue Book plan. The ultimate goal of all those projects was to further the growth and development of Omaha, and the nature of the proposals suggested a continued concentration on infrastructure improvements as the path to growth. Efficiency in the form of a solid infrastructure was a city's best argument on its own behalf. Apparently, the general public also shared that opinion. In November 1946 it voted on seventeen bond issues to finance the urgent projects; eleven were approved, six turned down. Approved were bonds for arterial highways, fire stations, police equipment, the aviation field, the river port and terminal, sewers, the auditorium, fire equipment, grade-crossing elimination, and parks. Rejected were an improved public market, parking lots (downtown and suburban), a new police headquarters, a new municipal garage, and the civic center.[24]

The vote on the Blue Book plans also involved approval of the creation of five commissions to supervise spending of the bond money. The commissions, appointed by mayor and city council, would ensure that the money raised was spent in the exact manner for which it was intended. Evidently the civic and business leadership had little faith in city hall's ability—or, perhaps, the traditionally inactive government's desire—to see the Blue Book plans through to completion. The idea of creating citizen-staffed commissions to supervise certain municipal activities was not new. Rachael Gallagher had long argued for an independent park board. The commissions dealt with parks, the airport, the auditorium, and sanitation. They were intended to be permanent parts of city government, continuing their authority over their municipal functions even after the bond money had been spent. The fifth commission, for improvements, was to be a temporary oversight body. It would make sure that the bond money for the aforementioned and other projects was spent according to the plan. Once the bond money ran out, the commission would disband. The five commissions were approved by the voters in the general election.[25]

Supporters of the commissions called their idea "a sweeping experiment in Omaha City Government."[26] The need for special expertise was an oft-cited argument on their behalf, and—perhaps in contradiction with that first argument—the commissions would be staffed by private citizens. Presumably, those citizens most interested in the various projects would be appointed. In that way, the private sector could keep a very close eye on the projects it favored and have expanded authority to act for them.

Another justification lay at the core of the matter. According to an editorial published in March 1946, city hall had serious fiscal troubles. In fact, the editorial referred to the "impoverished City Government."[27] The state legislature put a ceiling of 7.2 mills on the level of taxes Omaha could levy. Add to that an outdated and effficient assessment system and the city could not raise enough money to cover rising costs. The situation reached crisis proportion that year.

Police and firemen had been promised a raise in 1946. Early on in the year, however, the city found that it did not have the funds to cover the expense and canceled the pay hike. Not surprisingly, that action caused controversy. In late 1946 a court ordered the city to reinstate the increase. It could not. The business community was then forced to do something that reflected both its devotion to privatism and the weakness of city hall. Led by Robert Storz, it raised from private sources the $160,000 necessary to cover the cost of the raise.[28] That was hardly a tremendous sum of money, but the fact that city hall could not raise it spoke volumes about its weakness. The fact that the business community could and did come to the rescue clearly illustrated its far more powerful position and its adherence to privatism. Further, the private sector put its planning priorities ahead of city hall's needs. The same March 1946 editorial carefully separated the bonds from city hall's general money troubles and argued that one should not affect the other. The crisis did, however, push the Chamber of Commerce to sponsor a drive to improve Omaha's financial situation by modernizing the assessment and collection system.

All five commissions went to work but soon proved less of a method to expedite completion of the plans and more of an administrative headache. The commissions, especially Parks and Sanitation, had overlapping and conflicting authority with the city government. Their existence only fragmented and confused the situation further. In 1952, Mayor Glenn Cunningham led a fight to abolish the commissions.[29] The attempt failed, but the campaign brought to light many of the shortcomings of the commission system.

The Blue Book commissions were not the only governmental innovation to face opposition in the early 1950s. Frustration with the commission form of government was widespread by the late 1940s. At least as it worked in Omaha, the system was very weak and ineffective, especially in the position of mayor, which was largely honorary in nature. Seven commissioners were elected and decided among themselves who would be mayor. The position had no independent executive authority. The desire for a clear central authority and the efficiency it was supposed to bring led the civic and business community to propose that Omaha adopt the city-manager form of government.

The first postwar mention of the city-manager plan occurred in 1947. In October of that year the board of directors of the Omaha Manufacturers Association announced its resolve to see the city adopt that form of government. The campaign did not begin in earnest, however, until late 1949 and early 1950. The *Omaha World-Herald* backed the idea enthusiastically. In April 1950 a group of civic leaders organized to put the issue on the November ballot and popularize the plan. As with the argument for the Blue Book plan, supporters took up a booster theme. At the core of the issue was modernization of city government. A speaker brought into the city by advocates of the reform assured Omahans that "[t]he city manager plan is offered Omaha not as a reform movement, but 'as we would advocate trading in a 1912 automobile for a new model.'" The commission form was outdated and inefficient. The manager plan would give Omaha the strong executive leadership a modern city needed.[30]

Proponents of the city-manager plan encountered deep and immovable opposition led by Mayor Cunningham. Cunningham, a surprise choice for mayor by the commissioners elected in 1948, replaced Charles Leeman, who was defeated in the election although he was strongly backed by the *World-Herald*. Cunningham was never able to gain the support of the newspaper nor, apparently, of the business community. He did, however, have a strong political base in his native South Omaha, remarkable for the fact Cunningham was a Republican and South Omaha was heavily ethnic and Democratic. It was to working-class South Omaha and others suspicious of the attempt to alter city hall so radically that Cunningham addressed himself. He acknowledged the necessity of some type of reform, probably because of his frustration in attempting to exercise authority. He went on radio and declared that the mayor had to have authority but also had to be accountable to the people. That meant he had to be elected. A hired manager was not democratic because he was not accountable to citizens. In the early days of the Cold War, such an argument found an audience. In November the city-manager plan went down to defeat by a two-to-one margin. The overwhelming rejection of a civic and business community–sponsored idea foreshadowed the same type of old Omaha versus new Omaha political split that blossomed in the late 1950s and early 1960s.[31] The defeat of the city-manager plan and the subsequent challenge to the Blue Book commissions might have signaled an ebbing of the planning and reform momentum begun in 1946. In 1952, however, there occurred a crisis that helped put into motion the second wave of planning and reform. In the spring of that year, Omaha experienced its worst flooding in nearly a century.

The Flood of 1952 and the Omaha Industrial Foundation

Omaha had been flooded before, sometimes seriously. Almost every spring brought at least some lowland flooding. Thirty-six miles of levees and a mile-long flood wall along the industrial section of the riverfront protected the city against a flood crest of 26.5 feet. That figure represented the most flooding possible after completion of the Pick-Sloan series of dams, but in 1952, completion of the dams was more than two years away. In April of that year the Missouri River went on a rampage and at its highest crested at 30.2 feet. Only the dedicated efforts of thousands of volunteers, desperately sandbagging and otherwise building up and reinforcing the levees, saved the city's riverfront and held damage to a minimum. Most of the damage occurred in the low-lying areas of neighboring Council Bluffs, Iowa, which, despite its name, was built largely on a floodplain.[32] The flooding pushed Omaha businessmen into action. Omaha needed a lot more to recover from the flood than a receding of the waters. Omaha was a disaster area and its available industrial land along the riverfront tainted with the label "flood area." If the city was going to shake off the effects of the flood and move forward, the civic and business community needed to act.

The flood came at the same time Omaha's business leaders began to organize to promote industrial development. The Program of Work Committee of the Chamber of Commerce raised the issue in 1951. Investigation by the chamber's Industrial Department found a scarcity of available industrial sites within the city. The Work Committee declared that the chamber must make the solution of that problem a top priority. In doing so the chamber found support from the newspaper and from two young Omaha businessmen, Robert Storz, president of Storz Brewery, and Wray M. Scott, president-treasurer of Wray M. Scott Company, a plumbing supply firm. In typical fashion under the leadership of Storz and Scott, the civic and business leadership formed a committee to deal with the situation, known as the Committee of '52.[33]

The committee hired an industrial management firm to survey the situation. Cresap, McCormick and Paget recommended that the committee sponsor creation of a nonprofit organization chartered to develop industrial sites. In the meantime, the flood made the available riverfront sites highly unattractive and turned a difficult situation into a crisis. The flood did, however, galvanize the business community and it responded by establishing the Omaha Industrial Foundation, or OIF. Chartered as a nonprofit agency, the OIF had as its major task the purchase, development, and sale of industrial properties. It acted as a discreet real-estate agent for firms—those already in Omaha and those moving into the city—considering relocation. The OIF raised its initial capital from a bank loan and a private subscription campaign that netted nearly a million dollars.[34]

Its first client was Continental Can. Storz, a brewer and thus large customer of the firm, persuaded Continental to locate a new plant in Omaha. The first site available, however, was on the recently flooded riverfront. Storz told the company to come to Omaha, pick a new site, and he promised that the OIF would prepare it. The company chose a forty-acre site on South Seventy-Second Street along the Union Pacific right-of-way, at that time on the southwest edge of town. The OIF bought those 40 acres and 320 additional acres of farmland and prepared the entire site for industrial development. The action had several consequences. Continental Can located in Omaha, and Omaha's industries, factories and warehouses, both old and new, found a new home on the city's outskirts far from their traditional inner-city locations. The OIF eventually purchased 1,700 acres in five industrial districts stretching from Sixty-Eighth Street to 144th Street along the railroad right-of-way. It also facilitated the sale of two other suburban tracts, one on North Seventy-Second Street to Sperry-Vicker, a farm-implement manufacturing firm, and the other to Western

Electric at what became 120th Street and I Street, at that time near the small farming community of Millard. The latter plant opened in 1958 and employed seven thousand workers.[35]

As suggested, the OIF's activities facilitated the decentralization of industry in the city. Traditionally, industries either hugged the riverfront or grew alongside well-developed in-city railroad lines, but after the early 1950s they sought the spacious suburbs. Companies attracted to Omaha by the OIF helped diversify the industrial base, and the success of the OIF wedded a large segment of the business community to industrial development. Even as the service sector grew to surpass the industrial sector, people tied to the OIF continued to see industrial growth as the city's rightful priority. And an emphasis on industrial development meant continued emphasis on traditional booster themes of efficiency and quality infrastructure.[36]

The vigorous efforts on behalf of industrial development were coincident with renewed efforts to push forward with government reform and city planning. A. V. Sorensen, civic leader and owner of Midwest Equipment Company, and Mayor John Rosenblatt led a campaign to hold a city-charter convention. The Chamber of Commerce, the Improvement Commission, and the Omaha Planning Commission convinced those seeking government reform that it must be accompanied by renewed planning. The mid-1950s thus saw adoption of a home-rule charter providing for a strong-mayor form of government and the appointment of a second mayor's committee on city planning.

Home Rule and the Omaha Plan: Charting a Course toward the New Omaha

The campaign for the city-manager plan in 1950 and the vote on abolishing the Blue Book commissions in 1952, though unsuccessful, reflected growing frustration with the existing form of municipal government. Mayor Glenn Cunningham had opposed the city-manager plan but went on record in support of reform. His successor, John Rosenblatt, elected in 1954, also became frustrated by the weaknesses of the commission system. One year after Rosenblatt became mayor, the Chamber of Commerce chose A. V.

Sorensen as its new president. Sorensen launched a campaign called 'Let's Sell Omaha.'[37] As the most vigorous booster effort in years, it aimed to convince Omahans and prospective Omahans that theirs was a city on the move. Rosenblatt and Sorensen united to support programs that would move Omaha forward. The spirit of their partnership was manifested in two major thrusts: a city-charter convention and the appointment of a citywide planning committee.

The Nebraska constitution allowed cities of the metropolitan class, such as Omaha, to hold conventions and adopt home-rule charters. Omaha had last held such a convention in 1922. It revised the city charter but did not adopt home rule. The state legislature continued to retain a great deal of authority over the city, especially in tax matters. The weakness of the commission form of government, in addition to the desire to escape such close scrutiny by the state, led to the call for a charter convention in 1955. The election was held in 1956, and fifteen people were chosen to serve. Of that group of mostly prominent men and women, A. V. Sorensen emerged as the clear leader. The convention wrote a new home-rule charter that received voter approval in an election later that year.[38]

In 1961 Rene Beauchesne, a political scientist at Creighton University analyzed the nature and effects of the home-rule charter.[39] His analysis pointed to several important features. Those who drafted the charter wished to establish a stronger executive and a more professional administrative staff. They also wanted to attract better-quality candidates for elected offices—more educated, financially independent. They did so, however, at the political cost of pitting lower-income working-class eastern Omaha against higher-income white-collar western Omaha. From the late 1950s and well into the 1960s, the two sides were fairly balanced and the split between them defined much of the nature of local politics throughout that period.

The convention drafted a charter adopting the strong-mayor form of government, hoping to give Omaha strong executive leadership. Under the old charter the elected commissioners acted as department heads; the 1956 charter permitted the mayor to appoint professionally qualified candidates. The appointments did not need the approval of the city council, although it could remove department heads for cause. The position of the mayor vis-à-vis the council was even clearer on the issue of salaries. Under the old charter, each commissioner received $4,500 per year and the commissioner serving as mayor received an additional $500 per year. The new charter awarded the mayor a minimum salary of $17,500 per year and reduced council members' salaries to $3,000. A city council position was considered part time and the lower salaries, it was argued, offset the expense of the higher salaries paid the mayor and department heads.[40]

The salary discrepancies spoke more directly to the charter framers' desire to attract "better men" to local government. The low council salary, it was hoped, would discourage all but financially independent and "public spirited" candidates. The Beauchesne study analyzed the success of that policy. It examined the candidates and winners in the 1954, 1957, and 1961 city elections and in the 1956 charter convention and concluded that the charter framers elected in 1956 were far more educated and drawn more from managerial and professional ranks than those who normally participated in city politics. Over time, those elected to the city council began to resemble the charter framers in their educational and employment profile. Council candidates and winners did not duplicate the same degree of educational achievement and professional, managerial employment exhibited by the charter framers, but the movement toward that type of individual profile in candidates was clear.[41]

The charter revision also spawned two electoral coalitions. An anticharter coalition formed in the older eastern and southern sections of the city, areas of low-value, owner-occupied dwellings. It included both ethnic South Omaha and the predominantly black "near north side" (roughly Sixteenth to Thirtieth streets and Cuming Street to Bedford Avenue). A procharter coalition formed in the newer, high-value, owner-occupied residential sections in the western part of the city. With some modification, this situation persisted and influenced the 1961 mayoral election, in which blacks turned away to support the coalition that favored the charter.[42] The coalitions that appeared after the 1956 charter revision were significant in Omaha elections, but in many ways the split between them also represented a split between the old Omaha and the new. It helped defeat the Omaha Plan in 1958 and persisted into the 1960s.

Very closely related to charter revision was the second private-sector planning initiative of the postwar period. The two efforts actually over-lapped in at least one area. An important part of the new charter was the section that set up a planning department headed by a professional planner. The planning director also served as a member of the mayor's executive cabinet. The charter retained a citizen-staffed planning board, but its func-tion became even more advisory. General policy would be developed by the planning director and his professional staff,[43] a marked change from the past. The status accorded the planning director gave Omaha's planners more influence, but full recognition was not accorded overnight. The ability of city planners and city hall to influence the private sector increased gradually over time.

City hall and the planning director took an important step toward full recognition during the development of the Omaha Plan. The provisions of the new charter required the city to develop six-year capital-improvement plans that outlined proposed city spending on public works over the specified years. The purpose was to help the city budget capital improve-ments and determine whether adjustments were needed in taxes or bonded indebtedness. Accordingly, in 1957 the Rosenblatt administration devel-oped an eighty-two-million-dollar capital-improvement plan known as the Cabinet Plan. Supporters of the Omaha Plan determined that much of what they wanted in the way of infrastructure improvements meshed well with the recommendations in the Cabinet Plan. City hall and private-sector planners coordinated their programs and the final form of many of the proposed 1958 Omaha Plan bond issues represented a blending of the two. City hall proved able to assert its right to give direction to capital improve-ments, but it was still far from able to take fully independent action.[44]

In the 1950s planning was still very much a private sector activity. As early as 1954 the Chamber of Commerce came out in favor of a new planning initiative to revise and update the Blue Book. In mid-1955, Mayor John Rosenblatt turned to the chamber and from those of its members most actively interested in planning chose a new citywide plan-ning committee. At first glance the new body might seem merely a mirror image of the committee of 1945–46. From the beginning, however, the 1955–56 version was different, and in more than just personnel. The name given to it, Mayor's City-Wide Planning and Development Committee, suggested a difference. The new committee was interested in far more than updating the public-works program established by the Blue Book. It formally included among its recommendations an item on land use and fundamental planning. It greatly desired that the city adopt planning policies that would promote growth. Public works were only one side of the equation. Infrastructure improvements remained at the core of the planning activity, yet the committee also realized the necessity of more than just tangible public works. It must also address the issue of orderly development. Thus it advocated creation of a professionally staffed and adequately financed city planning department that would develop, as part of a master plan, those policies necessary to the promotion of orderly growth and development. In 1946 the private sector did not recognize a need for a development policy as a complement to the public works policy. By 1956 it had begun to see more clearly the other side of planning, the side reflecting a city planner's definition of planning.[45]

The 1956 committee also represented the emergence of a limited progrowth coalition. As described by John Mollenkopf, Herbert Molotch, and Carl Abbott, among others, a progrowth coalition was primarily an alliance of local politicians, corporate leaders, downtown real-estate interests, representatives of the construction industries, local institutions (hospitals, universities), and other local civic leaders. In northeastern cities, especially, such coalitions also involved the mobilization of labor and ethnic groups as a voting base. Progrowth advocates shared a metropolitan vision of their cities, and the coalitions, enticed by the possibilities offered by federal urban-renewal and redevelopment programs, came together after World War II and by and large orchestrated urban growth policies and practices in cities throughout the country through the early 1970s. Cities as different as Pittsburgh, San Francisco, New Haven, Chicago, Atlanta, San Antonio (Texas), and Portland (Oregon) all had such coalitions.[46]

Omaha had many of the elements necessary for a progrowth alliance. The heads of many of the larger local corporations were involved in planning and supported growth initiatives; groups were organized to promote downtown interests; representatives of the construction industries, Kiewit and Daly, were highly influential leaders; hospitals and universities supported growth policies and, when able, provided leaders and expertise. In

Omaha, however, the alliance operated on a very limited scale. The coalition of business and government represented by the Omaha Plan committee, led by Mayor John Rosenblatt and A. V. Sorensen did set a progrowth tone, but their success in establishing a strong, enduring alliance and obtaining results was very limited. City hall's weakness proved to be a major factor.

City government, as noted, was quite limited in power and fragmented in structure during the early postwar years. The new charter corrected many of the problems, but in the late 1950s a stronger city hall in practice was still many years away. Both the form of government and personal factors contributed to that situation. Charles Leeman came into office as a dark horse, was never very popular, and served only one term. Glenn Cunningham, though very popular in South Omaha, never gained the trust or support of the wider business community. Only John Rosenblatt had potential. He was very popular personally and worked well with the business and civic leadership, of which he was a member (he headed a very successful dairy firm). As the last mayor under the old system and the first under the new, he succeeded in easing the transition from one form to the other, and his political skill helped to establish the new firmly. He was a very visible booster of the Omaha Plan, frequently speaking on its behalf. He did not, however, direct the work of the planning committee, so in that way the committee was, like its 1945 predecessor, a mayor's committee in name only. His support of the plan did not translate into a vote for it. He was far enough removed from the planning initiative that its defeat was not a personal one. His work with the Omaha Plan, though limited, did demonstrate a potential for further leadership development, yet he never fulfilled it because illness ended political career. Rosenblatt left office in 1961, succeeded by antiplan leader James Dworak, a circumstance that further reduced the possibility of a strong progrowth coalition.[47] A progrowth booster theme underlay planning activity, but did not support a strong, enduring civic-political alliance.

Both the Blue Book and the Omaha Plan initiatives promoted growth, but the vision of the earlier planners was limited. The Blue Bookers still thought largely of Omaha proper, the city as defined by its corporate boundaries, rather than a metropolitan Omaha. The 1956 committee, in common with progrowth coalitions, had a far broader vision of Omaha and its place in a metropolitan area. That new, broader vision emerged clearly in the annexation issue. In the late 1940s and early 1950s, the civic and business community had a rather ambiguous attitude toward annexation. In 1952, two members of the city planning staff, Francis Green and Joe Mangiamele, appeared before the Municipal Affairs Committee of the Chamber of Commerce to advocate a program of growth through annexation, pointing out that most growth in the Omaha area occurred outside the city limits. Annexation became a serious issue the next year when the city proposed to annex an area known as East Omaha (near the municipal airport) and a tremendously large affluent area just west of the city limits (roughly between Seventy-Second and Nintieth streets and Blondo and Center streets). The scheme was very ambitious. The Municipal Affairs Committee supported it at first but rescinded the endorsement when it became clear that many chamber members opposed it. Many undoubtedly lived in the affluent western area and wished to continue living free of city taxes. The city backed down.[48]

Between that early defeat and the late 1950s, the Chamber of Commerce changed its thinking on annexation. How the change came about is not clear in the documents available. The city did annex territory in the 1950s, though at a level far more modest than that endorsed in its 1953 package. City planners continued to appear before the chamber to argue for annexations. In 1956, the chamber's new Urban Development and Planning committee favored a master plan to direct city growth and development in addition to the Omaha Plan then being proposed. One year later, the new city planning director, Alden Aust, announced an annexation program "which would provide for the annexation of small areas at regular intervals rather than large areas at infrequent intervals." Though not universally supported, the program had enough chamber support to make it successful. It directed Omaha's growth through annexation for the next decade and a half.[49]

Another indication of a more metropolitan view of Omaha was a 1952 intercity committee "for the consideration of problems of the Omaha metropolitan region." The Omaha and Council Bluffs chambers jointly sponsored it. The committee met and discussed issues of mutual interest to Omaha and Council Bluffs. Not tremendously active or very influential, it proved a far less hearty endorser of the metropolitan idea than supporters of annexation. It did demonstrate, however, that at least some members of the chamber were thinking of planning that transcended Omaha's corporate limits.[50]

The charter-revision campaign and the appointment of the planning committee were coincident with the launching of a very vigorous booster campaign known as Let's Sell Omaha. It was followed the next year by Let's Build Omaha and then by Let's Go and Grow. The strength and vigor of the campaigns suggested the strengthened progrowth attitude of the Chamber of Commerce. After three years of steadily promoting the growth and development of Omaha and its surrounding area, the effort peaked in 1958. In that year the chamber, directed by the keynote address of President-elect Fred Curtis, formally adopted the "area concept" as part of its philosophy:

> Omaha is the center of a metropolitan area comprising three counties and including several cities and incorporated villages. The problems relating to this metropolitan area are multiplying as communities grow and relationships become closer. The Chamber will therefore exercise its efforts to bring the communities of this area closer in spirit as well as in fact, will aid in the solution of common problems and will assist wherever possible in the resolution of difficulties experienced in the growth and progress of our neighboring cities.[51]

Adoption of this policy, acceptance of the annexation program, and support given to other city growth and development policies were important turning points in thinking about Omaha. Leaders thought of it as far more than the area within its corporate limits; they saw it as a metropolitan area and thought it must assert its claim to its proper place as the center and guiding force of that larger area.

In other ways, the Mayor's City-Wide Planning and Development Committee was remarkably similar to its predecessor. It had a slightly stronger connection with city hall but was in no way led by the mayor. Almost an exclusively private-sector endeavor, it fell very much within the familiar pattern of private-sector action. Most of its committees took up exactly the same issues tackled by the Blue Book, but the priorities assigned various projects differed somewhat, the most remarkable example being the high priority given urban renewal. As has been suggested, the plan exhibited a more metropolitan vision of the city, and its booster value received much emphasis.

As did that of the Blue Book committee before it, the 1956 committee's membership list was a who's who of Omaha leadership. Once again the president of the Northwestern Bell Telephone Company, a position then held by A. F. Jacobson, acted as the general chairman. The organization of the committee, however, was more complex than that of its predecessor. A special planning committee, advisory committee, steering and coordinating committee, and administrative assistants committee directed and coordinated the various project committees. The Special Planning Committee consisted primarily of top business executives from leading Omaha firms. The Advisory Committee consisted of second-level businessmen (up-and-comers) and public officials (chairman of the county board, two city commissioners, the superintendent of schools, and the city attorney). The Steering and Coordinating Committee drew its membership from the leading members of the Special Planning Committee. The most interesting group was the Administrative Assistants Committee. The Blue Book planners operated with very little staff support, but the Omaha Plan people had not only an administrative assistant but a staff of architects, public-relations officers, artists, writers, designers, and engineers. The staff came from two sources, Northwestern Bell Telephone Company and Leo A. Daly Company, suggesting these firms' close connection with city planning. The Minneapolis city planning director also served on the committee in an advisory capacity. His presence was a step away from the previous position of the civic and business community that it could do the planning without outside experts.[52]

The Omaha Plan committee also availed itself of other sources of not-so-outside expertise by calling on local universities and utilities to provide research assistance as they had for the Blue Book planners. Northwestern Bell was especially active in this regard. Its personnel served on the Administrative Assistants Committee. Northwestern Bell experts also compiled statistics on population growth, telephone use, retail sales, wholesaling, manufacturing, automobile registration and employment. The Omaha

Public Power District (OPPD)—Omaha's electric company—and the Metropolitan Utilities District (MUD)—the gas and water company (both public corporations)—provided statistics on, naturally, electricity, gas and water consumption. The two large universities and the Omaha Board of Education supplied the necessary information education. Further, the presidents of Creighton University and the University of Omaha acted as cochairmen of the bond-issue campaign. Carl Reinert of Creighton and Milo Bail of the University of Omaha were committed to the goals of the Omaha Plan. They were widely respected, and other supporters of the plan hoped their reputation would prove influential.[53]

For the most part, the project committees took up the same issues covered in the Blue Book. They included Air Terminals; Area Redevelopment; Armory; Civic Center and City Hall; Finance; Municipal Garage, Fire and Police Stations; Parking; Parks and Recreation Facilities; River-Rail Terminal and Transportation; Sanitation; Street Lighting; and Streets, Boulevards, Arterial Highways and Traffic Control.[54] Their existence indicated several factors in the planning process. First, the informal planning agenda set in the 1930s and 1940s continued to exert influence in 1956. Projects envisioned earlier under different circumstances still had strong supporters, which suggested a very human reason for the lag between change and policies based on the changed circumstances. Once a project becomes popular and gathers support, unless something happens to stop them, supporters will continue to push for it until they get it. People become identified with certain projects and their egos and reputations become intertwined with it. It is difficult to let go of something once one has invested time and energy. Changes may make a project out of date or inappropriate, but its supporters see their goals, not the changes, and thus continue to support a program long after the ideal time for its implementation has passed.

Boosterism again figured in the arguments for committee proposals, just as it had a decade earlier with the Blue Book plans. For example, supporters argued that the Omaha Plan was needed to show the outside world that Omaha was a progressive, modern, forward-thinking city. Omaha needed it to show businesses that here was an efficient, well-located, and convenient city in which to build a factory. Other cities were moving ahead, building new highways and airports, improving their streets and sewage systems. If Omaha was to keep up, it, too, had to work on its infrastructure, make it sound and up to date. Clearly, planning and promotion continued to be closely intertwined.[55]

The similarity of the 1946 and 1956 projects indicated the persistence of emphasis on infrastructure improvement. Such items continued to make up the bulk of proposed planning projects. The committees could also draw upon past plans and ideas, including those in the Blue Book. The committees common to both initiatives represented the degree to which, as the chamber had first envisioned it, the "Omaha Plan" was a revision and update of the Blue Book. Three other committees new to the process represented the emergence of concerns grown important under the conditions of postwar change: Business District and Building Improvement, Land Use and Fundamental Planning, and Public Educational and Cultural Facilities.

The Business District and Building Improvement Committee was one of the first acknowledgments that downtown had serious problems. Previous plans, both formal and informal, hinted at a concern for the downtown, but indirectly. Those plans involved a face-lift but never mentioned the downtown specifically as the target of planning concern. By 1956 the concern was apparent and focused. The recommendations suggested what the committee felt should be done and reflected its opinion of the downtown's role.

An early concern for the downtown's future was manifested in 1954 when a group of downtown merchants and businessmen organized the Omaha Downtown Parking Association. Fitting well the privatist mold, the nonprofit corporation had as its long-range goal the development of forty-five hundred additional parking spaces downtown. It called the parking situation "one of Omaha's most critical problems" and repeated this sentiment in 1957 when association President Louis Somberg described parking as the "number one problem." The association continued to purchase land for parking and to push for city action well into the 1960s. Concurrently, the downtown traffic system came under scrutiny. In 1954 the city adopted one-way streets to improve traffic flow, feeling it would alleviate congestion.[56]

Those twin concerns—parking and improved traffic flow and access—

were seized upon as the answers to downtown's problems by a large segment of the business community. They were at the core of recommendations suggested by the Downtown Omaha Association, a private-sector group formed in 1955 to promote the interests of the downtown area.[57] The idea of what was needed to address these concerns expanded over time. For example, the traffic solution expanded from one-way streets to the Interstate Highway System. Parking and improved access remained central in the thinking about downtown needs, however. Various Omaha Plan committees, including those on parking; on streets, boulevards, arterial highways and traffic control; and on business district and building improvement, took up both subjects.

Additional Business District and Building Improvement committee recommendations reflected other ideas for solving downtown's problems. Besides traffic control and parking, the committee proposed a pedestrian oasis, private redevelopment, an effective city planning department, and a public-relations program. Several cities had built pedestrian malls or squares; Omaha simply followed their example. It also followed the example of Kansas City, Missouri, which enacted ordinances encouraging private redevelopment. The Kansas City program involved a tax break for those willing to acquire land for redevelopment, not the use of federal redevelopment or renewal funds, which came with so many strings attached. The committee also urged creation of an effective planning department with adequate authority to prevent further erosion of the downtown and control growth at the fringe. It labeled that suggestion urgent. All the others were listed as merely necessary or desirable, diminishing their chances for implementation. The new city charter met the urgent recommendation, but the other recommendations received no further action. In that way, the committee's top-priority work was done almost as soon as it got started. The situation also indicated that perhaps concern for the downtown did not run very deep. Finally, to overcome downtown's poor image and promote plans for it, the committee suggested that the new planning department direct a public-relations campaign on behalf of the downtown.[58]

The committee's report gave voice to the prevailing idea of downtown's role. Obviously it still saw the downtown as Omaha's vital core, the same role it had played in the past and must continue to play in the future. In the words of the committee, "the business district of an urban community is comparable to the heart in the human body. From it flows the very life blood which stimulates and reinforces the continued growth and prosperity of our entire urban area. Without the business district, there could not be any worthwhile substantial urban development."[59] Clearly, the committee considered a strong downtown business district vital to Omaha's growth and development.

As the downtown was at the core of the city, so was retailing at the core of the downtown. Shopping was one of the primary activities that brought people downtown. Opulent department stores and specialty shops acted as magnets to draw people toward the city's center. By 1958 it was clear that downtown retailers were losing shoppers. Between 1948 and 1958 the percentage of retail sales declined steadily in relation to city sales and SMSA sales. In 1948, 39.6 percent of all city sales and 31.9 percent of all SMSA sales were made in the central business district. By 1958 the central business district accounted for only 28 percent of city sales and 22.4 percent of SMSA sales. In absolute figures, sales in the central business district, or CBD, increased 13.8 percent between 1948 and 1954, compared with a 27.5 percent sales increase in the city and a 27.7 percent increase in the SMSA. Excluding the CBD, sales in the city rose 36.5 percent and in the SMSA by 34.2 percent. An absolute decline in CBD sales set in between 1954 and 1958, when sales declined 4.1 percent. Sales in the city and the SMSA increased during that same period by 13 percent and 13.6 percent, respectively. Excluding the CBD from the figures, sales increased 21.5 percent in the city and 19.9 percent in the SMSA.[60] Downtown clearly declined in one of its traditional functions. The Downtown Parking Association and the Downtown Omaha Association were early private responses. Several sections of the Omaha Plan—business district and building improvement, parking, traffic plans—represented later responses. The situation had not yet reached crisis proportions. The assumption was that with some cleaning up, more parking, and better access, downtown would reverse its recent decline and continue in its traditional role.

The Omaha Plan proposed a city planning department headed by a professionally qualified planner; the 1957 city charter created it. The plan further recommended that the department have a budget large enough to carry out its responsibilities and that the budget be between seventy thousand and eighty thousand dollars, an increase of twenty thousand dollars over pre-1957 budgets.[61] This represented a moderate change in thinking for the civic and business community. Its leaders did not abandon their adherence to privatism, but they did seem to realize that a weak, ineffective city hall and planning department hindered progress. Charter reform helped correct the situation. Neither city hall nor the Planning Department emerged immediately as an equal partner with the civic and business community, but they could pass and enforce ordinances favorable to growth and development—subdivision regulations, annexations, tax incentives—and be consulted for expert advice.

Another section of the plan, the recommendations on public education and cultural facilities, anticipated the emergence of a new kind of boosterism. During the 1950s, John Merriam and Northern Natural Gas Company began a development campaign that focused on the quality of life in the Midwest. It emphasized the region's cultural and recreational resources to attract new businesses. In its content and focus, Northern's campaign was an unusual approach to boosterism. Merriam, chairman of the Public Educational and Cultural Facilities Committee, brought that theme with him and into the Omaha Plan.

A proposed central park and cultural civic center embodied the fresh philosophy. The plan was not entirely new, however. The area under consideration was much the same area designated as the possible site of a civic center in the 1930s (Twentieth to Twenty-Fourth street and Dodge to Davenport streets). It contained Central High School and Joslyn Art Museum. The civic center proposed in the 1930s and 1940s contained primarily public buildings: post office, city hall, library. The Merriam-backed plan had something very different in mind; it envisioned an area containing, besides Joslyn, a central park, a central museum (on the site of Central High), a new public library, a new amateur theater, a junior theater, an outdoor symphony, an outdoor summer theater, a planetarium, an aquarium, and an industrial-exhibits building. It also recommended a permanent fine arts planning committee to advance Omaha's cultural development.[62]

The argument for the project reflected Merriam's personal philosophy.

Son of a prominent political scientist, he was reared in a culturally enriched environment and was educated at the University of Chicago, where his father, Charles E. Merriam, taught. Charles Merriam has been referred to as "the father of the behavioral movement in political science." He helped develop the Social Science Research Council and was directly involved with the National Resources Planning Board in the 1930s. Although materials available did not say so, John Merriam's father probably had a hand in developing the younger man's ideas and strong interest in planning. John Merriam came to Omaha in 1930 to work for fledgling Northern Natural. He rose quickly in the ranks and in 1950, at the age of forty-six, was selected as the company's new president. Under his leadership, the company forged strong ties with the Joslyn Art Museum. Near it the company cleared a large area, considered blighted, when it built its corporate headquarters in 1950. (The move also indicated early interest in the idea of a civic center for the area. Northern Natural designed its new corporate headquarters to complement the civic center plans as presented in the Blue Book.)[63] The later Omaha Plan proposal reflected both the tie to the museum and Merriam's personal ideas on the relationship between business growth and the cultural enhancement of an area. A newspaper article summed up his view:

> John F. Merriam, a dominant figure in the immense gas industry; a hard-headed and eminently successful businessman, is also a student. He grew up on the campus of the University of Chicago, was the son of a nationally known scholar. His own search for knowledge and for some of the finer things in life has kept pace with his business achievements and is an integral part of the man. It would be inaccurate to say anything comes before business with Merriam; but it is a fair summary to say that he considers the cultural development of the "northern plains" as important as the industrial growth.[64]

The link between promotion of cultural facilities and promotion of growth and development in Omaha permeated the argument on behalf of the central park and cultural center. Cultural facilities, such as the Joslyn, had appeared in booster material before the late 1950s, but the material depicted the museum as more of a tourist attraction—often listed with Boys Town and the Union Pacific Museum—than an integral part of

Omaha life. The 1956 report viewed such facilities as a vital outlet for leisure-time activities of both urban residents and tourists and lamented the fact that "in the area of cultural facilities, Omaha scores zero." It said Omaha must provide such facilities to meet the needs of its residents. The Mayor's City-Wide Planning Committee felt that such facilities "would be an important asset adding materially in Omaha's stature in its trade area as well as in the nation"[65] and said Omaha needed to move forward, that it had been stagnant for at least thirty years in providing cultural facilities, and that it had fallen behind other cities, which were even then providing such facilities. The committee concluded:

> We cannot afford to be branded as a backward community in cultural and civic activities that are increasingly important in everyday life.
> We need something dramatic to attract attention to our City—and to eliminate one possible roadblock to the location of business here.[66]

The idea that cultural backwardness—a lack of cultural and recreational amenities—was a hindrance to development was a new idea in Omaha boosterism. How could the lack of an adequate symphonic hall rate with efficient roads and a favorable tax structure in the competition for new businesses? The civic and business community did not readily embrace the idea, and in that respect Merriam stood ahead of the crowd. Such a notion gained strength in the 1960s as demands for cultural and recreational amenities grew among the new middle class of the service economy.

Concern for providing an outlet for leisure activities may have provided part of the rationale for the civic-center project, but it did not extend to ideas for use of the river or riverfront. Actually, the Omaha Plan had very little to say about the river. More and better sewers were proposed, along with construction of the city's first sewage-treatment plant to help curb pollution. However, the River-Rail Terminal and Transportation Committee made no recommendations beyond a vague call for future maintenance and improvement of existing facilities. The committee continued to emphasize how important such facilities were to Omaha's industrial development, but seemed more or less satisfied with what the city already had. The riverfront was not targeted for urban renewal. As an important part of Omaha life, the river seemed to be fading quickly out of mind.[67]

Overshadowing most of the Omaha Plan's other recommendations was the area-redevelopment proposal. In 1946 slum clearance ranked low on the priorities list; by 1956 it was at or near the top. During the 1950s the civic and business community gradually embraced urban renewal as the answer to the problems of a run-down inner city. The Omaha Plan proposed a massive area-redevelopment scheme that involved most of the city east of Thirtieth Street between Y Street in the south and Bedford Avenue in the north. Understandably, the proposal caused much controversy. Combined with lingering resentment over the new charter and the concurrent announcement of Interstate Highway System plans, the area-redevelopment section all but assured total rejection of the Omaha Plan by voters.

Opposition to public housing or any type of large-scale clearance, especially if it involved residential properties, never abated among Omahans in general. After construction of additions to existing housing projects in the early 1950s, opponents successfully lobbied for a legislative bill requiring that all proposals for public housing be put to a vote of the people. Such a requirement almost ensured defeat of any housing measure. The enticements in the Housing Act of 1954, however, convinced a large segment of the business community that Omaha must participate in urban renewal. Within a year of the bill's passage, plans to bring urban renewal to the city were laid. The focal group involved was the Area Redevelopment Committee of the Mayor's City-Wide Planning and Development Committee. Its membership reflected many of the groups supporting urban renewal. On it were representatives from the Chamber of Commerce Urban Planning and Development Committee, the Omaha Housing Authority, the Omaha Health Department, the Omaha Board of Education, a real-estate firm, an architectural firm (Leo A. Daly Company), the Douglas County Tax Appraisal Board, and the Urban League (the league supported urban renewal into the early 1960s, at which time its emphasis shifted to open-housing legislation). Also supporting urban renewal were the Associated Retailers of Omaha, various labor organizations, the League of Women Voters, and the Omaha Planning Department.[68]

In 1954 the city created the Neighborhood Conservation Board. Its primary purpose was to collect data on housing conditions. Following passage of the Housing Act of 1954, the city abolished that office in favor of the Office of Urban Renewal, created in 1955. The name changed, but the primary purpose remained the same. The first positive step toward initiating urban-renewal programs was taken in 1956 with adoption of a required minimum-standards ordinance despite determined opposition from a group known as the Small Property Owners Association. That same year, the Omaha Housing Authority, partly financed by the Chamber of Commerce, studied a sixty-four-block area from Sixteenth to Twenty-Fourth streets and Dodge to Cuming streets. It aimed to create a redevelopment project that would meet the specifications of the Housing Act of 1954. Support for urban renewal became organized as the Health Department and a group known as the Nebraska Council for Urban Development held conferences to educate the public about the benefits of urban renewal. In that increasingly favorable environment within the civic and business community, the Area Redevelopment Committee commenced its work.[69]

The committee began by conducting its own survey of Omaha housing conditions. In doing so it was treading familiar ground. Once again it studied areas examined by its Blue Book predecessor, which had used data collected in the 1930s as a base, and the Omaha Housing Authority. It went far beyond that earlier work, however, and designated a massive area of concern that included almost all of Omaha east of Thirtieth Street. The committee then recommended that the city take the necessary steps to participate in the urban-renewal program: adoption of a master plan, appointment of an effective urban-renewal director, and enforcement of the minimum-standards ordinance.[70]

The committee's report sparked immediate and immovable opposition. Foes of the renewal scheme organized into a group known as the Taxpayers Plan in 1958, the year Omaha Plan bonds went to voters. Membership was similar to that of the Small Property Owners Association, which had opposed the minimum-standards ordinance. It attracted lower-income homeowners and many people, primarily ethnic whites, living in the areas targeted by the renewers.[71] The Taxpayers Plan's public argument centered on project cost. The Omaha Plan was far more ambitious than the Blue Book. The original recommendations called for spending nearly one hundred million dollars over a ten-year period. The scaled-down version submitted to voters proposed spending sixty-eight million dollars, still four times the amount recommended by the Blue Book plan. The opposition argued that Omaha could not afford such a lavish program.

The Taxpayers group drew heavy support from the area designated for renewal. Not coincidentally, it was the same area that had delivered the heaviest anticharter vote. Analysis of voting on the charter and the plan suggested that Omaha's civic and business community pushed for too much too fast.[72] Both the charter and the Omaha Plan represented major changes, and many Omahans apparently were not ready to accept so much change so quickly.

The concurrent announcement of the proposed Interstate Highway route in 1957 added fuel to the fire. Highway engineers envisioned a route through the southern section of the city, with north and south branches running along the western boundary of the area designated for urban renewal.[73] The people living in that area therefore faced a double threat. If the renewers did not get them, the highway engineers would. Not surprisingly, after the Taxpayers Plan helped defeat the Omaha Plan, it turned its attention to defeat of the Interstate Highway route.

Those people were truly threatened by the changes under way. The charter, which aimed at bringing "better" people into city government, meant that the civic and business community wanted affluent businesspeople living in the newer western areas of the city to serve. It no longer wanted politicians tied to the South Omaha machine to run city hall. The plan (and the Interstate) threatened their homes and their very way of life. The new city emerging west of Seventy-Second Street—however much those living there might have seen themselves still as part of the old Omaha—was quite different from the older ethnic working-class neighborhoods of the eastern and southern sections of Omaha. The struggle between those two groups, the former on the rise and the latter declining, helped define city politics well into the 1960s. Older Omaha was not going to disappear quietly.

Unlike the Blue Book planners, who trimmed their recommendations down to a fairly modest level, supporters of the Omaha Plan went for broke, making at least part of the Taxpayers Plan's argument seem quite valid. For fiscally conservative Omaha, sixty-eight million dollars was a tremendous amount of money to spend. Further, Omaha Plan backers urged support for their proposal as a package even more strongly than had

Blue Book proponents. The earlier planners were surprised when voters chose among the proposals, approving some but not others. Perhaps the heavy emphasis on the package nature of the later plan precluded voter selectivity. Seemingly, faced with approving the entire plan or voting it down, the people of Omaha chose not to approve it. The eastern and southern sections of the city returned the heaviest antiplan vote, the magnitude of which made the margin of defeat on some issues as high as five to one and in South Omaha as high as thirteen to one.[74]

Planning and the Image of the City

The fact that between 1946 and 1956 the image of the city—what it was and how it worked—remained consistent offers another explanation for the striking similarities between the Blue Book plan and the Omaha Plan. In 1946, as in 1956, Omaha thought of itself primarily as a food processor, a city of butter, eggs, cattle, and grain. Its future lay in its traditional industries, and boosters put much emphasis on how efficient and convenient Omaha was for industry. They paid tribute to the fine utilities, public and private, that served the city but viewed them largely as symbols of growth rather than important growth areas in and of themselves. Cultural and recreational facilities received scant attention. Retailing was accorded only a little more notice than insurance, medical facilities, and educational institutions as important segments of the economy, even though by the end of the 1950s the service sector equaled the traditional commercial and food-processing sector in employment. The fact was noted, but it did little to change the thinking of those most involved in articulating and promoting Omaha's image. The acceptance of a more metropolitan vision was the only significant shift in thinking. Despite all the changes of the 1950s, Omahans still thought of their city what it had been, not as what it was becoming.

In 1949, Arthur W. Baum of the *Saturday Evening Post* wrote a descriptive article on Omaha. He was not an Omahan but drew his images of the city from the impressions he received from local spokespeople. He emphasized Omaha's role as a processing center for the products of midwestern agriculture. He acknowledged that the stockyards and meatpacking plants of South Omaha gave the city much of its reputation, for better or for worse. He also stressed the influence of grain and dairy processing and described many of the Wild West elements still shaping the city's image: an abundance of saloons, the presence of Indians, the cowboy boots and straw hats on frequenters of both the grain and livestock exchanges, and the city's reputation as a railroad town.[75] These images harkened back to descriptions of Omaha written during the 1930s. Much of the Wild West angle might have been an exaggeration, but otherwise Baum was not wrong about Omaha in 1949. Food processing was still the dominant sector of the economy, and Omaha *was* a rail center. The Union Pacific was the city's largest single employer, and it still emphasized traditional railroad activities: hauling freight and passengers. Baum mentioned retailers, insurance companies, and the utilities (especially Northwestern Bell and Northern Natural Gas), but only in passing. They were not given credit as significant parts of either the local economy or the city's image.

When Baum turned to local attitudes about the river, he spoke of the hope that it would once again be a great traffic way. He mentioned local support for channelization and flood control without a single word on the river's recreational potential. He wrote of Omaha's cultural and recreational amenities, but again only in passing. His description of the Joslyn Memorial focused on the dubious background of George Joslyn, in whose memory it was built, as a peddler of patent medicine. He expressed surprise that the parks did not do more to curb juvenile delinquency. In that respect, he was probably not in touch with Omahans' feeling toward their parks because they were the source of immense civic pride. And Baum reminded his readers of Omaha's climate extremes, the blistering summers and frigid winters. While that might have upset some city boosters, his favorable descriptions of the cattle, dairy, and grain industries and the men who ran them more than compensated.[76]

Baum quite accurately depicted a city that ended at Seventy-Second Street on the west: "At the western city limit of Seventy-Second Street, Dodge [Street] breaks with great suddenness into treeless, rolling cornland. Here there is no question of what is beyond. There is an almost physical suggestion that the plains ahead rise and rise and become the boundless West."[77] Although Omaha boosters looked to growth beyond

Seventy-Second Street, even as late as 1949 that boundary largely defined the city.

Thus Baum's description of Omaha was not far from the mark and reflected the city's self-image. The accuracy of his reporting became clear in the mid-1950s when the Chamber of Commerce launched its big booster campaigns. Many of the same themes in the 1949 article were repeated in the campaign material. When the chamber looked to sell Omaha, it sold it as an industrial, transportation, commercial, and medical center. The idea of the city as a medical center was relatively new. The growing importance of the medical-health complexes—hospitals, clinics, professional services, medical schools—received recognition as early as 1951. The selection of new Bishop Clarkson Memorial Hospital as Modern Hospital of the Year in 1956 helped focus attention on Omaha's health-care role. The emphasis, however, fell on the services such facilities provided and the numbers of patients they brought to the city rather than the employment the facilities offered or their impact on the local economy.[78]

Those themes remained dominant into the late 1950s. In 1958, Omaha was selected as an All-American City, largely because of its recent governmental reforms. In response, the *Omaha World-Herald* produced a magazine telling Omahans and potential Omahans about the city. The similarities between themes developed in the 1958 magazine and earlier material about Omaha were striking. The 1958 material still pictured Omaha as an agricultural capital and the river as a source of transportation. Utilities and transportation were viewed as assets to attract industry alongside a report on the activities of the Omaha Industrial Foundation, while other segments of the economy received scant notice.

One of the longest articles in the magazine argued the validity of Omaha's claim to the title Agricultural Capital of the Nation. It outlined the extent of the food processing industry and emphasized the importance of Omaha's links with the agricultural hinterland. Another long article described attempts to use the Missouri River as an industrial resource for transportation and industries that used much water. "If you are looking for water," the article began, "Omaha has it." Omaha had it for industries, however, not recreation. Other articles spoke of the efficiency and abundance of public utilities and transportation. Northwestern Bell Telephone and Northern Natural Gas received special notice, but they were viewed as an asset for attracting industry, not as important segments of the economy in and of themselves. And just to make sure the message was clear, yet another article explained the work of the OIF, accompanied by maps showing the location of all available industrial sites.[79]

Conspicuously absent was anything about the insurance industry. Mutual and United had attained national if not international stature by the late 1950s, yet when Omahans wrote about themselves and their city, the insurance industry was not important. Universities and medical-health complexes did receive notice.[80] Again, though, the emphasis fell not on their role in the economy but on the services they provided. Of activities considered part of the service sector, only retailing received significant attention.

The article on retailing reflected the metropolitanism that had developed during the 1950s. It described the retail industry as a regional business serving nineteen counties in Nebraska and Iowa. A metropolitan theme permeated articles on the proposed highway system and annexation. The highway piece described a city reaching out along "10 points of the compass." To the east, north, west, and south, the city reached out into its hinterlands via new highways. With tables and a map, Omaha's growth through annexation was demonstrated and celebrated.[81]

In 1949, Arthur Baum could have concentrated his attention on the commercial and food-processing sector of the economy and would have been mostly correct in his assessment. By 1958, however, the service sector was rapidly approaching equity with the commercial and food-processing sector. In that year the former commanded 36 percent of total employment, while the latter held on to 37 percent. The service sector reached equity in 1960. It cannot be argued that civic and business leaders had no knowledge of the changes under way. In May 1958 the City Planning Department produced an economic survey that illustrated many of the changes during the preceding decade. It pointed out that the service sector was almost equally as important as traditional economic activities. However, it also predicted that manufacturing would be the important growth sector, echoing economic projections published in connection with the Omaha Plan. The charts supplied by the Northwestern Bell Telephone

Company showed manufacturing as an important growth area along with retailing and wholesaling. More telling, the Union Stockyards Company supplied figures that predicted a near doubling of the number of cattle processed between 1955 and 1975. Those who defined the city by what it produced and how it worked continued to emphasize the traditional sectors.[82]

While it can be argued that civic and business leaders knew about many of the changes under way, it can also be argued that they did not know what those changes meant to the life of their city. They continued to hold a vision of Omaha based on past experience. As yet they had no clear focus on the quite different city that was emerging under the influence of social and economic changes. So it was that they planned for a city rapidly fading into the past rather than one that was developing and changing.

Conclusion

The period 1945 to 1958 was one in which continuity rather than change was the theme. In the two private-sector planning initiatives developed during that time, the many similarities between them marked the era as one demonstrating the persistence of ideas on how best Omaha could promote growth and development; the emphasis fell almost entirely on infrastructure improvements. The similarities also called attention to the continuing dominance of the private sector in the planning process. City hall did take a few short strides forward, but it continued to operate largely in the deep shadow cast by the private sector. And the years saw very little, if any, change in the image of the city held by its civic and business leaders. Thus, although important social and economic changes were under way, they received little notice and were not understood by the image makers. Only the new metropolitanism, born in part of the more physically apparent suburbanization, represented significant alteration in thinking.

Change, though subordinate, proved significant as well. Social and economic changes were transforming Omaha. Most significantly, those sectors associated with the service economy equaled the importance of the traditional commercial and food-processing elements by the end of the period. The Omaha Plan largely put to rest the informal planning agenda, developed in the 1930s and 1940s, that was so dominant through the 1950s. Many of its specific proposals—the auditorium, the sports stadium, new sewers, the airport, park improvements—were already met or being met by existing programs. Some specific projects, such as a civic center and still more parks, did continue to find supporters in the 1960s, and boosters continued to emphasize infrastructure improvements. By and large, however, the informal agenda faded away after 1958 as private and public planners shifted their attention to the necessity of coming to grips with changes under way since 1945: suburbanization, the rapidly declining downtown, and federal government demands to clean up the river, to name a few. City hall had gained some measure of influence and was on its way to greater equality with the private sector. And the desire to bring urban redevelopment and urban renewal to Omaha, a desire that had grown in fits and starts from the time of the earliest slum-clearance legislation, reached a new level of intensity with the Omaha Plan. Rather than ending the urban-renewal thrust, defeat of the Omaha Plan seemed only to set the stage for an even bigger drive in the early 1960s.

While continuity in many ways dominated change from 1945 to 1958, in the next planning period, 1958 to 1966, those forces went head to head and marked those years as a time of important transition. And 1958 to 1966 also proved to be the time during which older Omaha and newer Omaha continued to battle for dominance. The former gained a few victories early in the period, but it could not escape the crushing weight of change represented by suburbanization, annexations, the highway program, and the decline of the traditional commercial and food-processing economy. Momentum favored newer Omaha. By 1966 it was ready to take the lead as new ideas began to remake its image.

1. This aerial view from the mid-1920s shows the compact size of the downtown area (center right), which did not grow much over the years. The horseshoe-shaped body of water at the top of the photo is Carter Lake. Also shown are the railroad tracks north and east of downtown. From the Bostwick-Frohardt Collection, owned by KMTV and on permanent loan to Western Heritage Museum, Omaha, Nebraska.

2. Pictured here are the lawn of the Douglas County Courthouse (bottom right), Old City Hall (first building from left), and the old Omaha National Bank Building (third building from left). City Hall was demolished to make way for the Woodmen Tower and the old bank building was renovated as office space. From the Bostwick-Frohardt Collection, owned by KMTV and on permanent loan to Western Heritage Museum, Omaha, Nebraska.

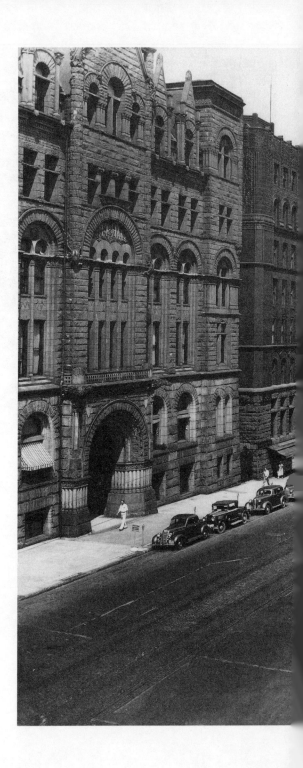

3. A view of downtown Omaha
before parking lots. From the
Bostwick-Frohardt Collection,
owned by KMTV and on permanent loan to Western Heritage
Museum, Omaha, Nebraska.

4. This is essentially the same
view as in photo 3, but after the
Omaha Downtown Parking Association began its work. From
the Bostwick-Frohardt Collection, owned by KMTV and on
permanent loan to Western
Heritage Museum, Omaha,
Nebraska.

5. Pictured here are Central High School and Joslyn Art Museum (top center), Civic Auditorium (below the high school and to the right), the Old Post Office (below the high school, with the clock tower), Union Pacific headquarters (below the Post Office), and the Hotel Fontenelle (top left, with sign). The photo was taken in the early 1960s before the Interstate cut across the northern boundary of the downtown (right of Civic Auditorium in this photo). From the John Savage Photography Collection, owned by Western Heritage Museum, Omaha, Nebraska.

6. The downtown skyline, circa 1970, with the Hilton Hotel (left center, site of the Old Post Office), next to it the First National Bank Building, and clearly the tallest structure, Woodmen Tower (with sign). From the Bostwick-Frohardt Collection, owned by KMTV and on permanent loan to Western Heritage Museum, Omaha, Nebraska.

7. This photo looks east from W. Dale Clark Library over construction of Central Park Mall in 1975. From the Bostwick-Frohardt Collection, owned by KMTV and on permanent loan to Western Heritage Museum, Omaha, Nebraska.

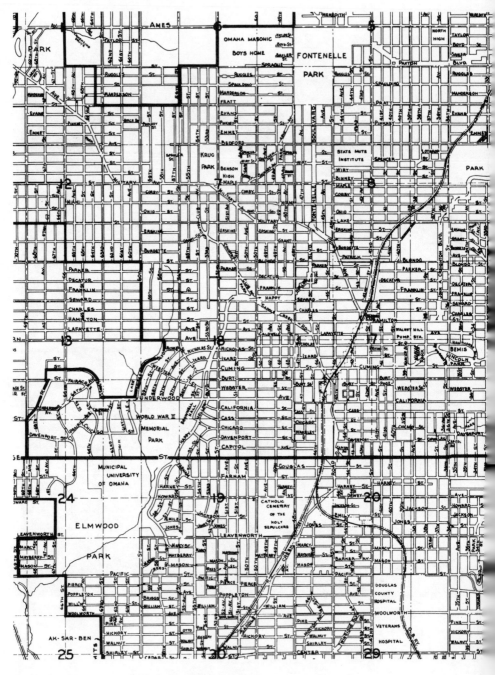

Omaha in 1950, courtesy Nebraska State Historical Society

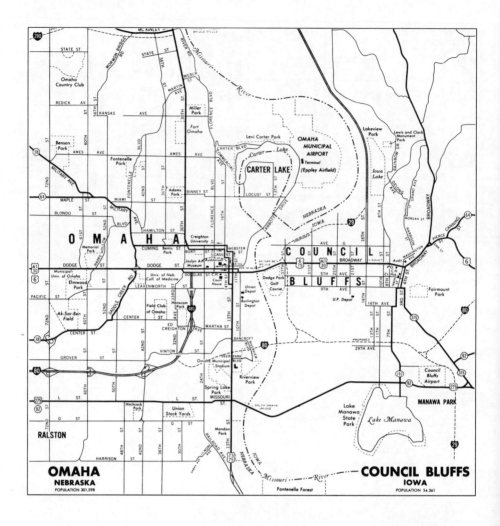

Omaha–Council Bluffs region in 1964, courtesy University of Nebraska Libraries

FIVE

A City in Transition, 1958–1966

Part 1: Continuity, 1958–1966

The years 1958 to 1966 marked a time when continuity with past planning practices and themes gradually gave way under the force of ever increasing change. Nonetheless, it did shape much of the planning activity during those years. The formal planning for the downtown and riverfront as outlined in the Central Omaha Plan of 1966 represented the continuing influence of older ideas about the city. Three programs that were introduced or had gained renewed popularity in the 1950s set planning priorities for the 1960s. The first of these, annexation, represented Omaha's major response to rapid growth in outlying areas. The second, an Interstate Highway System loop around the fringes of the city, with a direct connection to the downtown, promised to bond the newer areas with the central core. By affording easy access, planners hoped to reinforce the central role of the downtown. And in the third program, intended to shore up the city's center in its traditional role, public and private planners proposed to use urban renewal. In pursuing these priority programs, civic and business leaders faced two directions at once: decentralization and expansion, and the continued dominance of a traditional, viable downtown. They could pursue such seemingly contradictory courses because, as they saw it, they could have both.

ANNEXATION, THE INTERSTATE, AND URBAN RENEWAL: PRIORITIES FOR THE 1960S

The metropolitan-area concept adopted by the Chamber of Commerce in 1958 colored much of the planning activity from that point on. The recognition of a metropolitan Omaha brought increased focus on the growth occurring at the edge of the city. The civic and business leadership determined that Omaha must fully benefit from the expansion under way. To that end, it offered nearly full support for the development and annexation program carried out by the City Planning Department.

One of Alden Aust's first actions after he was appointed planning director was to develop an annexation program. As a necessary companion to it, the Omaha City Council passed its first subdivision ordinance in 1960. The ordinance established regulations concerning the provision of basic services to new subdivisions. It aimed to minimize the debt burden in those areas and minimize as well a potential argument against annexation. The program and the ordinance gave Omaha a vested interest in and a measure of control of development just beyond its boundaries. It added another layer of control with the land-use plan adopted in 1961. The tripartite expansion scheme represented a city aggressively seeking growth. The liberal annexation law determined that it was also a program following the path of least resistance. The relative ease with which the city could add both population and area determined that annexation would be its major response to growth and change.

As early as 1960, Aust and the City Planning Department forecast a bright future of growth through annexation. The department projected a population increase of eighty thousand in the fringe area just beyond the city's 1960 limits. And by that early date, planners assumed that Omaha would annex the area at the first opportunity. This is not to say that annexation met little or no resistance; on the contrary, a number of older established neighborhoods closer to and even surrounded by the city successfully staved off annexation for many years. Generally speaking, however, they proved the exception rather than the rule. The actions taken between 1958 and 1966 put Omaha's expansion policies into practice and set the stage for the massive annexations that were undertaken between 1966 and 1973.[1]

For each proposed annexation, the City Planning Department prepared a report explaining why a particular area should be annexed. Between 1958 and 1966 there were more than a dozen such reports. As a crude measure, they accounted for a little more than one-third of all the studies, plans, and programs issued by the department during those years.[2] It is difficult to compare an annexation report with a land-use plan, yet the sheer volume of the former indicated the department focused its energy on annexation.

The civic and business community also supplied a great deal of energetic support. In 1960 the Chamber of Commerce created the Metropolitan Area Committee. Following through on the already adopted area concept, its announced purpose was "to seek to bridge the barriers of city, county and state which run though the Omaha metropolitan area, and to promote the idea that we are one community." Two years later the committee proposed creation of a metropolitan planning organization to coordinate planning for the larger area. That idea came a step closer to fruition in 1966 with the appointment of a metropolitan development committee.[3] At the time, action on the metropolitan level was still at the quasi-official committee stage. Yet the appointment of the various committees indicated a real interest in promoting Omaha's position as the dominant force in a wider area. The support given the annexation program and the ideas behind the committees indicated a civic and business leadership eager to reach out and reap the benefits from all the growth and development occurring within the metropolitan area.

The relative ease of implementation associated with the annexation program contrasted sharply with the intense, emotional, and sometimes bitter opposition to a second major planning priority, the Interstate Highway. That massive program became embroiled in national, state, and local politics. When it was first proposed, Omaha's planners thought it would be completed in a few years' time, but it took more than a decade for it to reach a stage anywhere near completion.

From the very beginning the Interstate program faced opposition. At the local level, neighborhood groups and park supporters, among others, fought long and hard either to prevent construction or to reroute the Interstate south of the city. At the state level, supporters of a "Greater Omaha," who craved easy access to the city's hinterland, encountered strong opposition from backers of a "Greater Nebraska," a coalition of outstate politicians determined that the nonurban sections of the Interstate receive top priority (for purposes of this study, *outstate* means anything beyond Omaha and Douglas County). At the national level, the year-to-year swings in the level of appropriations disrupted even conservative construction timetables.

The section of the Interstate that involved the most intense controversy was Route 3, or I-480, the connecter between the main Interstate and the downtown. The route cut from the interchange at Thirty-Second and Grover streets north through older, heavily white ethnic neighborhoods past the western fringe of the downtown, where it swung eastward between Cass and Chicago streets along the northern fringe of the downtown toward the new bridge across the Missouri River. From the civic leaders' point of view, the route conveniently spanned two areas adjacent to the downtown: its western and northern fringes, long considered blighted and long involved in proposed civic-center projects some of them dating back to the 1930s. What city plans and urban renewal could not clear, the Interstate could.

While most of the civic and business community was thrilled with what I-480 could do for the downtown in terms of access and clearance, the people living in its path raised vociferous arguments against it. The focal group was the Taxpayers Plan, the same group organized to fight the Omaha Plan. Its activities centered in and around Immaculate Conception Parish, a heavily ethnic Catholic neighborhood severely threatened by construction plans. As the fight dragged on from 1959 into the early 1960s, battle lines were clearly drawn. On the one hand, opponents represented people trying to preserve and protect the familiar, small-scale neighborhood life they valued. On the other, proponents represented people with a metropolitan view of Omaha determined that the wider area be linked with lines of efficient transportation. In essence, therefore, it was a clash of basic values, a clash between those who put neighborhood first and those who valued the metropolitan area. That kind of deep division tended to make the struggle ever more bitter. In the end, metropolitan Omaha won, but opponents helped to ensure that clearance and construction were anything but quick and easy.[4]

In addition to neighborhood groups, supporters of Omaha's park system also offered strong opposition to the Interstate program. Several parks were threatened by construction, including Hanscom Park and Jefferson Square along the I-480 route and Riverview Park along the I-80 route.

Once the threats to those parks became apparent, longtime park advocate Rachael Gallagher rose to their defense, leading a group known as Friends of the Parks. At each and every point where Interstate and park met, Mrs. Gallagher drew battle lines, determined to fight it out to the end. As an indication of her strength and determination, she won more battles than she lost. Only Jefferson Square near the downtown was a complete loss. (However, by local custom, it had long since been given over to indigents and other so-called undesirables.) Once again the park issue proved to be a clash of values, parks versus roads, but it never became as bitter as the fight led by the neighborhoods.[5]

Opponents of Omaha's Interstate system were not confined to the local level. At the state level, Greater Omaha ran headlong into Greater Nebraska. The entire Interstate construction process became a protracted battle over funds. The issue was which section of the highway, urban or rural, should receive priority. Greater Nebraska, which included a coalition of outstate legislators, thought the rural section should receive priority, the idea being that the Interstate would help tie the large and somewhat sparsely populated state together.

In many ways the struggle lined up as the typical rural versus urban political battle so common to malapportioned state legislatures. Although Nebraska's unicameral legislature was less malapportioned than other states', nonetheless political battles often boiled down to Omaha, the major city, versus the rest of the state. Throughout the 1960s, Omaha interests led a frequently losing fight to obtain a bigger piece of the road-fund pie. In the end, the Interstate stretched from Omaha's outskirts to the far western boundary of Nebraska before it reached downtown from the suburbs. Add to the state financing battles the shifting pattern of federal appropriations and the Interstate ended up taking far longer to construct than its early supporters ever imagined.[6]

The construction delays and the disruptions caused by the sweeping clearance made the Interstate as much a part of the problem as planners hoped it would be part of the solution for a declining downtown. In 1960, Alden Aust spoke for many when he said the key to having growth and a traditional center was an Interstate Highway system to link the two. As long as the periphery had easy access to it, downtown would continue to play center stage in the metropolitan area. Further, many of the assumptions behind certain projects in the Central Omaha Plan of 1966 were based on rapid completion of I-480. Clearance and construction along the fringe of downtown made access more difficult. Photographs from the mid-1960s showed a downtown isolated from its surroundings by a swath of barren terrain. Hemmed in by the massive Interstate, downtown became a place where one went only with difficulty. This further diminished its chances of meeting competition posed by suburban shopping complexes springing up throughout the metropolitan area.[7]

The third priority program of the early 1960s, urban renewal, also met with stiff opposition. The Chamber of Commerce orchestrated a major media blitz on behalf of the program but was unable to sway public opinion or the city council. Hampered by unfavorable state legislation, the civic and business community failed to bring urban renewal to Omaha, but the single-mindedness of supporters revealed much of their thinking about the downtown and its fringe neighborhoods. By the early 1960s, the crisis was apparent and the desire to take positive action strong. The civic and business community saw downtown rapidly declining and was willing to propose drastic actions to preserve and protect it.

Defeat of urban renewal in the 1958 Omaha Plan election seemed only to intensify the efforts of its supporters. The campaign began in earnest in late 1960. At committee meetings and in the chamber's newsletter arguments in favor of the program appeared. The chamber adopted it as part of its 1960–61 Program for Progress, the yearly civic-improvement agenda. From that point until 1965 the chamber waged a vigorous battle. Throughout 1961 the chamber published articles favoring its use and tried to amend statutes concerning renewal authorities. Under a 1957 state law, cities had to obtain voters' permission to initiate a renewal project. Intense lobbying efforts headed by the chamber resulted in a 1961 revision of the law. Under the new legislation, the city council could create an urban-renewal authority empowered to initiate a project, but final approval of any project, including the issuance of bonds, was still subject to a vote of the people.[8]

Between 1958 and 1966 the urban renewal issue came before the council twice: in 1962 and 1965. Preceding each vote, the chamber sponsored intense media campaigns that included newspaper articles, television programs, and public speakers. In 1962 it established a community-improvement division responsible for directing all urban-renewal efforts and hired Jason Rouby, a professional renewal advocate from Little Rock, Arkansas, to head the division. The chamber was not alone in its support of the program. The Real Estate Board, the Associated Retailers of Omaha, the League of Women Voters, the administration of Creighton University, and several labor unions gave vocal support to the program, but the institutional support never added up to a majority among the general public or on the city council.[9]

An analysis of the urban-renewal movement in Omaha suggested that it represented a fight between business interests and city hall. Ignored was the fact that the councilmen were businessmen, though on a smaller scale than the leaders of the Chamber of Commerce. Urban renewal, which often threatened small businesses, naturally would not appeal to small, independent businessmen.[10] Further, although the council was elected at large, sectional differences were a factor. Those council members whose political bases were in South Omaha, the area of the city most opposed to urban renewal, invariably voted against it. (However, in the late 1960s those same councilmen favored a small renewal project to help the South Omaha business and industrial districts.) In addition, Mayor James Dworak firmly opposed renewal. By the time A. V. Sorensen, a supporter, became mayor in 1965, renewal was a dead issue. Opponents found gained strong corroborative evidence in early 1960s criticism of urban renewal elsewhere. The combination of opposition, unfavorable state legislation, and the late date at which renewal supporters began their campaign assured repeated defeats for the program. Thus Omaha did not participate in urban renewal.

The rhetoric of renewal supporters, however, indicated a deep and growing concern for the downtown. One of the early proposals involved an area, considered blighted as early as the 1930s, adjacent to downtown and the Creighton University campus. The university administration decided to stay at its in-town location in the late 1940s and from that point on was vitally concerned that the campus could expand its boundaries and not be threatened by the damaging effects of a deteriorating neighborhood. During the 1950s and 1960s, Creighton underwent rapid expansion that involved construction of many major buildings. Its president, the Reverend

Carl Reinert, proposed a pilot program that combined urban-renewal funds with the university's construction budget. It died with the failure of urban renewal. (Much of the problem was addressed otherwise as Interstate Highway routes cut through much of the area in question.) Even so, the proposal indicated the concern of downtown interests and a major institution about deterioration at the fringes of the city's center.[11]

Annexation, the Interstate, and urban renewal represented the planning priorities of both the public and the private sectors. Most of the formal planning of the early 1960s assumed implementation of the three programs. Plans for the downtown in particular depended on completion of the Interstate and the availability of urban-renewal funds. Those programs, further, set a very conventional framework for planning. The nature of the public-private partnership also indicated the continuance of a traditional framework, namely of private-sector dominance. Although city hall moved toward a position of more influence, the progression did not occur along a straight line. The relationship between the public and the private sectors was stressed.

THE PUBLIC-PRIVATE PARTNERSHIP AND PERSISTENT IMAGES: SETTING A TRADITIONAL FRAMEWORK

Mayor John Rosenblatt and A. V. Sorensen, president of the city council and former president of the Chamber of Commerce, worked well together. Both had firm connections to and good reputations in the ranks of private-sector leaders. While they occupied city hall, the relationship between the public and the private sector was relatively close. Much more than in the case of the Blue Book, the municipal government offered support to the Omaha Plan. That brief period of cooperation ended in the early 1960s when Rosenblatt was forced by illness to retire. Sorensen also left public office to concentrate his energies on behalf of one of his favorite projects, the Boys Club of Omaha. With those two prominent leaders gone, the 1961 mayoral election became a hotly contested race. It pitted an anti–Omaha Plan, anti-Interstate, anti–urban renewal candidate against the pro–Omaha plan, pro-Interstate and pro-renewal candidate sponsored by the civic and business community.

James Dworak was a young, brash politician known for his trademark bow tie. A mortician by profession, in 1957 he was elected to city council at age thirty-one. Those who opposed the Omaha Plan soon found a supporter in him: he led the fight against it on the city council. He even claimed to have his own plan, which, he said, would produce the same results at a much lower cost. Riding on the wave of his popularity with antiplan groups, he decided to run for mayor in 1961. His opponent, attorney James Green, was the unofficial candidate of the civic and business community. Green had supported the Omaha Plan and ran very much on a progrowth civic-improvement platform. In the election, a division remarkably similar to the one seen in the 1958 plan vote decided the outcome in favor of Dworak. Those who opposed and were threatened by the ambitious schemes of the civic and business leadership viewed Dworak's successful election as a victory.[12]

Dworak, only thirty-five years old, was a dashing figure and proved very popular with his constituents. However, his refusal to cooperate with various programs promoted by the civic and business community, most notably urban renewal, soon won him the latter's enmity. The relationship became particularly acrimonious between the mayor and Peter Kiewit, who had recently purchased Omaha's only daily newspaper. In 1964 the *World-Herald* broke a story involving the mayor, other city officials, a Chicago real-estate developer named John Coleman, and the solicitation of bribes, adding fuel to an already combustible situation. Eventually, Dworak, two city councilmen, a member of the Omaha Planning Board, and a real-estate man were tried on charges of bribery and conspiracy. Needless to say, city hall's reputation plummeted. The fact that Dworak was found innocent and the other defendants guilty did not help the situation. The scandal paralyzed city hall.[13]

Although he was under indictment, Dworak ran for reelection in 1965 against the well-respected A. V. Sorensen, who easily outdistanced the discredited Dworak, 59,525 votes to 35,636. Under Sorensen's leadership the city and the private sector began rebuilding their relationship. Sorensen had much experience. He was president of the Chamber of Commerce, led the campaign for a new city charter, supported the Omaha Plan, and advocated a businesslike attitude at city hall. Though not a member of it, he had connections with the top ranks of the leadership structure. He worked tirelessly to promote Omaha's interests and deserved credit for restoring city hall's image, but only after a long uphill battle. In 1966 the effort had just begun.[14]

The occupants of the mayor's office did not alone define city hall's role in the planning process. Throughout the 1960s, Planning Director Alden Aust sought a more prominent role for his department. When he came to the job in 1956, he found an understaffed and underfinanced operation and a poorly trained crew. Over the next decade he gradually hired more and better-trained planners and fought a budget battle that nearly doubled his department's appropriations. He also forged ties to the business community and continually insisted that the Planning Department have a voice in private-sector planning initiatives.

In 1959 the department had ten permanent employees: four people designated as planners and six in support roles (secretary, stenographer, draftsman). By 1966 there were seventeen. Of these, eight were planners; nine filled support positions. As the number of employees increased, so did the budget. It grew from just under $70,000 in 1959 to $131,882 in 1966.[15] (The total does not include grants for various projects.) The citizen-staffed Planning Board, touched by the Dworak administration scandal, had a sullied reputation, but there is no evidence that the Planning Department experienced any backlash.

In separate interviews, Aust and James Kelly, one of the first people Aust hired, suggested that in the beginning, department employees were poorly trained. Aust further suggested that the low salaries offered by the city prevented him from hiring the best-qualified people. As a result he had to spend a good deal of time training his staff. He created a departmental library and encouraged his people to acquaint themselves with the latest thinking in the planning field. He and Kelly both indicated that professionalizing the staff required much time.[16]

A combination of factors helped advance the role and reputation of the Planning Department. While developing the Omaha Plan, the civic and business community turned to experts for help. That represented a step away from the intense privatism of the Blue Book, which was developed with little or no expert help. The trend toward outside expertise continued with the Central Omaha Plan. The city hired several firms, including the Leo A. Daly Company, to conduct studies and prepare reports and plans. The fact that one of the firms was essentially an Omaha company indicated the limited nature of the search for outside assistance. Nonetheless, in the same vein the Central Omaha Committee turned to the Planning Department for technical expertise, and Aust aggressively asserted his department's right to direct planning initiatives. In general, by 1966 the larger-staffed and more adequately budgeted department found itself in a far better position to determine the course of planning than in the past. The relationship still favored the private sector—hence, it remained very traditional in nature—but the civic and business community realized, at least tentatively, that an active City Planning Department might be a helpful ally.

A third circumstance also helped to establish a very traditional framework for formal planning activity. Between 1958 and 1966 the image of the city, the image of the downtown, and the image of the riverfront remained defined in ways reminiscent of the past. The Chamber of Commerce presented Omaha in terms of how much it produced, how hard it worked, and how efficient it was for industry. Its booster arguments echoed previous campaigns that emphasized what a great city Omaha was to work in and thus in which to locate a factory. Within the traditional view of the city, the downtown and the riverfront continued in their customary roles. The downtown especially received attention, which increased as the disparity between the ideal image of the downtown and the reality of the situation grew. Although it was still described as the vital center, in actuality, the part downtown played in Omaha's economy shrank and it gained a somewhat unsavory reputation. The riverfront, on the other hand, received very little attention at all.

The early 1960s did not witness highly organized booster campaigns similar to those of the mid-1950s. The promotional material that did appear continued to describe the city in traditional terms. In 1960 the chamber published the first of several reports on Omaha's business activities, highlighting several growth areas, such as the number of building permits issued, livestock processed, retail and wholesale sales, the increased output of local utilities, and the value of manufactured goods. The report contained graphs illustrating these accomplishments. Other factors, such as

Omaha's role as a major medical center and the growth of its institutions of higher education, were mentioned but received little emphasis.[17] Obviously, the chamber still concentrated its attention on the efficient and hardworking aspects of Omaha's business life. Quite remarkable for its absence was any mention of the insurance industry.

The following year, much to the apparent delight of chamber members, an outsider, Louis Azrael, wrote glowingly of Omaha's "get-up-and-go." A newspaper columnist from Baltimore, Azrael wrote of Omaha's success in promoting growth and outlined the major points in the city's success formula. Those points, confirmed as important by chamber spokesmen, included the absence of a state sales tax, the power of local government to issue industrial revenue bonds, the work of the Omaha Industrial Foundation, and the state's right-to-work law.[18] In general, Azrael had endorsed the chamber's longstanding booster strategy and the article received prominent notice in the chamber's newsletter.

The chamber launched a new comparatively modest booster campaign in 1964. First, it created a new economic development committee and charged the group with developing strategies for bringing more jobs to the area. A number of local businesses offered technical advice, including Northern Natural Gas, the Metropolitan Utilities District, the Omaha Public Power District, Leo A. Daly Company, Bozell and Jacobs (advertising), and Northwestern Bell Telephone Company. It was a familiar lineup of the city's largest firms and its growth-conscious utilities. The City Planning Department and United Community Services also offered their help. The new committee conducted research, visited the Twin Cities, and forged close ties with the OIF in its efforts to find the best methods to promote Omaha and fulfill its primary purpose: attracting industry.[19]

The endeavour resulted in publication of a brochure describing Omaha to potential industries. The brochure emphasized very traditional factors, primarily infrastructure and the availability of labor and land, and the facts it presented included "utility rates, transportation, labor potential, financing, waste disposal, construction costs, [and] available land."[20] Nothing in the committee's report or in any of its early promotional material indicated departures in thinking about the image of the city.

Planners and boosters couched the image of the downtown in very traditional terms. When they spoke of it, they often referred to it as the "hard core" or "vital center" of the city, with the assumption that a growing metropolitan region needed a strong downtown. The downtown stood as the symbol of the city, the image that came to mind when one wished to picture the city. Not surprisingly, as downtown Omaha continued to have difficulties, planners directed much energy toward correcting the situation. Despite all efforts, however, the downtown continued to slip and its reputation, as well as its physical plant, deteriorated.

The civic and business community began to respond to downtown's problems in earnest in the 1950s. Private and quasi-public organizations were formed, and a section of the proposed Omaha Plan dealt specifically with the issue. Even as it began to acknowledge the problems, the civic and business community continued to think of downtown in traditional terms, which persisted even in the face of challenges. In 1959, J. L. Brandeis and Sons, Omaha's largest department store, announced plans to construct a branch in the city's first major suburban shopping center, Crossroads, at Seventy-Second and Dodge streets. A newspaper editorial admitted that such a move threatened downtown shopping but confidently predicted that "downtown will long remain the primary shopping area." This did not mean that downtown could stand quietly by; it and the city had to act. More parking, better transportation, a face-lift, and rehabilitation were needed to help it meet the suburban challenge. None of the suggestions were new. They all represented rather standard responses to common problems. The *World-Herald* editorial did emphasize, though, that the programs must be implemented when it said, "Every city needs a center to hold it together."[21]

City plans echoed such a sentiment throughout the early 1960s. In 1960 the Planning Department outlined a program to shore up the city's "hard core." It, too, centered on the two most popular answers: parking and easy access. And, as in the 1959 prediction, the department stated firmly that "[t]he central business district will remain compact, the 'hard core' of the city."[22] The central business district and the downtown were not synonymous. The CBD, in effect, was the center of downtown. However, when the general public thought of downtown, the functions performed in the CBD, primarily retailing and offices, came to mind most readily.

The same general theme was repeated in 1961 when Alden Aust said, "The downtown area alone is the best able to serve as the city's retailing, office, entertainment and hotel center." He also reiterated the need for adequate parking, better access, and a face-lift. Another old and familiar favorite project of the civic and business community also appeared on the list of proposed solutions. In November 1961 the Maenner real-estate firm announced plans to develop a civic center just south of the Douglas County Courthouse (between Seventeenth and Eighteenth streets and Harney Street and Saint Mary's Avenue). The proposal included a city-county office building, new police and fire headquarters, and parking for six hundred cars. Also, by demolishing the old city hall and police and fire headquarters the city could make room for other new development projects. Urban renewal received no mention at that time; rather, the proposal anticipated issuance of county revenue bonds and receipts from the parking facility to pay for the project. Although it involved a good deal of demolition and construction, it essentially involved a basic face-lift for just one small section of the downtown.[23]

Such assertions of the downtown's central role continued and that image permeated much of the planning. The image did not spur civic and business leaders to act, but hard reality forced them to initiate planning programs. Despite rather confident assertions to the contrary, the downtown continually and steadily lost out to the competition from suburban shopping centers. Surveys indicated that the percentage of Omahans shopping frequently in the downtown was relatively stagnant, while the percentage frequenting the major suburban shopping centers grew. These problems were concurrent with an increasingly unsavory reputation. Optimistic booster slogans aside, the downtown had real problems.

Between 1958 and 1967, downtown's share of city and metropolitan retail sales shrank substantially. In 1958 its share stood at 28 percent of city sales and 22.4 percent of metropolitan sales. By 1963 those figures had dropped to 21.2 percent and 16 percent, respectively, and by 1967 they had fallen to 16.4 percent of city sales and a mere 12.3 percent of metropolitan sales. Not surprisingly, during the same years in which retail sales increased in the city and metropolitan area, they declined downtown. In 1958, city sales were up 13 percent. They went up another 13.3 percent by 1963 and

had risen a dramatic 25.5 percent by 1967. In those same years, metropolitan sales grew 13.6 percent, 20 percent, and 26.7 percent, respectively.
By contrast, downtown sales declined. In 1958 they had fallen by 4.1
percent, declined a substantial 14.1 percent by 1963, and dropped another
2.9 percent by 1967.[24] Clearly, suburbia was replacing the downtown as
the site of the city's and the metropolitan area's major retailing activity.

World-Herald surveys conducted yearly after 1963 asked Omahans
about their shopping habits. The answers indicated that the downtown
managed to hold as frequent shoppers about one-third of the survey re-
spondents, but more and more people did their most frequent shopping at
the Crossroads. In 1963, 30.3 percent indicated they frequently shopped
downtown. The figure rose to 32.4 percent in 1964 and to 34.9 percent in
1965 but fell back to 31.2 percent in 1966. In contrast, the percentage of
frequent shoppers at the Crossroads grew over those same years from 18
percent in 1963 to fully 27.3 percent by 1966. There was a slight drop to
16.4 percent in 1964, but the figure rebounded to 23.6 percent in 1965.
Taking into consideration the figures on retail sales, Omahans might have
continued to shop downtown, but they did their major purchasing in the
suburbs.[25]

The economic figures and the shopping-habit survey data clearly indicated hard times for downtown. What many deemed the most critical blow
to the area came in 1965 when Burroughs Corporation opened women's
Job Corps centers in two former downtown hotels, the Regis and the
Paxton. At the least, it meant a loss of 450 hotel rooms, a circumstance seen
as a serious threat to the convention trade. More to the point, critics argued
that the centers brought young people—a large number of whom were
blacks—into the downtown. Almost immediately downtown streets gained
the reputation of being unsafe as shoppers viewed the Job Corps participants and their "male associates" as threats to public safety.[26] With the
opening of the centers, the downtown gained the reputation of being not
only difficult to get to and impossible to park in, but also dangerous. Until
they closed in 1969, the Job Corps centers carried much of the blame for the
decline of downtown shopping.

In sharp contrast to the intense attention paid the downtown, the river
and riverfront received little notice. The river did little to draw attention to

itself. With completion of the Pick-Sloan series of dams, rampaging floods like that of 1951 were a thing of the past. Spring flooding recurred periodically, but was more of a nuisance than a menace. The sewer bonds defeated in the Omaha Plan election later gained the favor of voters.[27] Sewage-treatment plants gradually corrected the worst of the pollution problems. Promoters' great expectations of barge traffic and river ports were never met. Generally, the river and riverfront became forgotten areas.

Despite any real improvements, the river, like the downtown, had a bad reputation. Memories of the devastating flood faded slowly. Before the construction of sewage-treatment plants, officials described the quality of the river water in stomach-wrenching terms. Occasionally the chamber newsletter printed a hopeful article on the prospects for developing river trade, but the only specific plans for the river surfaced in 1964. The Chamber of Commerce's Park and Recreation Committee announced plans to create a park along the river near the airport. The project foreshadowed a new attitude toward the river, but it languished as it failed to gain approval from the Airport Authority, which owned four hundred acres of the proposed one thousand-acre site. The old uses for the river—highway and sewer—had faded from prominence and new ideas had not yet come of age.[28]

The three priority planning programs, the nature of the public-private partnership, and the persistence of older ideas about the city, the downtown, and the riverfront combined to create a very traditional framework for the formal planning that was initiated during the early 1960s. In 1962, within the context of a growing concern for the downtown, the chamber established the Central Omaha Committee and charged it with creating a plan for the downtown. The Central Omaha Plan was published in 1966.

REFLECTIONS OF THE PAST: THE
CENTRAL OMAHA PLAN, 1966

The Central Omaha Committee fit well in the pattern of post-1945 planning activity. It began as a chamber committee but gradually evolved into yet another mayor's committee. There were, however, several important differences. It was not a citizen's committee in the ways that the Blue Book and Omaha Plan committees had been. Membership included civic and business leaders, as with the previous committees, but the committee itself did not do the planning. Rather, it hired experts to do so while it acted as an advisory and oversight body. The earlier committees gained the cooperation of the mayor with little or no difficulty. James Dworak, mayor at the time of the Central Omaha Committee's inception, offered his cooperation only reluctantly. In addition, the committee tried to underplay its ties with the private sector, striving to seem more like a quasi-official public-planning group than an extension of the Chamber of Commerce, which further demonstrated retreat from the intense privatism of the past. And the group took much longer to produce a plan. The Blue Book and the Omaha Plan committees produced theirs within a year or two, but almost four years elapsed between the appointment of the Central Omaha Committee and publication of the Central Omaha Plan. Despite the differences, the committee and its proposals represented the persistence of older ideas about planning and about the downtown and riverfront.

Within months of its creation, the committee approached city hall and proposed a plan to reinvigorate the downtown. Although supporters claimed it would be comprehensive, a plan for the entire city, clearly it aimed directly, if not exclusively, at the downtown. To help finance its development, the committee asked the city council to submit an application for a $120,000 planning grant. Under the requirements of the grant, the city had to supply $60,000, and the chamber offered to pay half that sum.[29] The proposal met immediate opposition, especially from Mayor Dworak.

Dworak's opposition centered on the grant application. He rose to political prominence on the strength of his battles against several federal programs, especially the Interstate Highway System and urban renewal. In fact, the central Omaha proposal came shortly after he defeated the chamber's bid for urban renewal. In general he proved quite reluctant to participate in any federal program, but he especially opposed those that appealed to the Chamber of Commerce. He could not gain enough support to block the new initiative, however, and it won the unanimous support of the Omaha Planning Board in November 1962 and the nearly unanimous support of the city council the following month. The mayor could delay the process, but he could not stop it. Finally, in 1963, he designated the chamber-sponsored group as the Mayor's Central Omaha Study Committee."[30]

Unlike previous mayor's committees, the group that was appointed did not do the actual planning. Rather, it acted as a citizens advisory committee. It participated in the decision-making process, but experts hired for the job did the research and designed the various projects. In a significant departure from the past—though not as drastic as it might have been—the city hired the Leo A. Daly Company, headquartered in Omaha, as the prime contractor. The company was involved in urban planning all over the country, so it had broad experience.[31] The first time Omaha's leaders fully entrusted planning to professionals, they looked to a source with strong local ties.

The Mayor's Central Omaha Study Committee also differed from its predecessors in the way in which it wished to appear to the public. Supporters presented the previous planning groups as citizens committees composed of private-sector individuals infused with civic pride striving to improve their community, and the Chamber of Commerce proved not at all shy about celebrating its own hand in the process. The 1963 planning group wanted a somewhat different image. According to committee minutes, it believed that "to achieve maximum validity and maximum public acceptance [the Central Omaha Plan] should be a program of the City Planning Department and not a private program sponsored by the Chamber of Commerce or any other private organization." The reasons for that conclusion were not clear. However, the Omaha Plan suffered condemnation as the product of a few wealthy private interests. Its association with the chamber was a source of some of the hostility directed against it. Perhaps memories of that recent, resounding defeat led members to believe that for the new plan to succeed, it must be seen as a public rather than private-sector project. And since Planning Director Alden Aust served as a member of the committee, it was relatively easy, through him, to establish a link with the city's official planning body.[32]

Preliminary research began in June. A subcontractor, Real Estate Research Corporation, conducted much of the research, which included pedestrian interviews, an extensive land-use survey, and employment studies. In 1964 the company published *Economic Survey and Market Analysis of*

Omaha, Nebraska, in which it described downtown's role in the city and the region, emphasizing the fact that it generated one-quarter of all employment in the three-county metropolitan area. The final planning document integrated many of the report's conclusions with its own. The Daly Company presented tentative design proposals to the committee in early 1965, and after more than a year of meetings and discussions, the final plan appeared on October 12, 1966. The Planning Board approved it in December.[33]

Similar to its predecessors, the plan was a lengthy document, but, unlike the others, it seemed to be more of a unified piece than a collection of individual committee reports. It first presented a detailed description of the downtown, then outlined the results of the extensive research and the needs defined by it. Finally, it presented the plan itself and suggested various ways to implement it. There were familiar themes throughout the document. It still described the downtown largely in traditional terms and the analysis focused on its familiar functions, but the plan concentrated primarily on the three major responses to the problems: easier access, more parking, and a face-lift. In general, it reflected the persistence of older ideas of what the downtown was and how it could be maintained in its traditional role.

The first section of the Central Omaha Plan contained a brief history of the planning initiative, an outline of the goals and objectives sought, and a general description of the downtown. After explaining who produced the various aspects of the completed work, it listed five major goals and objectives. They centered on preserving downtown's center-place role, protecting property values (and hence tax receipts), encouraging private investment in the area, further development of Omaha's economic role in the region, and relating preservation of the downtown to an overall scheme for the growth and development of the city. The goals were very general. As the planners themselves explained, since the plan was long range and general in nature, it must be seen as a guide, not a list of specific project goals. That in and of itself set the Central Omaha Plan apart from it predecessors, which in many ways were little more than collections of discrete projects.[34]

The planners were a bit more direct in describing the role of downtown in the region and the metropolitan area. In their view, the downtown, with its business, financial, and administrative functions, was the key to Omaha's regional influence. They further stated that expanded regional dominance and general growth and development depended on the continued centralization of the various functions in the downtown. Obviously, to those planners, expansion of the periphery demanded a strong, highly centralized core. Quite naturally, the downtown played a similar center-place role in the metropolitan area. Again the major conclusion emphasized the necessity of maintaining the position and functions of the core. The planners stated that the downtown must, through the Interstate Highway System and other improvements, be "the single most accessible location in the metropolitan area" to ensure continued centralization of its functions.[35]

After stating their basic assumptions about downtown, the planners presented a rather detailed description of central Omaha, defining it as that area "bounded by the Missouri River on the east, Leavenworth Street on the south, the Interstate Highway (at 29th Street) on the west and Cuming Street on the north." Planners divided the three-hundred-block area into three components: the inner core, the outer core, and the frame area. The inner core contained major retailing activity, most of the downtown's financial institutions, and other offices. Heart of the central city, it also had the highest assessed real-estate values in the region. The outer core contained less-important retail establishments, office buildings, transient facilities, personal service establishments, and parking facilities. Unless otherwise stated, the two core areas were referred to as a single unit. The frame area encircled the core and included a wide variety of businesses, institutions, and residential complexes: "Creighton University, Josyln Art Museum, Central High School, Northern Natural Gas Company, Civic Auditorium and high-rise apartment buildings such as the Rorick, Cox, Palms and the OEA [Omaha Educators Association] Manor." The frame area along the Missouri River contained "the wholesale, warehousing and distribution center of the city."[36]

Having defined the area under study, the planners then moved to general descriptions of the downtown's physical and functional characteristics and its traffic and parking systems. The physical description included "specific land use, condition of structures, number of housing units, employees, parking space, land area and other relevant data." A chart showed the number of acres given over to each use category—residential, retail, office, parking, and so on. A more detailed study outlined the core area on a block-by-block basis in terms of available general floor space, office space, and store space. Mostly descriptive, this section offered no conclusions, nor did it present analyses.[37]

The section on downtown's functional characteristics proved somewhat more analytical. It concentrated on the core but provided employment data for the entire downtown area, showing four major employment groups there. The largest, representing 22.8 percent of total employment, included transportation, communication, and utilities. Retailing finished a close second with 21.8 percent of the total, followed by finance, insurance, and real estate (19.8 percent) and government (16.8 percent). Fully 23,276 people worked in the core area, representing 48 percent of all downtown employment and "more that one-quarter of the entire metropolitan area (SMSA) employment." With 48,482 employees, downtown remained the major employment center. The planners offered a few brief descriptions of the workers, such as where they lived, whether they owned their own homes or rented, how many in each household were employed, how they traveled to work, and their average income. The descriptive survey also included interviews of pedestrians; they were asked primarily about their shopping habits.[38]

Completing the descriptive phase of the plan, its authors presented information on the traffic system and the parking situation. This lengthy section examined the street system, traffic volume, traffic speeds, parking, the transit situation, and patterns of pedestrian traffic. Parking received the most detailed attention. Downtown interests long had put heavy emphasis on more space for parking and the need to provide better access. The twin proposals offered relatively simple, easy-to-imagine answers to the problems faced by downtown, and as such they received the most support from the central city's business community. This group especially emphasized parking. In December 1963 at a meeting concerning the plan, the evening's discussions centered on the parking situation. It emerged as the number-one priority of participants. The businessmen touted free or very inexpensive parking as the answer for downtown problems. Not surprisingly, therefore, parking occupied a prominent position in the completed plan.[39]

Planners used information from the first section of the plan to support the analysis of the second. In summary, according to the planners, the data indicated an extensive need for new office and retail space, a doubling of the number of hotel and motel rooms, many new apartments, more parking space, and, crucially, the completion of Interstate 480. The planners' recommendations were based on projected needs to 1980. "Space demands, traffic volumes and parking needs" stood at the core of the "basic program" for the downtown. The underlying assumption was that downtown would remain Omaha's office and retail center, although the study acknowledged that its share of metropolitan sales would decline. And, as in the past, basic infrastructure improvements were given the highest priority. A spruced-up, accessible, efficient center place for the metropolitan area and the region emerged as the goal.[40]

According to the planners, downtown Omaha consisted of about three hundred blocks, each equaling 68,278 square feet, or 1.6 acres. The Central Omaha Plan called for development of 126.9 blocks, or 43 percent of the total area. The fact that the new plan directly involved almost half of the central city made it far more extensive than any of its predecessors. Earlier schemes, which usually revolved around some sort of civic center, had involved only a few blocks at the most and the various civic-center developments primarily proposed construction of new buildings: museums, city hall, post office, and so on. In comparison, while more than half of the proposed land requirements in the Central Omaha Plan involved new buildings, more than a third was devoted to the needs of the automobile. Expressways and street improvements demanded the largest amount of land. The next-largest involved apartments, followed by parking. One more land-use category appeared in the plan: open space.[41]

The background and analysis sections led into the section that contained the plan itself. Not surprisingly, it reflected the same basic assumptions just presented. It assumed a continued strong commercial core, the persistence of wholesale and light industry and railroad-industrial use areas, and the notion that downtown would play its center-place role in the metropolitan area and the region. The concrete proposals involved a good many new parking areas and extensive expressway and other street improvements to provide better access. Other construction involved civic buildings, improved convention facilities, and a face-lift for the major retail streets. The plan melded public action with private development schemes and was heavily dependent on the private sector for success.

The collection of proposals for the core area was the plan's centerpiece. They included the Executive Park, the Old Post Office development site, the Government Center, the Convention Center, the Sixteenth and Eighteenth Street malls, and Petticoat Lane. Because they were more concrete than the proposed new traffic circulation and parking systems, they more readily captured the public's eye. The Executive Park and Government Center ideas came from the private sector. A local development firm proposed construction of two downtown superblocks, one to accommodate private business office needs and the other to house governmental offices. In a clear demonstration of the connections between private and public planning, planners wove that private development proposal into the fabric of the ostensibly public plan. The Old Post Office, with its clock tower, was a downtown landmark, yet as early as the 1930s civic leaders targeted it for demolition. With construction of a new post office and Federal building in the early 1960s, pressure for its removal mounted. It sat on prime real estate, and downtown interests eagerly awaited an opportunity to put it to "better" use.[42]

A downtown convention center and more hotel space ranked among the longest-standing booster goals. Conventions brought in trade for downtown merchants and offered a chance to show off Omaha to prospective businesses and customers.

The public-investment side of the story involved the two malls and Petticoat Lane. The Eighteenth Street Mall project consisted mostly of new lighting and some landscaping. The Sixteenth Street Mall was somewhat more extensive. That street ran through the heart of the commercial core, and the plan called for construction of sheltered bus stops, street furniture, some landscaping, and new paving, all to make the street more attractive and convenient to pedestrians. In the same spirit, the Petticoat Lane scheme proposed construction of above- and below-ground pedestrian passageways so that shoppers could move from building to building, store to store, in environmentally controlled comfort, making the downtown a pedestrian place.[43] (That was still quite different from the later idea of making it a popular people place.)

The plan for the frame area also involved a melding of private and public money. Three large institutions with expansion or improvement plans—Creighton University, Lutheran Medical Center, and Joslyn Art Museum—were major factors. Each independently had announced extensive construction plans. They, too, became part of the public plan. The Central Omaha Plan also urged new housing in the frame area; planners wished to encourage prestige high-rise apartment complexes. That involved a good deal of clearance along the edge of downtown, an area long considered blighted and in need of extensive clearance.[44]

The wholesale-district plan proposed sweeping changes. Even though it predicted continued wholesale activity downtown, planners felt that the center of the wholesale district needed substantial alteration. They proposed closing off streets to create superblocks and removing "obsolete" structures. They acknowledged the historic character of the area but emphasized what would be new and more efficient rather than rehabilitation to preserve a sense of the past.[45]

Planners did not entirely forget the riverfront. Three paragraphs explained a proposed esplanade along the Missouri's banks, an idea harkening back to the 1930s and the proposed scenic river drive. In presenting the project, planners acknowledged the need to do something about the deteriorating riverfront, but it ranked last on their list of priorities in the final pages of the document.[46]

The last pages of the plan dealt with methods to implement it. As the planners saw it, the key to success was creation of an Omaha Central Area Association that would concentrate on following through with their recommendations.[47] It would represent the central city's interests and lobby for them. The association did not materialize, and the reason is not clear. Apparently, however, in many ways the Central Omaha Plan was dead on arrival. First, it depended heavily on completion of I-480 to provide the all-important easy access, and in 1966 completion was still several years away. Furthermore, although the planners did not specifically mention it, the tremendous amount of clearance called for in the plan almost assuredly demanded the use of urban renewal, which had been repeatedly and soundly defeated. Finally, the disruptions caused by Interstate construction delays, the decline of retailing activity, and the unsavory reputation of the downtown by 1966 combined to create a very complex problem with no easy answers, a situation not readily or eagerly addressed by a committee of civic and business leaders. One year after the plan was issued supporters acknowledged that little or nothing had been done to implement it. The Central Omaha Plan and its conventional framework offered too little too late to meet the mounting crisis in the downtown.

Perhaps more important, by 1966 the traditional views of the downtown and the conventional answers for its improvement began to give way under the pressure of new ideas. Broader changes in Omaha's social and economic base created an atmosphere in which new demands arose. These included the idea of beautifying the city by planting greenery or through a general cleanup of waste and garbage, the preservation of architecturally and historically significant older buildings, a desire for more and better urban amenities, and new roles for downtown and the riverfront. These new ideas emerged during the late 1950s and early 1960s and gradually overtook the more traditional ideas. By 1966 they were in ascendance and the old ideas, which formed the core of the Central Omaha Plan, were in decline.

Part 2: Change, 1958–1966

BEAUTIFICATION AND HISTORIC PRESERVATION: GREENING, CLEANING, AND PRESERVING THE DOWNTOWN

The drive to beautify the city by planting trees and flowers, then eliminating litter and other forms of clutter, began on a small scale during the 1950s. Single projects sponsored by individuals provided precedents for similar action on a larger scale. Eventually the effort reached a stage where supporters could successfully push for appointment of the Mayor's Committee on City Beautification in 1963. That group evolved into Keep Omaha Beautiful, Inc., a private-sector nonprofit corporation. But formation of the mayor's committee marked a blending of progreenery and antilitter forces. Their overall goal was a more physically attractive city, one of the major targets being beautification of the downtown. In the discussion of beautification, moreover, first mention was made of the need to provide amenities to attract people involved in high-tech industries to

Omaha. While only the antilitter campaign really reached large-scale activity by 1966, the idea of the need for beautification grew in importance.

Beautification. In 1954 a pair of real-estate developers planted trees and flowers outside a "workingman's hotel" at Eleventh and Douglas streets and from that time on, projects to beautify the downtown grew apace. Two years later the owners of the Aquila Court Building, a shopping area at Sixteenth and Howard streets, sponsored the planting of four Chinese elms. Although at that time city foresters hoped other businesses would sponsor similar plantings, further efforts to beautify the downtown before 1966 tended to concentrate on cleaning it up, freeing it from litter and other forms of clutter.[48]

In 1959 city and business officials issued a call to clean up the downtown. The suggestion came in the form of an individual reminder to building owners to take better care of their properties. During an October meeting George Wruck, manager of the Associated Retailers of Omaha, told assembled businessmen that "a clean area is more inviting to shoppers." The city public works director mentioned the possibility of stricter enforcement of trash ordinances, but mostly emphasized individual voluntary action.[49]

Following a long tradition of cleanup, fix-up campaigns sponsored by the chamber and the junior chamber, the Chamber of Commerce, especially its women's division, lent organized support to the cleanup effort in 1960. For the next several years the women's division conducted beautification programs. Its members adopted a mother kangaroo and her baby as their symbol and "Please Don't Throw It . . . Stow It!" as their motto. In 1961 they began presenting awards for architectural excellence to building owners. The primary focus, however, remained keeping Omaha clean. The chamber's campaign undoubtedly publicized the effort to clean up the city, yet large-scale, broader-based citywide action on beautification came only after a 1963 proposal to establish a permanent private-sector organization to promote beautification.[50]

City Planning Director Alden Aust proposed the permanent organization in April 1963. His training as a landscape architect made him quite amenable to the idea of improving the city by removing old run-down buildings and planting trees and shrubs in parking lots. In speaking of the city's older warehouses and industrial districts, he cited as examples suburban industrial parks and their "fine green lawns" as models for improvement.[51]

The article announcing Aust's proposal also contained a statement indicating awareness of the growing demand for amenities. Aust reportedly told the Omaha Real Estate Board that in order to attract industries and research and development facilities, the city "must present a better face and more amenities." He described the employees of such firms as "a different breed of people. They want more schooling and recreational facilities and all sorts of amenities. They have a whole gamut of interests into which fall such things as beautification, education and a high level of public facilities and services." He noted that "these people are very mobile, not tied to one firm or one area. They won't stay in a city that doesn't have plus factors." In 1963, Aust's was something of a lone voice, but it indicated at least some early recognition of the necessity of new planning and boosting ideas.[52]

In May, Aust's beautification proposal received support from the chamber's women's division. More important, however, the call for a permanent organization gained the support of energetic and devoted Mrs. Les Anderson, chairman of the new Mayor's Committee on Beautification. She promised swift action and stressed that beautification was not just a women's project but must proceed on a large-scale, city–wide level.[53]

Omaha beautifiers were well aware of the national beautification drive that got under way in 1964 with support from the president's wife, Lady Bird Johnson. Thus Keep America Beautiful undoubtedly inspired the incorporation of Keep Omaha Beautiful that spring. The nationwide scope of the campaign spawned a spirit of competition among cities vying for the title "most beautiful." Omaha jumped into the fray. In fact, the article announcing formation of the organization mentioned San Antonio, Texas, as the winner of numerous national beautification awards. Said Keep Omaha Beautiful President Anderson: "They have little natural beauty there. Think what we could do here with our lovely trees and rolling hills." The fact that Omaha won a national award the following year served to entrench beautification as a civic priority.[54]

The chamber's beautification drives and those sponsored by Keep Omaha Beautiful involved the cooperation of small civic organizations, such as neighborhood groups and garden clubs. Recognition of the desirability of green-space amenities also reached into Omaha's corporate world. In 1964, Northwestern Bell Telephone Company built a small park "for the convenience and relaxation of visitors and shoppers" on vacant land near corporate headquarters at the corner of Twentieth and Douglas streets. The design included "trees, an attractive sundial, benches, serpentine brick wall, grassy areas, flowers and ornamental lamps for night lighting." Announcements described the park as fitting within the overall goals of the Central Omaha Plan, then under development. Possibly the small oasis provided inspiration for the brief, vague mention of the need for downtown open spaces in that plan.[55]

Perhaps more important, the announcement of the park's construction included a statement offering a somewhat different perspective of downtown. Real-estate man Alfred C. Kennedy said: "A city and especially its core can be attractive as well as functional; it can have beauty as well as efficiency."[56] Similar to Aust's statement on the "different breed of people" involved in the new service and high-tech industries, Kennedy's was something of a singular voice, yet it indicated rethinking of how best to improve downtown and promote Omaha. And support for the park represented acknowledgement that green open spaces downtown for rest and relaxation were desirable.

Finally, in 1966, downtown beautification received the imprimatur of longtime Omaha leader Robert Storz. He reached the peak of his personal influence in the 1950s, but well beyond that point his support lent considerable weight to any proposal. Storz, whose family was involved in the brewing industry, entered broadcasting in the early 1960s, taking over a company founded by his son, who died while still a young man. In 1966, Storz told the chamber president he was concerned about the appearance of downtown. He thought it was meager compared to the central areas of other cities he visited during his business travels. He suggested that a beautification project be undertaken.[57]

Historic Preservation. The efforts to beautify the city were not limited to providing green space and cleaning up litter. Others sought to preserve

Omaha's physical beauty by saving architecturally significant buildings from the wrecking ball. Historic preservationists came to the fore in the campaign to save the Old Post Office. Their efforts soon broadened to include Old City Hall, which was later sold for demolition to make way for new commercial construction. After both fights ended in defeat, the original organization, Landmarks, Inc., temporarily faded from view. Subsequent preservation and restoration work in the downtown, however, indicated that instead of a unique occurrence, the drive to recapture the spirit of Omaha's past would be a growing phenomenon.

As early as the 1930s civic leaders identified the Old Post Office as a likely target for demolition. Many considered the huge nineteenth-century structure a white elephant, its presence not fitting a modern, efficient downtown. Moreover, it sat on prime real estate that many felt could be put to better commercial use. The chamber's executive committee held that sentiment and recommended that the Central Omaha Committee plan for the razing of the building and "the re-use of the land for private commercial purposes."[58] Very shortly thereafter, the battle lines were drawn between those wishing to demolish the building and those wishing to save it.

The Central Omaha Committee, the Mayor's Post Office Committee, and the chamber supported demolition. They wanted the General Services Administration to declare the "ancient building" surplus, tear it down, and offer the cleared site to private enterprise for development. Support for preservation of the building, or parts of it, came from Rachael Gallagher's Friends of the Parks and Landmarks, Inc. The park group wanted to save the clock tower and several archways to provide entrance to a park. In many ways, the Post Office project was part of the larger politics of parks in the city. Downtown's only park, Jefferson Square, was sacrificed to Interstate Highway construction. In 1964 the Central Omaha Committee, trying to deal with opposition from the park group, considered the idea of a trade— a Post Office site park in exchange for Jefferson Square. As committee Chairman A. F. Jacobson observed, Friends of the Parks exerted tremendous influence. In fact, his statement indicated that the parks group won most of its political battles. The committee hoped that by supporting the Post Office proposal it could end the conflict over the fate of Jefferson Square. A committee member described that strategy as "sacrificing a bishop to capture a queen."[59]

The chamber favored the park proposal in February 1964, but it seemed to have been an empty endorsement. Supporting the park group's application to the GSA did not raise the funds necessary to bring the project to fruition. Funding proved the major obstacle for any group seeking to preserve the building, and none overcame it. By 1965 the Central Omaha Committee reasserted the civic and business leadership's original recommendation and called for demolition of the post office and sale of the site for commercial development.[60]

The other group supporting preservation, Landmarks, Inc., was headed by several prominent Omahans, including architect Nes Latenser, Josyln Museum Director Eugene Kingman, and the dean of adult education at the University of Omaha, William Utley. Also involved were two executives of Northern Natural Gas, David Carson and David Peterson. Their participation reflected that company's continuing support of educational and cultural endeavors. Landmarks proposed transforming the Post Office site into a western center that would include a hotel, outdoor restaurant, plaza, museum, and offices for the National Park Service (which had a regional office in Omaha). The group did not narrowly focus on that however, because it sought to preserve much of Omaha's downtown architectural heritage, including Old City Hall, another target for demolition.[61]

Landmarks had an example of successful restoration to cite in support of its position. Developers in Chicago had created an economically viable renovation of Old Town, an area of shops and offices in a run-down section on the north edge of the Loop. Landmarks hoped to create a similar area in the eastern section of downtown Omaha. Its proposal pointed out the considerable differences between the newer ideas for downtown and the more traditional plans. The area marked by Landmarks for renovation had been targeted for extensive clearance by the Central Omaha Committee. The Central Omaha Plan proposed closing off streets, creating superblocks, and tearing down obsolete structures. There was only one point of similarity between the two proposals: both Landmarks and the formal plan acknowledged the historical character of much of the district.[62]

The Old Post Office and the City Hall were sold to make way for private development. To some extent, without urban renewal, selling off surplus government property was the only way Omaha could clear significant parcels of downtown land for private development. After this, Landmarks quietly faded for several years. It had, however, identified preservation of historic buildings as an important issue, for the Central Omaha Plan acknowledged, though briefly, the desirability of at least some historic preservation. Further preservation action continued at an individual level. For example, an Omaha businessman converted a former downtown warehouse into living quarters. After 1966, downtown development—most prominently in the Old Market—initiated largely by individuals, demonstrated the value of providing a sense of the city's past while projecting a forward-looking image as a potential function of the downtown.[63]

CULTURAL INSTITUTIONS AND UNIVERSITIES: NEW DEMANDS, NEW GOALS

More support for cultural amenities and broader recognition of the role of Omaha's two universities in the community and in the economic development process joined the growing concern for urban aesthetics. It is difficult to measure a community's level of cultural awareness with precision. Most cities of any size display some degree of cultural activity, be it a museum or a civic opera or literary groups. Omaha long had had any number of cultural institutions and groups, the most prominent being Joslyn Art Museum and the Omaha Symphony. So cultural activity was neither new in the 1960s nor a sudden awakening of cultural sensitivity. However, Joslyn and the orchestra grew in size and importance during that decade, indicating a greater demand for cultural amenities. The museum enjoyed civic and business support from its very inception. In the 1960s, however, its director, Eugene Kingman, promoted his goals to civic and business leaders. The symphony had grown steadily during the 1950s and by the early 1960s it, too, had attained a central role in Omaha cultural life.

The universities became higher-profile institutions. Much of the attention still focused on their contributions to Omaha business life in terms of payroll and employment, but other contributions—research, expertise, leaders—gained more recognition. The level of support for higher education in the early 1960s was unprecedented, indicating increased recognition its importance and the need for better-educated individuals in the work force. They, in turn, would be more likely to support cultural facilities.

The chamber's 1961 Program for Progress included an item pledging its support for cultural and recreational activities. Kingman took the announcement as an opportunity to speak to the chamber on "Cultural Goals for Omaha." He proposed that museum visiting be considered as one of the recreational activities available to Omahans. The chairman of the chamber's Parks and Recreation Committee, J. A. C. Kennedy, Jr., endorsed Kingman's statement saying, "The chamber will support those endeavors in the arts and sciences which can make Omaha 'the Athens of the Midwest.'" While that statement was tinged with booster hyperbole, the new level of support for Joslyn and the arts was real, if not yet spectacular. Community gifts and steady membership growth accompanied a slow but consistent increase in the museum's assets throughout the 1960s.[64]

John Merriam of Northern Natural Gas Company made a strong commitment to the museum in the 1950s. The company built its headquarters across the street from Joslyn and Merriam led the unsuccessful campaign—part of the Omaha Plan—to turn the entire area into a cultural center. Support continued, however, and in 1962, Northern purchased the extensive Maximilian-Bodmer Collection and put it on permanent loan to the museum.[65] The collection consisted of drawings and paintings by Karl Bodmer, an artist hired by Prince Maximilian to record his visit to the American West in the 1830s.

In 1966 the museum repeated a familiar theme when it announced another expansion plan, this one involving clearance of land just north of it: Twenty-second to Twenty-Fourth streets between Capital Avenue and Davenport. As early as the 1930s supporters had pushed for general clearance of the area around the museum.[66] The additions envisioned in 1966 were not constructed, but a full block of older structures was demolished and the space provided more parking for patrons. Major renovation awaited the 1970s, but, during the 1960s, with its growing assets and its major collection of western art, Joslyn expanded its role as a cultural asset in the city and the metropolitan area.

The Omaha Symphony also enjoyed increased support and recognition by the early 1960s. It had begun growing slowly in the late 1940s. Under the energetic direction of Richard Duncan, it introduced youth concerts and evening outdoor pops concerts. The symphony added members throughout the 1950s and by 1960 had received recognition as a metropolitan-class orchestra. In 1958, Joseph Levine took up the baton and eagerly boosted both the symphony and his adopted city. His article "Why I Love Omaha" in the *Saturday Evening Post* received a great deal of attention. He continued the pops and youth concerts initiated by Duncan as the budget and concert schedule increased. The symphony did not professionalize until the 1970s, but even as an amateur group, by the mid-1960s it was a widely-recognized, well-supported cultural organization.[67]

Omaha had other cultural organizations as well, most notably the Community Playhouse, known as the theater that gave Henry Fonda and Dorothy McGuire their start in acting. The playhouse moved from an urban location to a suburban site in the 1950s. Although it continued to serve the entire metropolitan area, it was not involved directly in the expansion of cultural amenities downtown.

Expanding in perhaps the most dramatic fashion were the University of Omaha and Creighton University. Their plans gained the immediate and enthusiastic support of the civic and business community. Both had enjoyed community support in the past. Omaha leaders secured W P A funds to build a new campus for the municipal university. Creighton, founded by two successful early businessmen and their families, received bequests from many prominent individuals over the years. The level of support beginning in the early 1960s, however, was virtually unprecedented. Both schools, especially Creighton, undertook ambitious building programs headed and heartily endorsed by corporate leaders.

During the early 1960s, colleges and universities throughout the nation reported large enrollment increases as the so-called baby boomers reached college age. Omaha's two schools were no exception. By 1963 both had impressive expansion programs. In that year the University of Omaha, still a municipal entity, depended on taxpayer support, so its expansion program needed community endorsement. In April 1963 it asked voters to raise its tax levy from two mills to four. The Chamber of Commerce, never known as an advocate of higher taxes in any form, came out enthusiastically in favor of the proposal. The editorial outlining the organization's position on the issue emphasized the fact that good educational facilities at all levels—elementary, secondary, college—attracted business and industry.[68] Early arguments boosting Omaha's universities emphasized payrolls and the number of people employed. The later endorsement also included that element, but it was one of the first acknowledgments of higher educational facilities' contributions to the general business environment. Universities provided specialists and helped create a well-educated work force.

By far the largest expansion program belonged to Creighton. It announced twenty-four-million-dollar, eight-building construction goal, "the largest civic building program in the area's history." The campaign enrolled the financial and organizational support of numerous leading corporate figures. James B. Moore (vice-president, Northwestern Bell), Leo Daly (Leo A. Daly, Company), Willis Strauss (president, Northern Natural Gas) and Richard Walker (president, Byron Reed Real Estate) headed the fundraising committees. The article announcing the new program made note of the fact that Creighton produced many Omaha professional, civic, and business leaders. According to the article, 46 percent of the physicians, 46 percent of the attorneys, 75 percent of the dentists, 58 percent of the registered pharmacists, and 47 percent of the certified public accountants in the Omaha area were Creighton graduates. The conclusion asserted: "Leadership is the product of higher education."[69]

Individual leaders were not the only product of higher education. The expanded enrollment in colleges, coupled with the changing economic structure in Omaha, produced an increase in the percentage of the adult population with a college education. During the 1960s, college enrollment more than doubled from 6,416 in 1960 to 14,501 in 1970. The percentage of the adult population over twenty-five with a college diploma increased from 7 percent in 1950 to 9 percent in 1960 and to 12.4 percent in 1970.[70] A more highly educated population, moreover, provided a larger audience, hence greater demand, for cultural amenities.

Another important endorsement of higher education's role in promoting development came in 1966. The chamber's new Economic Development Council announced the funding of an "Area Research and Data Center" in the Urban Studies Center at the University of Omaha. Previous to 1966, the various citizen planning committees or a firm contracted by them undertook most planning and economic research. It proved rather narrow and confined to the limits of the specific projects under consideration. The new center was designed to conduct broad, ongoing research projects. Potential research topics included economic growth and change; trends in social factors, such as population, age, income, and education; land-use analysis; and requirements for education, police, and fire protection, other government services, and transportation. Creation of the center also indicated more reliance on experts and their advice in the planning process. The Economic Development Council expected to use data provided by the center to attract business and industry.[71]

STUDY TRIPS: LOOKING BEYOND THEIR OWN BACKYARD

The civic and business community also sought useful knowledge through a series of study tours. The first occurred in 1963, and over the next decade they grew in importance. The trips represented a significant change in local leaders' operating procedures. The booster element, always prominent in planning and economic development, had inspired a certain degree of imitation. For example, as cities throughout the nation built new civic auditoriums, Omaha simply had to build one, too. That type of response represented imitation from afar, but the plans and booster strategies produced were still based primarily on local experience. In the 1960s, Omaha leaders began to reach out directly to other cities and learn from their experience. Civic leaders wanted firsthand knowledge of improvement and development schemes. They did not then simply try to replicate the other city's ideas in Omaha; rather, the trips gave them a broader awareness of the variety of ideas used in planning and development programs. They were exposed to the new ideas as economic changes then occurring in Omaha became more obvious, but they did not give up the older perceptions until a series of crises in the late 1960s forced them to do so. Yet by 1966, rethinking of their image of Omaha was in fact under way.

On the first tour, forty-six Omahans headed north to the Twin Cities. The roster read like a who's who of Omaha's leadership and included most of the city's corporate leaders and some top local government officials. The agenda for the two-day visit consisted of very conventional items. Smaller study groups were formed to examine "industrial advancements, highways and streets, downtown rehabilitation, urban renewal, dock facilities, business climate, over-all metropolitan planning and related matters." Whether the expedition returned with new ideas is not clear. The article reporting it was not followed up by announcement of significant findings. The travelers were evidently impressed, however, because the following year the chamber invited the mayor of Minneapolis to speak at a public-affairs luncheon.[72]

A far more influential trip was made in 1965. In visiting the Twin Cities, Omaha leaders had chosen an urban area that in many ways was quite similar to Omaha. Minneapolis–Saint Paul was also an older urban area traditionally dependent on its agricultural hinterland. The trip to Dallas, Texas, in 1965 represented a visit to a somewhat different city that had experienced rapid growth as part of the post–World War II Sunbelt phenomenon. The second study group definitely was exposed to new ideas.

The Dallas trip included tours of privately developed industrial tracts, a modern wholesale market center, and high-tech Texas Instruments Corporation, which had twenty thousand employees. A seminar conducted for the Omahans by Dallas business and civic leaders was the highlight of the trip. Its major theme was the importance of education and research to economic development. Said a Dallas spokesman: "Research brings the products into existence but education has to supply the trained manpower to get the assembly lines rolling."[73]

Faced with mounting unemployment problems as rural Texans flooded into Dallas looking for jobs, that city's business leaders decided the answer was to encourage scientific and technological research and create new industries. (Though not identified, the military and nascent space industries in Texas and other southern states undoubtedly were examples for Dallas leaders.) In 1961 the city's businessmen pledged five million dollars to create a research center that would inspire a "spirit of innovation" to develop new products and create new jobs.[74]

The Omaha group did not return determined to transform their city into another Dallas. However, they learned the growing importance of high-tech industries and the vital need to encourage education and research in order to attract out-of-state companies to their area. The enthusiasm with which the new ideas were greeted indicated a high level of receptivity for them. By the mid-1960s, the changes in Omaha's economic structure that had been at work since the 1950s were more evident. Not ready to discard their perception of the city as the stockyard and meatpacking capital of the nation, Omaha leaders nonetheless recognized the obvious declines in that sector and the increases in the service sector. Only a series of crises could dislodge the old ideas. Yet, the process of rethinking was beginning.

Omaha employment changed dramatically during the first half of the 1960s. In 1960 the traditional employment sectors (manufacturing, transportation, communication and public utilities, and wholesaling) held a share of total employment that equaled the 35 percent held by the service sector. Within five years, however, the traditional sectors' share had dropped to 33 percent and the service sector's share had jumped to 40 percent of total employment. The shift was the result of a 2 percent drop in manufacturing employment, accompanied by a 1 percent rise in retailing and 2 percent increases in both services and governmental employment. Much of the manufacturing employment decrease resulted from the loss of more than thirty-three hundred food-processing jobs, the vast majority of them in meatpacking.[75]

Despite a booster philosophy that tended to accent the positive, the declines were far more evident than the gains. The stockyards and meatpacking industries were in trouble. Furthermore, concern about the viability of Omaha's traditional industries had generated much of the urgency in Interstate Highway construction. In 1959 City Planning Director Alden Aust had warned that without the easy access the Interstate could provide, several major packers would leave the city.[76]

ON THE THRESHOLD OF CHANGE

In 1966 the image of Omaha as perceived and promoted by civic and business leaders was on the threshold of rapid and substantial change. The older ideas embodied in the Central Omaha Plan had failed to meet the downtown crisis. Infrastructure improvements and clearance continued but no longer dominated. New ideas began to take hold, and with them came rethinking of downtown Omaha's role and image. "Efficiency" and "center place" receded into the background, replaced by "ambience" and "amenities."

In 1966, Omaha still saw itself as the stockyards and meatpacking center of the nation. After 1966, things changed rapidly. Beginning in 1967 the big meatpackers began closing and business at the stockyards declined. Death and retirement decimated the ranks of Omaha's upper leadership and opened the way for younger men to rise to the top. One by one, most of the major downtown department stores closed. In the resultant crisis atmosphere, new ideas with new promises for success took hold. But most important perhaps, a dynamic new leader named Eugene Leahy pushed his dream for Omaha and its downtown. By 1973 the pieces were in place.

SIX

A "New City," a New Image: Planning, 1966–1973

T he newer ideas in planning introduced in the early 1960s were on the rise by 1966. A tentative reshaping of Omaha's image was also under way. Neither the new ideas nor a fresh image could push aside the traditional ideas and image, however; an economic crisis and broad social, economic, and political changes were necessary before significant transition could occur. Three factors helped to speed up the process in the late 1960s. First and foremost was economic change, symbolized by the nearly total collapse of the meatpacking industry. Concomitantly, the service sector gradually gained recognition as the driving force in the city's economy. Second, between 1966 and 1973, there were a tremendous number of changes in Omaha's leadership structure. This opened the possibility for changes in attitudes and ideas, and the possibility became reality with the introduction of the third important factor: a dynamic, influential leader with fresh ideas. Eugene Leahy, elected mayor in 1969, came to office with a number of innovative ideas for the city. His administration marked the beginning of an unprecedented level of prestige and influence for city hall and further equalization of the public-private partnership. Under his leadership, a new image of Omaha was firmly established. Although he was not directly responsible for all that happened, he proved to be the necessary spark to ignite many of the changes.

Within the context of economic change and new leadership, city planners and boosters began searching for new ways to promote the city. They needed to find other aspects of the city they could use to present its case to the outside world. Slowly they built a new image reflecting the importance of ambience and the growing demand for cultural and recreational amenities. New middle-class values and attitudes (such as concern for the environment), the multifaceted importance of higher education, and the desire for an abundance of diverse leisure-time activities and other so-called quality of life issues influenced the shaping of the new image. An important turning point came in 1970 when the Chamber of Commerce declared that its top priority was enhancement of Omaha's quality of life. As the city took on a new image, so did the downtown and riverfront.

The planning proposals of the late 1960s and early 1970s reflected the new images of both the city as a whole and the downtown. Their melding climaxed in a collection of related planning proposals generally grouped under the title "Riverfront Development." In a reversal of past trends, the long-neglected Missouri River suddenly emerged as the focus of a wide-ranging and ambitious scheme championed by Eugene Leahy that, in his words, aimed at building a "whole new lifestyle" along the river.[1]

Change and Crises: Economic Transformation and New Leadership

The final curtain came down very quickly on the meatpacking drama in Omaha. The industry did not cease to exist altogether, but three major packers—Armour, Swift, and Cudahy—closed in as many years. It was the end of Omaha's role as a meatpacking center. In 1968, Chamber of Commerce President J. Allan Mactier (Nebraska Consolidated Mills) referred to the Swift plant's closing as regrettable and understandable.[2] A few years earlier, it would have been viewed as devastating and unthinkable. By 1968, however, the economic changes under way since World War II were plain enough that civic and business leaders could absorb such a loss without much panic.

The unemployment produced by the plant closings was, relatively speaking, minimal. That factor undoubtedly helped ameliorate any sense of panic. Studies of the closings' effects indicated that although they produced pockets of unemployment, their impact was short term. Large numbers of packinghouse workers, especially the unskilled, were old and near retirement. Unemployment and retirement benefits thus cushioned the blow.

Other segments of the economy were growing; young, skilled workers appeared to move into these and other jobs with relative ease.[3] While the collapse of meatpacking was by no means inconsequential, it did not produce the same devastation that, for example, the collapse of the steel industry caused in Pittsburgh in the late 1970s and early 1980s.

This is not to say that Omaha's closings precipitated no feeling of crisis. The crisis was not economic, however, but more of a psychological nature. With the plant closings and the decline of the stockyards, Omaha lost major components of its corporate identity. Even as local landmarks the old symbols of economic power virtually disappeared. The stockyards consolidated operations until it almost shrank from view; only the massive Livestock Exchange Building remained to stand in mute testimony to former days of glory. More dramatically, in 1971 a demolition expert's explosives reduced the old Armour plant to rubble in eight seconds.[4] The fading of the old symbols forced civic and business leaders to develop new symbols of Omaha's economic strength and corporate identity, and the expanding service economy provided many of the components.

The expanding service sector helped soften the blow of plant closings and abate the sense of crisis. By 1970 the service sector supplied 44 percent of total employment. In contrast, the traditionally strong commercial-industrial sector provided only 33 percent.[5] As late as 1967 (before the plant closings), however, local economic surveys failed to recognize fully the service sector's importance.

Three economic surveys appeared in 1967, all prepared by the new Center for Applied Urban Research at the University of Omaha. Each noted declines in the traditional commercial and food-processing sector. In fact, each study concentrated on explaining exactly what was happening there. They presented far more information on manufacturing and food processing than on any other segment of the economy. One reason for the primary focus on this traditionally important sector could have been the fact that none of the studies viewed service-sector employment as a unit. They recognized growth in each of the parts but failed to put them together as a whole. The service economy was a relatively new concept. Evidently, it had not yet taken hold enough to influence the way local researchers looked at the economy. By the early 1970s, however, civic and business leaders were more comfortable with the idea that the service sector was the driving force in Omaha's economy. And in 1975, for the first time, an economic study acknowledged that the service sector was and had been the major source of employment growth in the metropolitan area. Thereafter, economic surveys assumed as a matter of course that Omaha had completed the transition to a service economy.[6]

Certain sociodemographic changes also provided evidence of economic transformation. In the late 1960s there were further increases in educational achievement levels and the emergence of white-collar workers as a majority of the work force. Service-economy labor demands contributed to the higher level of educational achievement. The median level and the percentage of high school and college graduates in the over-twenty-five age group rose throughout the postwar period. In 1950 the median level of education stood 11.4 years of school. It was 12.0 in 1960 and reached 12.3 in 1970. The increase anticipated growing percentages of high school and college graduates in the twenty-five-and-over age group. In 1950, 45 percent of that group had a high school diploma and 7 percent had a college degree. By 1960 the number with a high school diploma rose to 51 percent and with a college degree to 9 percent. In 1970 the percentages stood at 61.6 with a high school diploma and 12.4 with a college degree.[7]

Concurrently, the percentage of white-collar workers among all workers rose from 49.1 in 1960 to 54.6 in 1970 (figures are not available for 1950). A breakdown of white-collar figures for 1970 indicated that 24.7 percent of all workers occupied professional or managerial positions, while 29.9 percent held sales and clerical positions.[8] The better-educated white-collar workers made new and different demands on the city, especially with regard to cultural and recreational amenities.

The economic transition tended to bring with it changes in the leadership structure. Human factors, such as death and retirement, of course, played major roles, and broad changes in the economic structure also were significant. Between 1966 and 1973, a large number of deaths and retirements caused rapid turnover in the leadership structure. Of the twenty men whose names appeared on the *Omaha Sun Newspapers* leadership list in 1966, five had retired and two had died by 1971. Another was promoted to an out-of-town job, and five others faded from prominence as their companies moved elsewhere or decreased in local importance.[9] These personal and impersonal forces resulted in fourteen openings at the top of the leadership structure.

Most of the men who had moved into the top spots by the mid-1970s did so by succeeding retiring leaders. Seven new men reached the top via that route. They were associated with companies whose ranking executives had long occupied established positions of influence. The companies included Bozell and Jacobs (advertising), Northwestern Bell Telephone, U.S. National Bank, First National Bank, Omaha National Bank, the Omaha World-Herald Corporation, and Union Pacific. Four new men came into the ranks from companies not previously associated with the leadership list: Commercial Federal Savings and Loan, Paxton-Vierling Steel, ConAgra (formerly Nebraska Consolidated Mills), and Woodmen of the World Life Insurance Company. The four remaining men on the tentative mid-1970s list included three individuals at the very top of the structure and a fourth very popular leader. V. J. Skutt of Mutual of Omaha had been influential since the 1950s, Peter Kiewit and Leo Daly were perhaps the two most powerful men in the city, and John Diesing of J. L. Brandeis and Sons was very influential.[10]

It is also interesting to note the companies that, for one reason or another, ceased over the years to put their ranking executives in the top leadership structure. Most of them engaged in Omaha's traditional economic activities. No single pattern marked the decline in importance of any of them. Some ceased operations; some were bought out by national firms, shifting important leaders out of Omaha; some were supplanted by growing competitors; and for some it was a function of the personality of new leaders.[11] Cudahy (meats), Reynolds-Updike (coal), Storz Brewing, Swanson Frozen Foods, Butler-Welch Grain, John Deere, Fairmont Foods, Carpenter Paper, Byron Reed Real Estate, Bekins Van and Storage, Meridith Broadcasting, and Omaha Loan and Building Association, all of which had provided influential leaders at one point had ceased to do so by the mid-1970s. By then only the Union Pacific and ConAgra continued to provide leaders who represented in any way the traditionally strong economic sectors. The representation was almost symbolic, however, because by that time both companies were quite different from what they had been in the 1950s, having long since expanded beyond their traditional boundaries of economic activity.

Fourteen openings within a few years undoubtedly created some measure of instability in the private leadership structure. During those years of rapid turnover a new leader from an unusual source stepped forward. Eugene Leahy, elected mayor in 1969, quickly emerged as an influential and popular public leader. Of all Omaha mayors between 1945 and 1973, he unquestionably displayed the most vigorous and dynamic leadership, and he transmitted his personal enthusiasm for projects to the civic and business leadership. It is difficult, however, to assess how much power he wielded, but while serving his lone term as mayor, he obviously exercised tremendous influence. He set much of the style and precedent for the future of the public-private partnership, and his dynamic leadership increased the role and importance of city hall. While the momentum never swung totally in favor of city hall, after Leahy the partnership proved far more balanced than it had ever been in the past. After voluntarily choosing not to run for a second term, though, he gradually but steadily faded into the background.[12] Regardless, his administration marked an important turning point the public-private partnership and in the approach to city planning and boosting.

Leahy reached the apex of his influence in 1972 when both the *Omaha World-Herald* and the *Omaha Sun Newspapers* named him Man of the Year. At the end of his tenure he enjoyed enormous personal popularity, part of it stemming from the fact that he was one of the most colorful mayors Omaha had. He was known for his sense of humor and his willingness to be his own puckish self, even if it meant reading the Sunday comics on television and showing up in a bunny suit to sign an Easter Seal proclamation, to cite only two of his more notorious high jinks. On a more substantial note, he brought unprecedented dynamism and a sense of vision to the office. He pushed forward a vigorous annexation program, expanded the role of city government by prodding for a substantial increase in the city's budget ($42 million in 1969 to $70 million in 1972), financed by a city sales tax; increased city spending on federal programs to more than $5 million; spearheaded the campaign to capture a $4.8 million Economic Development Administration grant to create the South Omaha Industrial Park; and negotiated the purchase of failing private bus lines and creation of city-owned Metropolitan Area Transit. Most important, he championed the sweeping Riverfront Development scheme.[13]

As Leahy's predecessor, A. V. Sorensen, put it, "Gene Leahy was the right mayor, in the right place and at the right time."[14] Leahy came to office at a time when the full impact of economic changes was finally recognized. It was a time of rapid turnover in the private leadership structure, and it was a time when civic and business leaders were beginning to seek new ways to promote Omaha. That, perhaps, was one of the most significant factors. The city was ripe for new ideas. Leahy's innovative ideas, new faces in the corporate leadership, and social and economic changes created the broad context within which a new image of Omaha was created and a new planning agenda established.

Promoting a New Omaha: More than Old Wine in a New Bottle

A promotional thrust introduced in 1967 began on a rather traditional note, but within a few short years, prominent themes emerged. Promotional material began to extol not so much the virtues of working in Omaha, but the virtues of living there. The transition was obvious in the tone of advertisements in national magazines to attract business and industry, and it proved to be not just a public-relations campaign created for the benefit of strangers. The newer themes caught on at home as well. They were evident in Chamber of Commerce annual messages, in the stated goals of citizens groups, in the choice of cities for study tours, in statements made by local civic and business leaders, and in materials produced for tourists.

In 1967 the Chamber of Commerce introduced its first major promotional campaign in several years. The theme was "Omaha Can Do." The slogan, in a very traditional vein, connoted a hard-working and efficient city. The catch phrase caught on almost immediately and soon appeared on windows, doors, stationery, advertisements, and brochures. As popular as the slogan was, the civic and business leadership was already reshaping Omaha's image.[15]

That same year, civic and business leaders received an empirical lesson in how to attract high-tech industries. In April, Control Data Corporation, a blue-chip computer and electronics firm, announced its selection of Omaha as the site for a new plant. An article describing the company's reasons for coming to Omaha indicated that factors other than infrastructure requirements influenced the decision. Inexpensive electrical power and ample, affordable land were part of the picture, yet other factors also played an important role. Control Data wanted to locate in an area with skilled labor, schools, parks, and a cultural climate.[16] The need for skilled labor indicated the importance of educational institutions and an educated work force. Availability of schools and parks was a rather standard wish, but a cultural climate was not so standard. Cultural institutions had been mentioned in promotional material predating 1967, but they had received little or no credit as attractions for new businesses and industries. From that point on, however, they achieved unprecedented prominence in such publications.

The new themes were evident in a promotional campaign launched in 1968. Known as Awareness Omaha, the effort was a direct attempt to create a favorable image for Omaha. Its stated objective was to "build a desirable image for our community and stimulate interest and awareness among those who influence industrial plant, service or office expansion." The campaign was directed by Charles D. Peebler, a youthful new member of the leadership structure. He was then thirty-three and president of Bozell and Jacobs, having succeeded Morris Jacobs in 1967. Awareness Omaha focused on local and national audiences. Locally it sought to retain industries and encouraged them to expand in Omaha. The chamber hoped to reach a national audience through an advertising program and publication of a quarterly magazine, *Dateline: Omaha*. According to Peebler, the magazine focused on industrial Omaha and its point of view. Therefore, it would deal primarily with business matters. The magazine also had a new twist. Besides the business-oriented pieces, in order to "balance out the magazine," Peebler planned articles on "the cultural, civic and educational communities."[17]

The advertisements, which appeared in a magazine published by United Airlines, were rather traditional at first. If they demonstrated anything new at all, the four 1968 ads at least showed the nation that Omaha had a sense of humor as they promoted the city in lighthearted fashion. The first two lampooned the city's outside image: "You've heard of Omaha. It's that place you skipped on your way to Knott's Berry Farm." And "You've heard of Omaha. It's under the crack in the middle of your road atlas." The new tone did not, however, mean a complete break with the past. The first two photographs depicted life in Omaha: the annual Ak-Sar-Ben coronation and the lights of downtown. The other two pictures clearly stressed working Omaha by showing the Fruehauf and Sperry-Vicker plants. Only the small print at the bottom of the advertisements publicized such assets as an opera company, theater, pro baseball, hockey and football (minor league), and, of all things, miniskirts.[18]

The four 1969 ads were strikingly different. They focused on Omaha's virtues as a place to live. Compared to the rather muscular campaigns of the 1940s and 1950s or even the Omaha Can Do drive of the 1960s, they marked a significant departure from the past. Each ad favorably compared Omaha with one of four national urban giants: New York, Chicago, San Francisco, and Los Angeles. Rather than proclaiming that Omaha offered the same attractions, they pointed out what the urban giants had that Omaha did not, namely, overcrowding, airway and freeway congestion, and "sophistication." (The sophistication San Francisco had that Omaha had much less of was depicted in a photograph of San Francisco's flower children.) Further, Omaha's lack of such features was what was good about it. The city had breathing room, easy access by air and uncongested freeways, and a cultural environment large enough to please yet small enough to invite participation. The photographs of Omaha in the advertisements showed someone walking a dog in a wooded area, a child flying a kite, people riding bikes, and a woman on horseback in an open field. The copy at the bottom of the advertisements reinforced the image of Omaha as a desirable place to live.[19]

The increasing prominence of the newer themes peaked in 1970. In that year the Chamber of Commerce declared that its priority for the year would be enhancement of Omaha's quality of life. The chamber seemed to define it as a combination of several broad categories of concern, including the "environment, political responsibility, pollution, education, transportation and a broad spectrum of 'people problems'" The article was not very specific. Another later that year suggested more clearly what was involved in the new attention on promoting Omaha as a place to live. "Omaha's 'Good Life' Pleases Citizens Transplanted Here" described a recent issue of *Dateline: Omaha* devoted to testimonials from non-Omahans about the desirability of living there. They came from several businessmen, and each concluded that he had "found a life style compatible with his profession or business with cultural and educational enrichments usually available only in the larger metropolitan areas."[20]

Clearly part of the quality-of-life picture were the antipollution campaigns of the late 1960s and early 1970s. A 1971 article described the various citizens groups and nonprofit organizations founded to promote cleaner air and water. Some of them were established organizations that took up the pollution issue as concern about the environment grew. They included the Fontenelle Forest Nature Center, which taught ecology, preservation, and conservation to schoolchildren, and Keep Omaha Beautiful, which moved beyond a narrow concern with litter to projects for improving the environment, including construction of a recycling center (antilitter, however, remained the solid core of its program).[21]

Most of the groups concerned with the pollution issue were new, founded in the wake of the enthusiasm generated by Earth Day 1970. The largest and most active was the Quality Environment Council, or QEC. It was "a non-partisan, non-profit organization . . . dedicated to informing and educating people about how to achieve and maintain a quality environment." Other groups included the Sarpy County Environmental Advisory Committee, small ecology clubs in the universities and larger clubs in the high schools and junior highs, and environmental committees formed by professional organizations such as the Nebraska chapters of the American Institute of Architects and the American Institute of Chemical Engineers, as well as the Professional Engineers of Nebraska.[22]

The number of groups established to deal with the issue indicated both the high value placed on a clean environment by many people and the fact that Omaha had very real problems with air and water pollution. The problems were mild, though, compared to those in older, highly industrialized cities or the automobile-choked cities of the West Coast. Omaha's relative lack of severe pollution became part of the booster argument. A promotional advertisement declared that Omaha was "located smack dab in the middle of the U.S., where pollution is a dirty word." A statement by Willis A. Strauss, chairman of Northern Natural Gas Company, further indicated the links between economic development and a clean environment. He declared that "The people of Nebraska and of the Omaha metropolitan area are committed to a common goal: balanced economic growth and a better quality of life in a cleaner environment. They have indicated this through their legislators in the establishment of the State Department of Economic Development and in councils on water and air pollution control."[23]

Not all of the promotional material was directed at business and industry. Another Chamber of Commerce group sought to promote Omaha's cultural and recreational amenities to a somewhat different set of people: tourists. In 1969 the chamber's Tourism Committee helped sponsor publication of "Gateway City Trail Map," which highlighted various activities in the area. Aimed at both out-of-town tourists and natives, the program publicized such attractions as Joslyn Art museum, the Omaha Playhouse, the Omaha Symphony, the Union Pacific and Strategic Aerospace Museums, Mormon Cemetery, Boys Town, the Ak-Sar-Ben racetrack, Henry Doorly Zoo, the Old Market, and parks, playgrounds, and professional sports.[24] The Gateway City project was the first extensive promotion of leisure-time activities in the Omaha area.

Civic and business leaders also played tourist as they continued study trips to various cities. In 1969 the Chamber of Commerce ventured to Hartford, Connecticut. That trip held a certain symbolic importance. In the late 1960s the burgeoning insurance industry began to replace meatpacking as a primary component of the city's image. The giants, Mutual/United of Omaha and Woodmen of the World, and nearly two dozen other insurance firms with headquarters or offices in the city put Omaha in a position to rival established insurance centers, such as Hartford. Virtually the only thing young midwestern Omaha had in common with old New England Hartford was the insurance industry. The choice of that city for a study tour suggested recognition of the insurance industry's vital role in Omaha life.[25]

The tour that represented the most significant departure from the past, however, was the 1971 trip to Toronto, Ontario, Canada. It indicated that civic and business leaders were ready and committed to move forward with newer themes. The trip came at a time when Toronto was completing Ontario Place, a ninety-acre, $23 million "entertainment and exhibition complex of islands, lagoons, canals, parks, beaches and buildings" constructed on man-made islands in Lake Ontario. In addition, Toronto had plans for a $190 million residential-industrial complex along the lakeshore. The tour was made just as Omaha planners and boosters were formulating their own riverfront-development plans.[26]

The trip revealed a civic and business leadership ready to look far afield for planning and development ideas. The localism that had characterized early postwar planning had eroded even further, and the retreat was indicated as well in another subject of interest on the tour: Toronto's metropolitan government structure. In 1967, Toronto and its suburbs engaged in a consolidation that reduced the number of municipalities from thirteen to six, which were then placed under the jurisdiction of a metropolitan council. Omaha, then facing the first stiff opposition to its annexation policy, showed keen interest in the Toronto model for extending political boundaries.[27]

In 1970, Thomas S. Nurnberger, Jr., the new president of Northwestern Bell Telephone Company, granted an interview in which he indicated the importance of higher-education facilities and cultural and recreational amenities in attracting business. "After all the primary considerations like labor and raw materials and market are considered," he said, "quite often the top man starts rationalizing and his recreational interests have a way of getting into the picture." Seven years later a *Fortune* magazine survey of facility locational decisions over a ten- to fifteen-year period concluded that "personal preferences of company executives" and "style of living for employees" were major factors in the decision-making process. A *Dateline: Omaha* advertisement that appeared in *Fortune* in mid-1974 indicated clearly that the civic and business leadership had recognized and accepted the new forces influencing Omaha's development and had reshaped the city's image to harmonize with the newer themes.[28]

The multipage advertisement used testimonials from business leaders to tell Omaha's story. Some of the testimonials dealt directly with the newer themes. Others dealt with more traditional concerns—transportation and communication, availability of land—yet the tone of the descriptions reflected the newer themes. The advertisements first described Omaha as "The People City." Dale TeKolste of Northern Natural Gas Company and the Chamber of Commerce emphasized the friendliness and warmth of Omahans and stressed that the business community and local government worked in partnership to provide the amenities necessary to enhance the quality of life. He described Omaha as having small-town openness and a big city's cosmopolitan outlook.[29]

Leo Daly echoed TeKolste's sentiments in a section of the ad headed "People Have Time to Live." It quoted Daly as saying Omahans have "time to do things" because they are free of the "worry about getting to work and surviving the daily grind that can consume a person's vitality and interest in his job." One reason, apparently, that Omahans had time to live was the fact that they did not have to spend a large part of their work days commuting. Another unidentified business leader described Omaha as a "20-minute city," saying, "I can get anywhere in the city in 20 minutes. That's important to me, to my family, and to my clients. This is a major reason why it's a pleasure to live in Omaha."[30] Easy access long had been booster material, but previously the emphasis was on the efficiency it produced, not on the increased time it allowed to enjoy life.

The advertisement spoke briefly of the riverfront program, emphasizing the recreational and industrial facets of the development scheme. Finally, it concluded that the people of Omaha had "an enviable lifestyle." Residents enjoyed a wide variety of educational and cultural opportunities in the form of colleges and universities, ballet, opera and symphony companies, dinner theaters and community playhouses, museums, and a renowned zoo. They also had the security of living in "the medical center for mid-America" and could enjoy sporting events ranging from top-ranked college teams to minor-league professional teams to the "sport of kings," horse racing.[31]

The choice of subjects and the tone of the ads indicated that civic and business leaders had forged a new image of their city. Quality of life replaced efficiency as the focus of booster material; cultural and recreational amenities supplanted infrastructure improvements as the measure of progress. Concurrently, they reshaped the image of downtown Omaha as well. Reflecting many of the same themes, civic and business leaders began to see the downtown not so much as the center of working Omaha but as an office, entertainment, and cultural center that provided many of the amenities necessary for living well in the city.

New Ideas for a New Omaha: Reconstructing the Downtown

The deterioration of the downtown was evident by 1966 and accelerated after that. Retailing continued to fall off drastically, and in 1969 one of the large department stores announced it would close. In 1968, Westroads Shopping Center had opened its first stores, sealing the fate of large-scale downtown retailing. Located near Omaha's western fringe, Westroads was the nation's eighth-largest shopping center. The rather unsavory reputation downtown had acquired after the Job Corps centers were opened continued to dictate the popular view, and by 1973 fewer than half the families surveyed by the *World-Herald* said they ever shopped downtown.[32]

Under way at the same time was a movement to reconstruct the downtown both physically and in the mind of the general public. Beginning in the late 1960s, a series of projects was attempted, all directed at giving downtown a new flavor. The private sector sponsored some of the projects, the public sector others. More important, however, those involved in planning and boosting began to speak of downtown in new and different terms. Often they referred to it as the hub or vital center of the city. More and more, however, they referred to it not as *the* center but *a* center—a center of offices, of entertainment, of cultural amenities. The new attitude provided the context within which innovative ideas for the downtown could gain acceptance.[33]

The downward trend in the central business district's share of retail sales in the city and the metropolitan area continued. In 1967 the CBD held only 16.4 percent of city sales and 12.3 percent of metropolitan sales. It faced competition from five major retailing centers in 1967, up from four in 1963. Between 1967 and 1972, retail sales in the CBD dropped off a little more than 20 percent. By 1972 it held only 8.7 percent of city sales and 6.7 percent of metropolitan sales. And the number of competing major retail centers increased from five in 1967 to seven in 1972.[34] Studies of Omaha's shopping habits echoed the dismal tale told by retail statistics. Available data indicate a steady erosion in the percentage of Omaha families shopping downtown (see table 16).

Table 16: Shopping Habits

	1966	1967	1968	1969	1970	1972	1973
% Shop Regularly	31.2	29.3	26.9	31.6	27	17	15
% Shop Occasionally	49.4	45.2	40.8	37.0	41	28	30
% Little or none	19.3	25.2	31.9	30.8	31	n.a.	n.a.
% No answer	.1	.3	.4	.6	1	n.a.	n.a.
% Regularly/occasionally	80.6	74.5	67.7	68.6	68	45	45

Source: *Omaha World-Herald* annual market surveys, 1966–70, 1972–73. Reprinted by permission of *The World-Herald*.

Despite slight improvements in 1969, cumulative figures indicated that the number of shoppers frequenting the downtown was decreasing. The reason for the sharp dropoff between 1970 and 1972 is not clear. Further development of Westroads Shopping Center and the opening of competing centers undoubtedly were factors. Although the 1972 and 1973 surveys did not provide specific figures, they suggested that nearly 55 percent of Omaha's families did little or no shopping downtown.[35]

The decline in sales and the percentage of shoppers using the CBD came, not surprisingly, as the image of the downtown reached its nadir. In what seemed a cruel jab, in 1968 the *World-Herald* told Omahans that "[o]ne way to avoid crowds this Christmas is to shop downtown during the evening hours." It went on to detail the decline in downtown bus ridership at night (down 20 to 25 percent) and in business at parking lots (down 12 to 15 percent). Retailers attributed much of it to the opening of Westroads Shopping Center but also acknowledged that the perception of downtown as a high-crime area was a significant factor. They put much of the blame on the women's Job Corps centers. Said one retailer: "The centers draw male youths downtown and simply the presence of groups of youths deters shoppers."[36]

When facing crises, Omaha's civic and business leaders generally responded by forming a committee, and their response to the downtown crisis was no exception. In early 1968, downtown business interests transformed the old Downtown Parking Association into Downtown Omaha, Inc. The former, founded in the 1950s, owned and operated a number of parking lots in the downtown area. The renewed organization of 1968 proposed a broad range of activities, including intensified marketing of downtown office and store space, the use of new development laws (specifically the Sanitation and Improvement District Ordinance) to finance improvements, such as "a mall, a park or a small skating rink, lobbying for urban renewal and urging new construction." A 1969 editorial further explained the aims of the new organization, saying that Downtown Omaha, Inc., emphasized the availability of shopping, theaters, hotels, and restaurants. "The idea is to let people know that the new downtown is an exciting place to visit and in which to work. It's a show as well as a shopping place, a banking center, an office center, a government center, a convention center." The key was the notion that there was a new downtown that needed fresh ideas and a new image.[37]

In 1970 the organization launched its first big promotion, Downtown Day. Promoters described the event, held on a Saturday in November, as a combination of free entertainment, free parking, and shopping bargains, all intended to bring shoppers downtown. There was a first-of-its-kind outdoor art fair. Nearly forty artists displayed and offered their works for sale as part of the festivities. Many activities were for young people and young families. Rock bands provided much of the entertainment, and special movies were available to the twelve-and-under crowd for a dime. The organizers stated bluntly that they designed the event as an introduction to the downtown. As one official put it, "some people haven't been downtown in a year or two. We have a lot of exciting things to show them—new buildings, better lighting, planters."[38] Downtown, as it operated in its glory days, no longer existed. Boosters had to acquaint Omahans with the new one.

Part of the new downtown image was promotion of the area as an entertainment center. In 1971, so-called after-five businessmen—theater owners, restaurateurs—proposed an eighteen thousand dollar public-relations campaign to "tell Omahans we're here." Earlier that year, a newspaper article had assessed the "cultural and entertainment scene" and suggested that older "fixtures" were doing well while newer attractions, such as

Megan Terry's avant garde Magic Theatre, were still fighting for an audience. The civic opera, the civic ballet society, and the symphony all anticipated growth in the coming year. While in certain areas entertainment in the downtown grew in importance, one standard fixture disappeared rapidly. The ornate movie palaces, on the decline since the 1950s, withered and eventually died in the face of competition from multiscreen suburban complexes. Although the entertainment picture was mixed, by the early 1970s planners and boosters were referring more and more to the downtown as an entertainment center, especially in relation to cultural events. A booster pointed out in 1972: "The major musical, ballet, opera and touring stage shows [were] presented downtown."[39]

The promotional schemes of Downtown Omaha, Inc., and the growth of entertainment activities helped brighten the new image of downtown, but two other projects were the most influential. The first was construction of Woodmen Tower, a new headquarters building for Woodmen of the World Life Insurance Company. The second was the successful development of the Old Market. One gave the downtown a highly visible centerpiece, and the other lent a certain cosmopolitan flair.

The Woodmen Tower project was announced in 1965. Soon thereafter, as negotiated, the insurance company bought the site of Old City Hall and the city moved its operations to an interim location (plans were already under way for construction of a new city-county building).[40] The thirty-story structure, completed in 1969, was by far the tallest building in Omaha. Its clean, elegant lines and white marble-faced base set it apart architecturally. Its height, accentuated by its placement on higher ground, made it visible for miles. That visibility soon made it an important landmark on Omaha's horizon. As a showcase and centerpiece, it gave downtown the distinct and captivating symbol it had lacked.

Unlike the Woodmen Tower, which received much attention after the announcement of construction plans, the Old Market project began very quietly and on a very modest scale. The "old market" was a twenty-block area between Douglas and Jackson streets and Eighth and Thirteenth streets. Its heart was Howard Street between Tenth and Eleventh. The area had been known in the early twentieth century to most Omahans for its public markets, where one ventured to buy the freshest fruits and vegetables. That activity had long since faded in the wake of competition from neighborhood supermarkets. The area caught the attention of planners as early as the 1946 Blue Book. It was already in decline by that time, and planners hoped to clean up and upgrade the public-market facilities. Little was done. It received attention from planners once more in the 1966 Central Omaha Plan. At that point, they called for extensive clearance of older structures to make room for superblocks, parking lots, and new construction. Again, because of Omaha's rejection of urban renewal, nothing was done. The area remained largely intact and, as it turned out, was fertile ground for the private, small-scale redevelopment that began in the mid-1960s.[41]

The Mercers, a wealthy, long-established Omaha family, owned most of the buildings in the market area. Sam Mercer, a lawyer practicing in Paris, needed to find a way to fill the increasingly vacant buildings, so he invited artists and artistically minded entrepreneurs to set up studios, boutiques, bookstores, and restaurants in former warehouses. He personally provided the financing for what he hoped would become a premier restaurant, the French Café. The Mercer family was not willing or perhaps was not able to commit large sums of money to a massive project. Unlike the Old Town project in Chicago, the Old Market began very quietly and development proceeded slowly and incrementally. Once fully under way, however, it caught the attention of planners and boosters. In 1968, Mercer met with the Chamber of Commerce Executive Committee. (At that time he considered naming the project Gaslight Square and announced that Northern Natural Gas had volunteered to provide gaslights.) He explained the process of restoration and rehabilitation that was under way. Once it became known, the area grew in size and popularity. By the early 1970s, although it was sometimes decried as a haven for hippies, it was something of a tourist attraction, drawing people who were seeking something new, different, and "urban" in the downtown.[42]

The Old Market was one of a growing number of projects that demonstrated increasing interest in historic preservation. Much of the early push for it came from the state and federal government. Following passage of the National Historic Preservation Act (1966), the state legislature empowered the Nebraska State Historical Society to carry out a survey of historically significant properties. The survey covering the eastern part of the state was published in 1971 and listed fourteen buildings or sites of historic significance. Several were in or near downtown Omaha, including the sites of the first and second territorial capitols, Joslyn Art Museum, the old Omaha National Bank, the main branch of the Omaha Public Library, and the Union Pacific depot. Two of the buildings, Omaha National Bank and Union Pacific Station, had received attention from preservationists by 1973. In 1970 private developers reintroduced the old bank building, renamed the Omaha Building, as "one of Omaha's oldest and yet newest downtown office locations." The advertisement further stated that "the charm of one of Omaha's oldest and most sophisticated buildings will make your business transactions more pleasant." Although another decade passed before restoration was complete, the early interest shown in preserving that historically significant, charming, and sophisticated structure saved it from the wrecking ball. While private developers were ready to act on preservation projects, the city followed quite slowly. Its only major venture into the field was made in response to the donation of Union Pacific Station to the city.[43]

The city of Omaha was rather late in establishing a municipal historic preservation agency; the Landmarks Heritage Preservation Commission was not created until 1977. As early as 1973, however, the city prepared to act on a rather extensive preservation project. In the early 1970s, Union Pacific offered to give the city its railroad station on the southern edge of the downtown. Passenger traffic had declined significantly, making the huge depot, built in the 1930s, functionally obsolete. Architecturally and historically, though, it retained a great deal of significance. It was listed in the National Register of Historic Landmarks in 1972 and in 1973 the City Planning Department developed a proposal to restore the station. The plan envisioned its use as a museum with displays celebrating Omaha's transportation, communication, business, industrial, and Indian heritage. The Western Heritage Museum, a nonprofit organization founded in 1973, established headquarters in the station. The project got off the ground slowly and nearly two decades passed before it began to live up to its highly publicized promise. However, it represented Omaha's first major commitment to historic preservation.[44]

The growing interest in historic preservation was closely tied to the increasing and widening effort toward city beautification. Much of the focus remained on litter, but, as in the early 1960s, the package also included green space, aesthetics, and natural amenities. The drive to enhance Omaha's natural and man-made amenities accelerated in the late 1960s and early 1970s. Open and green spaces in the downtown began to gain considerable notice in the early 1970s. Small parks, plazas, and garden spots received attention as favorable additions. Although the city did some of the beautification work, much of it was done through the efforts of individuals. Architect Nes Latenser and F. Phillips Giltner, president of First National Bank, sponsored small plazas. The projects worked no major transformation, but taken together they established open and green spaces as necessary components of downtown improvement.

The city confined its actions primarily to the planting of trees and flowers. In 1968 it applied for and received a beautification grant from the federal government. Part of the money was used to plant trees in the downtown. A grant the following year helped pay for landscaping around public buildings. The largest downtown beautification project undertaken by the city was construction of the Eighteenth Street Mall, which had been proposed in the 1966 Central Omaha Plan. The project was not that extensive, mainly involving new paving, some landscaping, and the installation of ornamental lights. The city had completed one block of the mall west of Woodmen Tower by late 1969. Once in place, that single block provided an important example of what could be done to improve the appearance of the downtown. Omaha City Council President H. F. Jacobberger, who had opposed the project, changed his mind when he saw this small example of the finished product. "Sometimes," he said, "you don't realize how beautiful something is until you actually see it." Soon thereafter other projects provided more examples of what could be done.[45]

The small park created in 1965 by Northwestern Bell Telephone Company proved popular but was short lived. It was sacrificed to expansion of the headquarters building. Two other small plazas soon appeared to take its place. In 1970, Nes Latenser and Downtown Omaha, Inc., created a twenty-by-sixty-six-foot park at the southwest corner of Sixteenth and Dodge streets. It came under fire from the City Permit and Inspection

Department when a café opened on the site, but Planning Director Aust defended it and urged more development of that type. Both Latenser and Aust emphasized the project's "humanizing" aspects.[46]

Another small plaza opened in January 1971 in open space between two new buildings, First National Bank and the Hilton Hotel, across the street from Latenser's park. The plaza was designed to function as a gathering spot for shoppers and downtown workers during the day and a "hub of cultural activities" at night. As a location for open-air concerts and art fairs, F. Phillips Giltner of First National hoped it would "create an atmosphere of joy, pleasure, culture and color" in the otherwise drab and cold downtown. The plaza never became a hub of cultural activities, yet it served as another example of a different kind of vision of the downtown, one that emphasized cultural and recreational amenities.[47]

Greenery was added to the downtown to soften its appearance and inject that increasingly important humanizing element. In 1972, Alden Aust returned from a trip to Europe and renewed the call for more greenery and open spaces. Using Rotterdam as his model, Aust declared that "[e]very city needs greenery and open space for contrast to buildings and roads." He concluded that the downtown was "woefully deficient" in such amenities, yet, a newspaper article later that year noted that several areas of "garden beauty" were present, including Aquila Court (restored in 1970), a rooftop patio at the Medical Arts Building (an extension of the Central National Life Insurance Group boardroom), Latenser's minipark, the garden at the Scottish Rite Temple, the recently landscaped lawn of the Douglas County Courthouse, the First National Bank plaza, a fifth-level patio at Woodmen Tower, and planters filled with trees, shrubs, and flowers lining a number of downtown sidewalks.[48]

Between 1966 and 1973, certain individuals and business groups gradually forged a new image for the downtown. The cumulative result of the various projects, many of which were small in scale, was a definition of downtown that emphasized its role as an office, entertainment, and cultural center. Parks, plazas, and green space aimed to humanize the area, making it more attractive and inviting. Better access and more parking clearly had not fulfilled their promise of revitalizing owntown. The long-awaited Interstate Highway link finally opened in early 1970, yet the decline in retailing, a prime indicator of business activity, continued unabated. If downtown was to survive, it would do so performing a function quite different from that of its heyday. Gradually, the new image came into focus. It reflected the demands of the service economy and the educated and amenities-oriented individuals associated with it, and it harmonized with the new image of the city. Concurrently, the demands and concerns that were transforming the image of Omaha and its downtown moved into and influenced the formal planning process.

Riverfront Development: Planning a New Image of the City

Within the context of a new image of Omaha and the downtown, planning ideas introduced in the early 1960s rose to ascendancy in the late 1960s. A beautification plan produced in 1968 was the first clear indication that such concerns as beautification, historic preservation, cultural and recreational amenities, and quality of the environment had assumed prominent places in the formal planning process. The trend continued into the early 1970s as various plans associated with riverfront development began to focus on ambience and amenities. The wide-ranging scheme set the tone for a different style of planning. The process that produced the plans of the early 1970s was somewhat less business-community dominated, more reliant on outside expertise, and clearly a melding of the new image of the city and downtown with planning. The old civic-improvement agenda, which had focused heavily on efficiency and infrastructure, faded far into the background as a new agenda emphasizing beautification, preservation, amenities, and the quality of life replaced it and guided subsequent planning activity.

The beautification movement of the 1960s involved several groups, each focusing on a small part of the larger picture. In 1968, Alden Aust produced the "Beautification Master Plan for Omaha, Nebraska," which provided a comprehensive outline of the various projects involved with beautification. And since the master plan described most, if not all, local efforts associated with each of the projects, it provided a summary of action to date. The plan outlined fourteen "interrelated and interdependent" areas of concern, including community housekeeping, blight eradication, a discordant-features program, neighborhood improvement, commercial-area improvement, industrial-area rehabilitation, street and freeway beautification, park and public-building beautification, central-business-district beautification, enhancement of natural attractions, codes and ordinance modernization, a design standards program, a works-of-art program, and historic preservation. It did not present an overall picture of any kind of comprehensive, coordinated approach to beautification. Rather, it detailed many activities, often still independent and small scale, that, when added together, amounted to a significant and growing concern for the enhancement of the natural and man-made attractiveness of the city.[49]

Several of the proposed programs had been operating at the local level for several years. They included community housekeeping, blight eradication, neighborhood improvement, design standards, and park and public-building beautification. Community housekeeping long had been and largely remained the purview of Keep Omaha Beautiful, Inc. That organization remained very active in the antilitter campaign and put heavy emphasis on changing people's attitudes toward litter and fostering the idea of the value of a litter-free environment. Blight eradication also was a long-standing goal. The repeated failure to introduce urban renewal prevented widespread clearance other than that necessitated by Interstate Highway construction. The beautification plan indicated that the goal of finding some means to create a clearance mechanism was not yet abandoned. It also admitted, however, a certain ambiguous attitude toward clearance. By 1968 the experience of other cities demonstrated that urban renewal's success at correcting problems of the central city had "fallen far short of expectations." While mildly insisting on the desirability of some clearance, the plan seemed to emphasize rehabilitation and preservation as ways of revitalizing it far more than clearance.[50]

In the spirit of rehabilitation, the report suggested an extension of the city's efforts to improve older neighborhoods. Technically, it had been involved in neighborhood rehabilitation since 1956 and the passage of the Minimum Housing Standards Ordinance. Positive results awaited the 1960s, when the City Planning Department began working with neighborhood organizations. In 1967 the department and a group from a black neighborhood produced an improvement plan for the area known as Kellom Heights. The department continued to work with neighborhoods and in 1971 issued a "Neighborhood Planning Guide." The document demonstrated appreciation for the vitality of many older neighborhoods and the desirability of rehabilitating and preserving older buildings and homes. Moreover, it stated in no uncertain terms a new planning and boosting priority: making Omaha more livable.[51]

The planning guide's introduction concluded: "The challenge that we face is to turn the city from something that must be endured to something that can be enjoyed and appreciated." Furthermore, it said, "it is possible to take advantage of the peculiar aspect of the urban environment, the fact that the city brings a large number of people together in a relatively limited area for the purpose of living. It makes sense to use that characteristic to make life better and more interesting for everyone." The guide concluded with a bibliography directing readers to such urban-life proponents as Jane Jacobs, Victor Gruen, Kevin Lynch, and Lawrence Halprin. It also suggested that readers turn to *The Last Whole Earth Catalogue: Access to Tools*, described as having "more tools for affecting and interacting with the environment than any other book ever published." The emphasis placed on neighborhoods and the philosophy expressed clearly indicated a vision of the city as a place to live.[52]

The 1968 plan also described two other closely related and ongoing programs: design standards and park and public-building beautification. The women's division of the Chamber of Commerce presented awards recognizing "meritorious new and remodeled buildings," and the plan gave the program credit for creating interest in design standards. Mayor A. V. Sorensen "directed architects designing all future public buildings to include fountains, murals, statues, etc., in their plans." Neither program was very extensive, but they reflected the growing demand for aesthetically pleasing buildings and other public areas.[53]

A relatively new program, discordant-feature diminution, had as its core a concern for aesthetics. Early in 1968, Alden Aust proposed an ordinance to set certain standards for the appearance of service stations and suggested more restrictive zoning to prevent the use of sites zoned for filling stations as used-car lots or junkyards. The major argument against the proposal was that "governments may not legislate aesthetics." That argument must have carried some weight because the planning report indicated that very little was being done to eliminate the "blatant ugliness" blotting the urban landscape. Yet the city initiated a small program to haul off junked cars, commissioned a study to investigate solid-waste disposal, and moved to put telephone and power lines underground.[54]

Discordant-features diminution was closely related to a proposal for street and freeway beautification. As Aust put it, "it costs very little more to build an attractive highway than an ugly one." The Public Works Department replanted trees uprooted by street widening in an effort to keep the roads lined with pleasant greenery. And aesthetics evidently entered into the design of the I-480 segment that ran past the downtown. Aust reported that federal and state roads officials had "gone to considerable effort to design more attractive structures on Interstate 480 in Downtown Omaha." Clearly, efficiency was no longer the singular quality by which municipal improvements were judged. They had to be attractive as well as functional.[55]

The desire to use municipal ordinances and zoning to establish at least minimal aesthetic standards also appeared in what might have seemed a very technical and legalistic category: codes and ordinance modernization. Once again, however, that section expressed new appreciation for Omaha as a place to live. It described planning innovations that permitted new kinds of land subdivision, including cluster plans and planned unit developments, both of which freed developers from single-lot zoning restrictions and gave the City Planning Department more control of large-scale developments. Aust concluded that the innovations answered the needs of developers and "the planner's desire for a better living environment."[56]

Three programs that dealt specifically with certain areas of the downtown included commercial-area rehabilitation, industrial-area redevelopment, and central-business-district beautification. (Although the commercial rehabilitation program concentrated on South Omaha, it implied rehabilitation of the city's other commercial areas, such as the downtown.) All three aimed to make one part of the larger downtown more attractive. Central-business-district beautification received the most extensive attention. The report emphasized the seventy-five million dollars worth of construction in progress and in a clear indication of the priority given the central business district made the hopeful prediction that the CBD portion of the beautification plan would be the first completed.[57]

The beautification plan expressed concern for the preservation and enhancement of Omaha's man-made and natural amenities. The plan called for more historic preservation and admitted that much of the city's architectural heritage was disappearing and that very little was being done to prevent further destruction. It reported that the only preservation activity under way involved the Old Market. Planners hoped it would serve as an example and inspiration for future projects.[58]

The section of the plan that proposed enhancement of natural attractions foreshadowed the future of downtown. Attention focused on the city's long-neglected, almost-forgotten riverfront. The plan described a student project on riverfront development that, while not the single origin of the Riverfront Development program, was an important harbinger of subsequent events. A group of senior architecture students from the University of Nebraska had drafted a multiuse plan for redevelopment of the riverfront. It immediately caught the attention of the Chamber of Commerce, the U.S. Army Corps of Engineers, and the railroads that owned much of the riverfront property. The Chicago, Burlington and Quincy announced it would clear the property it owned and redesign its freight yards to make them more attractive. Predicted the planning report: "This new development will unquestionably result in a total change of attitude toward this area which will, in turn, facilitate future redevelopment along more beautiful lines than ever before."[59]

The student project, presented to the chamber's Convention and Tourism committees in 1967, did stir up a great deal of enthusiasm. The architecture students had been asked by their teacher, at the behest of planner Aust, to develop an innovative plan for the riverfront. They created a proposal for "a convention, hotel and shopping center, high- and low-rise apartments, a riverfront marina and traffic ways connected with Downtown Omaha and Eppley Airfield." The design took into account the scenic view available east of downtown and suggested the construction of a parkway, elevated walks, and observation areas. Aust responded enthusiastically. He felt that the area had to be improved because it was the "front door to Omaha," the first part of the city seen by motorists entering it on

I-480. He further suggested the construction of a city landmark similar to the arch in Saint Louis. Other civic leaders responded favorably. Mayor Sorensen and two council members felt the area could become a tourist attraction. The mayor even went so far as to announce a contest for the design of a city symbol.[60]

The chamber's Tourism Committee also displayed interest in the project. Shortly after the student presentation, a special subcommittee examined the student plan as well as one prepared by the Leo A. Daly Company. Planner Aust spoke in favor of a waterfront project and insisted that for the sake of economic viability it must include apartments and shops and not simply be turned into a park. In an interesting rebuttal, David Carson of Northern Natural Gas Company stated that "we did not have to justify such a project solely on economics but should consider the demand for beauty in our environment."[61]

Carson's statement and the fact that the Tourism Committee dealt with the issue were significant. Both suggested a very different attitude toward the downtown and a new set of ideas for improvement of the area. The downtown as a tourist attraction in and of itself was a relatively new idea. Certain landmarks, such as Joslyn Art Museum and the Union Pacific Museum, had been promoted to tourists. The downtown itself, though, had not been the object of such attention. The notion was even clearer in a 1968 meeting of the Tourism Committee. At that time it endorsed the actions taken by the railroads to clean up their riverside trackage and expressed enthusiasm over the tourist potential of developing the nearby Old Market area.[62] The idea of revitalizing downtown by developing its natural, cultural, and recreational amenities was gaining support. Further, Carson's remark was a clear statement of the growing demand for a better-quality environment that included the enhancement of natural amenities. Those concerned with planning for the improvement of the downtown were beginning to respond to such demands.

Despite the initial enthusiasm, very little was done on riverfront development for several years. The proposal struck a responsive chord but failed to spark an organized effort to see it through. The Central Omaha Plan, introduced the previous year, failed to bring about much positive action. That could have dampened immediate renewal of formal planning.

Retirement and death were beginning to take their tolls in the private leadership structure by 1967 and 1968, and Mayor Sorensen, beset by a number of problems—not the least of which was unrest among the city's black population—was unable to provide much leadership.[63] By 1970, however, several pieces began to fall into place, making possible a sustained drive for riverfront and downtown improvement. Eugene Leahy was elected mayor. He had the necessary leadership qualities to organize and motivate people. Civic and business leaders were open to ideas that would promote progress. The City Planning Department had enough expertise that it could play a more prominent role. And in 1970 the almost forgotten East Omaha Drainage District transferred thirteen miles of riverfront property to the city.

According to Aust, Leahy became aware of the East Omaha Drainage District during his campaign for mayor. A supporter acquainted him with the entity, which had become obsolete in the wake of successful flood-control efforts on the Missouri. Reportedly, all it did was collect a small tax and throw a banquet once a year. Those involved saw it more or less as a nuisance. Leahy promised to do something about the situation. Accordingly, at his urging, the state legislature passed a law giving the city control of the district.[64] Very suddenly Omaha had possession of thirteen miles of riverfront property just north of the downtown and an opportunity to develop it. The Missouri River, long thought of as a sewer, flood threat, or highway, was by the early 1970s cleaned up, tamed, and an avenue for pleasure boats more than barges. It was somewhat ironic that the almost-forgotten riverfront inspired sweeping plans for revitalizing the city and the region.

In August 1970, Leahy appointed the Mayor's Riverfront Development Committee. It differed from its predecessors in a number of ways. First and foremost, the mayor played a major role. Whereas the previous committees had been mayor's committees in name only, Eugene Leahy took part in directing the activities and promoting the plans of the committee. Further, membership reached beyond the confines of Omaha's business leadership. Because the riverfront project itself stretched beyond Omaha and Douglas County, any committee concerned with comprehensive development had to involve individuals outside the immediate area. Accordingly, the committee included municipal and county officials from Washington, Douglas, and Sarpy counties in Nebraska and Iowa's Pottawattamie County, but Nebraska city, county, and business representatives dominated the committee, both in number and in influence.[65] The Nebraskans could not act, however, without the cooperation of the other officials. If they wanted a broad-ranging project stretching across several political boundaries, they had to involve more people than Omaha's private-sector leaders.

Finally, the riverfront committee demonstrated far broader vision than its predecessors. The earlier planning committees had been rather limited in their vision and approach. They tended to concentrate on a relatively narrow range of topics and to emphasize a small number of discrete projects. In contrast, if any planning body ever followed the advice of Daniel Burnham to make no little plans, it was the Mayor's Riverfront Development Committee. Its first reports, issued in early 1971, indicated that the committee thought big. In January of that year a newspaper article outlined the general contours of its plan. At that stage, it involved a thirty-six-mile stretch of the river on both the Nebraska and Iowa sides. The committee envisioned commercial, industrial, and residential projects plus recreational development that included "marinas, lakes, parks, hiking and biking and riding trails, fishing and picnic areas, motels, restaurants and amusement parks." According to committee spokesman Aust, the riverfront development would provide a recreational outlet for metropolitan residents and attract tourists.[66]

The January article also indicated that the committee was responding to the new demands of the amenities-oriented middle class. Aust said the project was "an outgrowth, at least in part, of a society that [was] becoming increasingly oriented to leisure time activities."[67] He went on to say that it recognized the increased use of and demand for recreational facilities. Clearly, by the early 1970s recreational amenities ranked high on the list of attributes a city needed to promote growth and development.

Factors other than the demands of the new amenities-oriented middle class also made the riverfront project a possibility. The Corps of Engineers had the authority not only to improve harbors and build dams, but also to support recreation development along rivers and related lakes. The corps provided much technical expertise during the early stages of riverfront project planning. Further, the federal government encouraged planning on a regional level and made available funds for a variety of projects when such planning occurred. That carrot prompted creation of the Omaha–Council Bluffs Metropolitan Area Planning Agency, or MAPA, in 1966. After the initial committee work, MAPA coordinated much of the funding effort. In October 1972 the riverfront committee, by then formally a part of MAPA, received a one million dollar grant to continue planning for the riverfront.[68]

The far-ranging Riverfront Development program, despite all the enthusiasm, despite the strong and inspirational leadership of Eugene Leahy, and despite its broad base of support, had a rather short career. Talk about it continued after 1973, but supporters accomplished little. The centerpiece fifty-four-mile-long park was never completed. The Omaha Industrial Foundation did acquire riverfront land north of the downtown and promoted its commercial and industrial development, but its efforts were far from successful.[69] Perhaps most important, the Riverfront Development spirit increasingly became focused on one part of the larger project: revitalization of Omaha's downtown.

Almost from the beginning the broad Riverfront Development project and efforts to revitalize the downtown followed related but separate paths. The Riverfront Development concept was in many ways an umbrella for a wide range of planning initiatives; commercial, residential, industrial, cultural, and recreational projects all fell under it. At first the major concern focused on finding a way for Omaha's downtown to profit from the larger scheme. Once the ideas took hold, however, the downtown project began to move forward under its own momentum. Though technically still part of the bigger picture, plans for the downtown began to take on a separate identity and develop an independence from other parts of the Riverfront Development scheme. By 1973 as the energy generated by the Riverfront proposal began to wane and plans for the large-scale development began to fade into the background, the downtown plan moved forward, propelled by its own energy and the commitment of the city and its civic and business leadership to see it through.

The model proposal for riverfront beautification issued in 1971 contained a small section on the downtown. The committee drawing it up said it realized the need to address the problem of "the aging, decaying, industrial/warehouse/rail yard development along the riverfront in Downtown Omaha." The issue was crucial because the area was "at the midway focal point of the entire concept." To deal with the problem, the committee called on the local chapter of the American Institute of Architects. Volunteers from that organization developed a proposal to harmonize and connect downtown development with the broader riverfront proposal. They designed "a residential/commercial mega-structure along the river's edge, an urban park, bordered by in-town housing, connecting the riverfront area with the newly revitalized CBD." The plan also envisioned "[a] downtown campus for the University of Nebraska continuing studies program, the expansion of the Old Market historic development and space for more travel oriented motel and commercial land uses adjacent to I-480." Once those initial ideas were down on paper, there began a planning process that by 1973 resulted in yet another plan for downtown and commitment to a whole new agenda for improvement.[70]

Of all the projects proposed in 1971 the key element became the urban park connecting downtown and the riverfront. The park concept met a host of needs and demands. Civic and business leaders had tried for more than a decade to clear out blighted sections in and near the downtown. Urban renewal was out, but the city did have the power of eminent domain to acquire land for parks, and by the early 1970s it could turn for both technical assistance and grants to numerous programs in several departments of the federal government. The Department of the Interior offered matching grants to help meet the cost of acquiring historic sites and developing outdoor recreation projects and also offered technical assistance. The Department of Agriculture sponsored "resource development projects including public, water based recreation" and offered credit to rural landowners willing to develop recreational projects on their farms. The U.S. Army Corps of Engineers offered technical assistance, and the Department of Housing and Urban Development offered matching grants to aid in the acquisition of parkland. Not all of those programs applied to the downtown situation, of course. They meant, however, that both the amount and variety of money available to Omaha had increased, and because the money was not tied to the discredited urban-renewal program or the locally rejected public-housing program, the city pursued such funds with more freedom.[71]

The park also met demands for more open and green space downtown. From the telephone company's tiny park to First National Plaza to all the individual efforts to soften and humanize the appearance of the downtown through the addition of greenery, there was a clear message: that many people employed downtown wanted a working environment that was not only efficient but pleasing and relaxing. They wanted the area to provide places where they could take a stroll or enjoy an outdoor concert at lunchtime. They wanted a touch of the same quality environment of open space and greenery they sought in the suburbs, where they lived, to be present in the downtown, where they worked. It was no longer enough for downtown to be accessible; it also had to be a pleasant and inviting place in which to work. Because the park offered so much and because supporters obviously hoped it could be a catalyst for other improvement projects, the linear park connecting the heart of downtown and its long-forgotten riverfront became the priority. Planners took the first step toward meeting it in late 1972 when "Central Omaha Park" appeared as project 43 in the "Open Space Plan and Program" produced by MAPA.

As noted, one of the many new programs available to cities by the early 1970s was the Housing and Urban Development Department's Open Space Land Program. HUD offered matching grants to acquire open-space parkland but required that planning for open spaces be done on a regional level. Enticed by the opportunity of acquiring money for parks, MAPA (rather than the City Planning Department) developed a regional open-space plan.[72]

The Open Space Committee began meeting in September 1971. Its membership represented a very diverse group of people. They included city, county, and state officials; leaders of citizens groups; technical experts; and even a college student. Its members included Mrs. Les Anderson (Keep Omaha Beautiful, Inc.), Alden Aust, Mrs. Paul Gallagher (Friends of the Parks), Larry Holcomb (biologist and environmentalist), Lee Simmons (director of Henry Doorly Zoo), Martin Kivett (Nebraska State Historical Society), Willard Barbee (Nebraska Game and Parks Commission),

James Malkowski (Fontenelle Forest Nature Center), Mrs. Ricky Salisbury (League of Women Voters), and Gene Svenson (a planner with Gollehon, Schemmer and Associates). Previously, planning-committee memberships were fairly well limited to the business community. The range of people involved by the early 1970s was far wider and they represented a much broader cross section of the urban leadership. It was still by and large planning by elites, but the elites came from sources other than the business community. The committee met over several months to formulate a comprehensive plan for the "Omaha-Council Bluffs Metropolitan Area which [would] meet the recreational needs of the area as well as preserve and protect valuable natural resources." The completed plan contained sixty-seven projects. For purposes of this study, the most important was project 43, Central Omaha Park.[73]

The brief description of the project spoke much of the planners' aspirations. After explaining that the park would serve "as the major pedestrian connection and open space from the River to the central core," the planners expounded on its promotional value: "Extensive landscaping will be done, and fountain, sculpture, lighting and other improvements will help draw people to this area. This park will serve as a stimulus for other major redevelopment of the area." In the renewed effort to revitalize the downtown, the park became the key. With it as the core element, by 1973 those concerned with planning for the downtown developed a whole new agenda for improvement.[74]

The new agenda consisted of a number of projects, some directly related to the park proposal, some unrelated but in harmony with its basic goals. They included a residential development known as Marina City, a downtown campus for the University of Nebraska at Omaha, a new main branch for the Omaha Public Library, restoration of the Orpheum Theatre, expansion of the Old Market, and eventually a new headquarters building for Northwestern Bell Telephone Company. Each of the projects was important individually, but their real significance lay in how they worked together to demonstrate the new image of downtown. The 1973 plan, which drew many of the elements together, reflected that new image (the plan was developed in 1973 but not issued in published form until later).

The 1973 plan also indicated the more balanced relationship between the public and private sectors in the planning process and more reliance on outside experts. Local private leadership and money remained crucial, but the city played and continued to play a far bigger role in reshaping downtown than it had in any of the previous planning initiatives.

When it was announced in 1971, the Riverfront Development initiative immediately inspired innovative proposals for downtown development. The committee drawing up the model encouraged local architects to develop a plan for the area. The plan included a domed stadium, a downtown campus for the University of Nebraska at Omaha, a loosely defined megastructure, a linear park, motels, and office buildings. Many of the ideas, particularly the domed stadium, fell by the wayside. Other elements gained considerable support and by 1973 comprised the important elements in the Central Business District Plan prepared by the City Planning Department (technically the plan was part of the Riverfront Development scheme but was not dependent on the larger project).

The Central Business District Plan of 1973 differed from the other major postwar plans. It could not trace its origin to a Chamber of Commerce committee. It had chamber support, but, like the Riverfront Development scheme, it was a product of the two Omaha planning agencies, the City Planning Department and MAPA. The process did include a citizens advisory committee known as the Central Business District Task Force, which drew its membership from the "business community, downtown merchants, public officials, representatives of downtown organizations, major land owners in the study area, the Corps of Engineers, and people from various educational institutions in the city." Thus it had a somewhat broader membership base than previous committees in that one did not necessarily have to have direct ties with the Chamber of Commerce to belong. The major difference was the expected role of the task force. Previous committees had done much of the planning, even as late as the 1966 Central Omaha Plan. The task force had no such envisioned role. The section describing it concluded: "One important aspect that has to be remembered is that the Central Business District Task Force is an advisor to the City of Omaha, and that the City is the governmental agency that has to act on the plan." The planners expected the task force to help coordinate private and public investments, but much, if not all, of the planning was now out of the private sector and in the hands of professional planning experts in city hall and their hired consultants.[75]

Not only were city planners more directly involved, but for the first time outside experts were brought in to help develop the plan and provide fresh ideas. In 1973 the city hired nationally known architect and planner Lawrence Halprin to design the linear park, by then known as Central Park Mall, and provide general advice. Halprin or his firm designed Nicollet Mall in Minneapolis and a multilevel fountain in Portland, Oregon, and converted a New York warehouse into apartments and a similar structure in Cleveland into stores.[76] That knowledge and expertise was brought to the Central Park Mall project. Halprin was the first real outsider brought into the planning process in Omaha.

Halprin told business leaders his goal was creation of a downtown that would act as "a viable, interesting place for people of all ages." That ideal came through in descriptions of the central business district in the 1973 plan. It defined the downtown in terms of eight neighborhoods or major land uses: auditorium-government, financial core, retail core, UNO (the proposed downtown campus), recreation, Old Market, warehouse residential, and Marina City. By focusing on these diverse and relatively new downtown functions, the planners obviously had adopted the new image of the downtown that had developed by the early 1970s. Within each of the neighborhoods, they hoped to attract people back downtown. The plan they produced aimed at increasing "the social and economic viability of the CBD by providing new people-oriented amenities such as malls, parks, greenways, plus new activities and attractions such as figure skating rink, conservatories, conference centers and library." They still mentioned efficiency, especially in relation to transportation and transit, but it had clearly taken a backseat to ambience and amenities as the primary focus of planners.[77]

The description of Central Park Mall attested to the importance of creating an inviting ambience: "The open space system [primarily the mall] is intended to provide places in the Central Business District where people can go in their leisure to find relaxation, entertainment, sports, and even solitude at little or no personal expense." In order to attract a wide variety of people, the plan proposed a wide variety of attractions for the open spaces, including "[f]ountains, outdoor galleries, restaurants, theaters, skating rinks, boating lakes, play spaces, and quiet landscaped areas." In its overall concept, the mall fit squarely within the new image of the downtown, with its emphasis on ambience and amenities. "If the open space system, which includes the pedestrian network and the streets, is designed to a high level of excellence and aesthetic quality," the planners said, "it will not only produce a people-oriented Central Business District but it will also provide a fabric in which even the poorest building will take on a new ambience." Besides the open spaces, the Central Business District Plan also dealt with transportation and circulation, commercial revitalization, residential development, construction of educational facilities, community and cultural facilities, and the Old Market.[78]

The description of the transportation and circulation concept contained few new ideas. It did put emphasis on creating a "highly accessible pedestrial network." Moving people was evidently as important as moving automobiles. The section describing the commercial concept more clearly highlighted the new approach to planning for the downtown. Previous plans concentrated on ways to retain the large-department-store style of shopping. The "CBD Plan" focused more on small-scale shops and diversity. The idea was to create a number of mall-like areas—along Sixteenth Street, in Marina City, and in the Old Market—housing "boutiques, galleries, restaurants, etc." The Sixteenth Street Mall project was described as "a pedestrian transit mall providing people facilities all along the street and creating an environment which is conducive to strolling and enjoying the shopping experience in safety and comfort." The planners did not precisely define what they meant by "people facilities," but their plan obviously introduced a new approach to shopping downtown and aimed at creating a different and inviting ambience.[79]

The plans for residential development also emphasized the importance of ambience. The planners saw housing as crucial to the revitalization of downtown. The area needed its own resident population to give it vitality. Frequently, Alden Aust made hopeful projections of a "return to the city." Planners sought to attract people into the downtown housing, specifically Marina City and converted warehouses, "by providing a variety of stimulating and desirable urban living environments." They hoped to provide an alternative to suburban living and entice people back into the central city by offering them housing with an attractive urban ambience.[80]

The CBD Plan also concentrated on providing a wide variety of desirable amenities. The sections dealing with education and community and cultural facilities suggested some of the planned cultural amenities. The education concept consisted of two projects, a downtown campus for the University of Nebraska at Omaha and a new main-branch library. In 1970 the University of Nebraska Board of Regents published a report, "The Urban University in the '70s," declaring that UNO must reach out into the community and decentralize its operations. Almost at once a downtown campus appeared on plans. The CBD Plan envisioned development between Twelfth and Fourteenth streets on either side of the mall: on the north between Douglas and Dodge streets and on the south between Harney and Farnam streets. (The plan was later scaled down to a single building, a combination university–state office building, on the south side of the mall.) The other component was the new library. The original main-branch library, built in 1894, was considered inadequate as early as the 1940s. In 1973 the Omaha National Bank and the *World-Herald* donated $250,000 toward construction of a new library in honor of longtime civic leader W. Dale Clark. (Clark served as president and chairman at the bank and on the board of the newspaper.) The planned building stood at the west end of Central Park Mall and provided an important anchor for the project. Both the campus and the library were seen as sources of "cultural enrichment."[81]

The community and cultural facilities concept envisioned a variety of cultural and recreational amenities, including the education center and Central Park Mall, in addition to the Orpheum Theatre. By the early 1970s the Orpheum was a fading ornate movie palace and former vaudeville theater that had seen better days. Faced with overwhelming competition from suburban multiscreen complexes, the Orpheum closed in 1971. Concurrently, several individuals and organizations involved in the performing arts proposed restoration of the Orpheum as a concert hall. Thomas Nurnberger led the drive, which was well under way by 1973. Ak-Sar-Ben and a "city-sponsored, non-profit organization," the Omaha Performing Arts Center Corporation, raised the necessary funds. One of the first CBD Plan projects completed, the Orpheum opened as a performing-arts center in 1975, and the planners expressed their expectation that such cultural facilities would "attract people from all parts of Omaha to visit the Central Business District regularly."[82]

The plan included a section on the Old Market praising the work that had been completed and encouraging more development along the same lines. It described the area's role as "a haven and a testing ground for those who felt ill at ease with their ideas and styles in suburban Omaha" and a "fertile ground for the beautiful new ideas, expressions and ways of living." The planners hoped the area would not be ruined by commercial success and declared, "Selectively, the improvement of aesthetics, atmosphere, produce and the search for originality can and must go hand in hand with financial success." They desired that it remain a "sophisticated and innovative neighborhood."[83]

The plan developed in late 1973 had one important characteristic in common with plans of the past: many of the projects it described were already under way by the time it was published, even before the formal planning process began. On June 20, 1973, the city council unanimously approved a $2,375,000 appropriation to begin construction of Central Park Mall. The library gift from the Omaha National Bank and the *World-Herald* came one month later. Commitment to other projects soon followed. In 1976, Peter Kiewit donated $2,500,000 toward construction of the downtown education center. Later that same year, Northwestern Bell Telephone Company, which had been planning a new headquarters building for several years, formally announced plans to construct it just north of Central Park Mall.[84] Following the agenda that had been developed by 1973, Omaha began the long process of rebuilding its downtown to fit its new image.

Conclusion

A decade after development of the CBD Plan, the *Omaha World-Herald* declared, "Omaha's Downtown Rises Again." Articles supporting the declaration described the dozens of construction and renovation projects, costing $470 million, that had changed the face of downtown. Of all the projects, Central Park Mall received credit as the most important. It was the centerpiece around which the rest developed. Other crucial factors included the Old Market; the commitment of the civic and business leadership; outside investors; and local, state, and federal tax incentives. During the decade, reconstruction of the downtown proceeded in the spirit of the agenda set in the early 1970s. Priority fell on projects that enhanced ambience and provided amenities. These included the mall, the new library, the Northwestern Bell building, the new offices of the Chamber of Commerce, the Central Park Plaza office complex, the renovated Burlington Building and Orpheum Theatre, and several projects in the Old Market. Historic preservation, a concern for beautification, and the goal of creating a quality environment (broadly defined) also informed the process. The goal was development of a downtown that projected an image that appealed to the values and preferences of the new amenities-oriented middle class. As an image, it emphasized the idea of a city as a place to live first, then as a place to work.[85]

In that goal, Omaha was not unique. Any number of recent publications have proclaimed an urban renaissance in the 1980s. They have reported the rebirth of downtowns in cities throughout the nation. The Omaha case suggests that the seemingly sudden reawakening was part of a much larger process linked to changes in the socioeconomic structure. The transformation from an industrial or commercial economy to a service economy tended to influence the creation of a new middle class that made new demands on the city. Downtowns lost their center-place dominance and only gradually acquired a new role as office, cultural, and entertainment centers. Underlying both the socioeconomic changes and the changes in the role of downtown was the significant reshaping of the image of the city. Once the image changed to reflect the new circumstances, the values and attitudes inherent in the view of the city as a place to live paved the way for the celebrated urban renaissance.

Epilogue

In the decades following World War II in Omaha, and in cities across the nation, planners and boosters had to come to grips with the large-scale changes that were reshaping urban America. Omaha grew from a city of 40.7 square miles in 1950 to 76.6 square miles in 1970. Its population expanded steadily from 251,117 in 1950 to 347,328 in 1970. In the 1940s and 1950s, the economy centered on meat and grain processing, transportation and wholesaling. By the early 1970s, retailing, finance, government, and services had completely supplanted the earlier sources of economic strength. No longer the livestock and meatpacking center of the nation, Omaha functioned as a regional service center. Those economic changes brought with them important demographic changes as the population became more educated and more white collar with the rise of the service economy. As the physical, economic, social, and demographic changes occurred, planners and boosters gradually reshaped their image of Omaha to fit their perception of the changed circumstances.

The process of rethinking the image of the city was not unique to Omaha. Nationally, elite planners, planning theorists, and other influential urban spokesmen began reevaluating what a city was, how it worked, and how best to plan for it in the early 1950s. As the United States entered the postwar period, the "city efficient," with its heavy emphasis on center-place structure and infrastructure improvements, stood as the basic model for planning action. That urban vision identified the city as a place in which to work, one that worked efficiently. Beginning with the introduction of the concept of urban design, and through the articulation of such ideas as open space, historic preservation, and beautification, planners developed a new agenda based on the vision of the city as a place to live, a place in which to enjoy the cultural, recreational, and environmental amenities that make possible a higher quality of life. Much of the concentration focused on the downtown and its waterfront. As both the oldest areas of the city and in many ways its most visible symbols, the downtown and waterfront and the plans for them reflected the city as planners and boosters saw it.

Introducers of new ideas at the national level moved forward in their reevaluation of the city more quickly than their counterparts at the local level. Local planners and boosters, composed largely of civic and business leaders, had their own perceptions, ideas, and agendas. They held a vision of their city based primarily upon local circumstances, and once a firm vision formed, it proved difficult to dislodge. Omaha's planners and boosters began the postwar period with an image of Omaha and an improvement agenda rooted in social and economic conditions undergoing significant change. Only gradually did they fully understand the transformations under way. Once they did, they developed a new agenda in a context of selective involvement with national planners. As they worked to reshape Omaha's image and decide on the best way to plan for it, civic and business leaders turned to the national planners and selected from the many ideas available those that best fit their perception of Omaha's situation.

The civic agenda taken up in the first decade after World War II had originated in the 1930s and early 1940s. Anxious to capitalize on public works and defense spending to achieve urban greatness, planners and boosters compiled a lengthy wish list of projects, including a civic auditorium, new sewers, better streets and roads, and a civic center. Their agenda emphasized basic infrastructure improvements, projects to demonstrate that Omaha was a modern city; it reflected well the model of the city efficient. Not only did their plans fit that mold, so did their image of Omaha. They promoted Omaha as a hardworking city with a congenial tax structure and the necessary infrastructure to support significant industrial activity. The downtown stood as the city's center, and the nearby river had valuable commercial potential. That agenda and that image held sway until the late 1950s.

At the close of the 1950s, social and economic changes were already well under way. By the end of the decade, the service sector equaled the traditional commercial-industrial sector in terms of employment; each employed 35 percent of the total labor force in 1960. Yet the old image of Omaha remained uppermost in the public mind. Promotional activities in the 1950s centered on Omaha's role as a meat and grain processor and continued to proclaim the hardworking nature of the population, the congenial tax environment, and Omaha's suitability as a location for industrial activity. Although planners and boosters realized the downtown had problems, they continued firm in their belief that it would remain the vital center of Omaha. The river and riverfront largely faded from popular view, and plans produced in the first decade after World War II clearly reflected this. Both the Blue Book plan of 1946 and the Omaha Plan of 1956 concentrated heavily on basic infrastructure improvements. In addition, civic and business leaders latched on to two national programs that promised to improve access to and within the city and preserve its center-place structure. The Interstate Highway System offered to tie Omaha into a national transportation system and improve access between the burgeoning suburbs and downtown. Urban renewal promised the opportunity to give downtown Omaha a needed face-lift, to make it more attractive to both Omahans and outside businesses seeking to relocate. Despite significant change, planners and boosters remained transfixed with their traditional vision of the city and a traditional planning agenda.

As Omaha entered the 1960s, the weight of the changes at work gradually pushed forward a reevaluation of the city and of how best to plan for it. Insurance, retailing, and services grew in size and prominence. Planner Alden Aust opined that the city must do more to attract the new high-tech industries and to do that, he said, Omaha must provide the cultural and educational amenities sought by individuals involved in those new industries. A study trip to Dallas, Texas, gave the civic and business leadership the opportunity to see firsthand a city that had aggressively sought growth through high-tech industries. Concurrently, new shopping centers challenged downtown Omaha as the decline begun in the 1950s continued. Largely unheralded, the Missouri River improved as new sewage-treatment plants corrected the most serious abuses.

As in the case of the city's image, so in the formal planning process did traditional ideas have the upper hand through 1966 and publication of the Central Omaha Plan. That document reflected continued emphasis on infrastructure improvements and depended on successful implementation of urban renewal and the completion of the Interstate Highway System within the city. Again, beneath the formal planning process, informally and on an individual basis, new planning ideas and strategies found expression in Omaha. Beautification, historic preservation, open-space development, and cultural and recreational amenities all had champions and to a very limited extent began to inform the planning process. After 1966 the new ideas supplanted traditional planning strategies.

After collapse of the meatpacking industry in the late 1960s, it became painfully clear that Omaha no longer functioned as the stockyards and meat-processing center of the nation. Once that realization took hold, civic and business leaders determined that Omaha needed a new image to fit its new role as a regional service center. A sense of crisis pervaded thinking about the downtown as its decline accelerated. Beginning with a promotional campaign in 1968, the boosters gradually forged a new image based on the quality of life metropolitan Omaha offered. Promotional materials highlighted the city's cultural, recreational, and environmental amenities and described its economic life in terms of the service sector, centering on insurance, finance, retailing, health complexes, educational institutions, and professions. The materials bespoke the values and expectations of the new middle class the service economy had created.

The civic and business leaders also developed a new planning agenda. Anxious to match the activities of cities elsewhere, they turned to national planning ideas and selected those that fit local circumstances. Open space, beautification, cultural and recreational amenities, and to a lesser extent historic preservation and environmentalism, informed the new agenda. Quality of life replaced efficiency as the most sought-after characteristic. Planning activity climaxed with the Riverfront Development initiative of the early 1970s.

The long-neglected river and riverfront, now valued for their amenities potential, provided the inspiration for an aggressive planning initiative. The ambitious scheme never came to fruition, but it begot a number of vitally important projects that set the stage for rebuilding downtown. Central Park Mall proved to be the key element. Once the city committed to construct that massive oasis of greenery and water in the heart of the downtown, a flurry of construction followed, including a new headquarters for Northwestern Bell Telephone, the Central Park Plaza office complex, a new main-branch library, a combination state office building and conference center, and many large-scale renovation projects. The downtown, once the vital center of Omaha, now functioned as one of many centers. It provided multiple services, offered cultural and recreational amenities, and gave Omaha a decidedly urban ambience.

Throughout the postwar planning process, the public-private partnership perhaps exerted the most influence. The private sector dominated. It initiated or was behind nearly all postwar planning. The public sector, represented by city hall, became a stronger member of the partnership, but it did not reach a sustained level of equality. Eugene Leahy, mayor from 1969 to 1973, provided important leadership in the Riverfront Development program but depended heavily on private-sector cooperation, and his leadership proved more an outgrowth of his personality than an increase in the authority of his office. And once he was out of office, his influence waned. Political and planning power thus remained largely in private hands, and private-sector perceptions and demands shaped Omaha's image and the planning agenda. Besides the dominant business-community boosters, park supporters and beautifiers also proved capable of advancing their programs. Urban renewal and public housing, on the other hand, never overcame strong public opposition and failed to become factors in the planning process. The lack of urban renewal, however, spared downtown Omaha the ravages of the "federal bulldozer" and left intact many areas and buildings that later were successfully renovated.

With a new agenda in place, downtown Omaha has witnessed a remarkable physical transformation since 1973. In January 1984 the *Omaha World-Herald* declared that "Downtown Rises Again." The accompanying articles described the results of investing $470 million in the area since the early 1970s and outlined the prospects for an additional $169 million worth of investments. A map showed fifty-nine major projects, including new construction and renovated buildings completed and projects under way or planned. Central Park Mall received credit for sparking the turn-around. The following June, the downtown business community sponsored *Discover Downtown*, a newspaper supplement. It described the area as a fit and feisty "people place" and gave the Old Market credit for spurring planners to think of downtown in a different light. And *MetroGuide*, also produced in the summer of 1985, clearly echoed the new image Omaha and the downtown established in the early 1970s.[1]

Between 1974 and 1983, nineteen new buildings significantly altered the downtown skyline, the most important of which were the Central Park Plaza buildings, the Chamber of Commerce headquarters, Lutheran Hospital, the City-County Building, W. Dale Clark Library, the State Office Building–Kiewit Conference Center, and the new headquarters of Northwestern Bell Telephone Company. During the same years, fully twenty-four structures were renovated, the most important being the Braiker-Brandeis Building, the old main-branch library, the Campbell Soup plant (directly across the street from Central Park Mall), the Douglas County Courthouse, the Metropolitan Utilities District building, the Orpheum Theatre, and the Old Market Passageway. Projects under way in 1984 included construction of a new Federal Reserve branch bank, the Park Fair Retail Building (behind the Central Park Plaza buildings), the Sixteenth Street Pedestrial Mall, and renovation of the Omaha Grain Exchange Building, the Flatiron Hotel, the Farm Credit Banks Building, and the old First National Bank Building.[2]

City planners interviewed for the *Discover Downtown* promotion piece suggested important changes in the approach to downtown planning since the mid-1960s. After briefly describing the premises of the 1966 Central Omaha Plan, the article explained the differences between the approach of the mid-1960s and planning for the downtown in the 1980s. The downtown envisioned in 1966 "was Omaha's employment, shopping and hotel center." Planners assumed that the major department stores and hotels would remain, and the 1966 plan was aimed at shoring up the traditional functions of the area. The stores and hotels closed, however, causing an acute crisis. The turnaround began with the Old Market restoration. The project's success surprised planners as "[t]he Central Omaha Study hadn't predicted it." The market offered a new approach to planning and a new image for the downtown. Said Steve Thompson, redevelopment specialist for the Greater Omaha Chamber of Commerce: "The common misconception of that era [the 1960s] was that downtown would remain the city's only major economic center." Once planners moved beyond that image, they adopted a new agenda for the area. The article summed up the results: "Today's downtown has fewer new office buildings, less retail activity, more open spaces and, in general, a less massive appearance than envisioned in the 1964 study."[3]

In 1985 condominiums joined the list of projects reshaping downtown. Six projects involving investment of $27.4 million suggested significant interest in making the area an attractive place to live. Marty Shukert, Omaha city planning director, was enthusiastic about the new direction, declaring that "[d]iversity is becoming a strength of the downtown. . . . It is becoming a place where you can live, shop, work, see trees and flowers and have a good time." At the time of publication, the downtown had about six hundred residents; the new projects added 436 living units.[4]

Just as *Discover Downtown* demonstrated its new image, so did *Metro-Guide*, also published in 1985, reflect the new approach in boosting Omaha. The introduction to the newspaper supplement touched on many of the booster themes first emphasized in the late 1960s and described the city as "the hub of a metropolitan area of 600,000 people who enjoy the advantages of bigness without a lot of the hassles." Omahans lived free of major commuting frustrations in a city of "broad, tree-lined streets and well tended yards" with plenty of room for gardens. They have the opportunity to enjoy professional sports, "a symphony orchestra, a ballet company, an opera organization, a children's theater, community playhouse, dinner theaters and a performing arts theater called the Orpheum that is a visual joy and an acoustical marvel." In addition, they could seek recreational outlet in the city's museums, zoo, parks, tennis courts, golf courses, and racetrack and on the Missouri River or any one of many area lakes. As the article concluded, boosters promoted the city as having "some of the advantages of small town living with the opportunities inherent in a city."[5]

Perhaps the new Omaha came across most clearly in the section describing its largest private employers. Mutual of Omaha with 6,364 employees stood atop the list and easily outdistanced the rest. American Telephone and Telegraph ranked second with 5,800 employees, followed by the Union Pacific (5,200), First Data Resources (4,800), Northwestern Bell Telephone (4,519), InterNorth Inc. (2,300), Richman Gordman Stores (1,900), J. L. Brandeis and Sons, Inc. (1,800), and Control Data Corporation (1,300). The list excluded Offutt Air Force Base, with a work force exceeding 14,000, and the city's nonprofit organizations, such as hospitals and universities. It also excluded local, state, and federal government employees. The list of private employers, however, clearly indicated the new sources of strength in the Omaha economy.[6] Insurance, telecommunications, and retailing have completely replaced meatpacking, wholesaling, and transportation as the major sources of employment. (Change remained a constant in the employment picture, though. Since 1985, InterNorth twice changed its corporate name, then moved its headquarters to Houston; Union Pacific instituted large-scale layoffs in its middle-management ranks; and a regional retailer, Younkers of Des Moines, Iowa, purchased J. L. Brandeis. The loss of jobs was heavy, but not enough to alter significantly the city's overall employment structure.)

By 1973, Omaha was a very different city—physically, economically and socially—than it had been in 1945. The many changes occurred at varying rates, yet by the early 1970s all had made their mark. The most significant change, however, was in the minds of those responsible for articulating Omaha's image. The civic and business leadership—Omaha's planners and boosters—reevaluated their city. In the late 1960s and early 1970s, taking cues both from local circumstances and national planning ideas, they developed a city more in tune with the changed circumstances.

As this study has shown, city planning ideas often come about as reactions to change rather than in anticipation of change. In the nearly twenty years since the inception of the Riverfront Development initiative, Omaha—as indeed cities throughout the United States—has witnessed more change and the emergence of new issues. Homelessness has risen to the level of national concern, and all cities have had to decide how they will respond to this human tragedy. Omaha is fortunate in that the problem seems to be at a rather manageable level, at least for now. It is in the enviable position of having an excess of shelter beds. And yet it still needs to come to grips with housing-related problems. As the city enters the nineties, the future direction of public housing is emerging as an issue of major concern.[7] And the nation must soon address its mounting infrastructure needs. It is not so much a matter of needing to build more. Rather, the question facing cities today is how to repair and maintain the existing infrastructure so that the livable cities may remain both livable and accessible. It seems time once again for planners, civic leaders, and those concerned with urban America to take a hard look at the once-again new American city of the 1990s.

Notes

CHAPTER ONE

1 Mel Scott, *American City Planning since 1890* (Berkeley: University of California Press, 1969), 473–74, 477–80, 561–62.

2 Ibid., 542–43, 637.

3 Ibid., 542–43.

4 Ibid., 492–93, 611, 623.

5 Quoted in ibid., 481.

6 Ibid.

7 See Charles Haar, "The Content of the General Plan: A Glance at History," *Journal of the American Institute of Planners* 21, nos.2–3 (Spring–Summer 1955): 66–70.

8 Scott, *American City Planning*, 481–83.

9 Ibid., 528–29.

10 Quoted in ibid., 595.

11 Ibid.

12 Ibid.

13 Quoted in ibid., 596.

14 Quoted in ibid., 615–16.

15 Ibid., 616–18, 637.

16 Ibid., 533.

17 Jeanne R. Lowe, *Cities in a Race With Time* (New York: Random House, 1967), 337–39.

18 Samuel Zeitlen, "Waterfront Planning and the Master Plan," *Journal of the American Institute of Planners* 11, no.3 (Summer 1945): 28.

19 T. H. Abell, "A Shoreline Master Plan for Los Angeles," *Journal of the American Institute of Planners* 12, no.3 (Summer 1946): 26.

20 Ruth Layton, "St. Louis Riverfront Revisited, 1933–1964," *Landscape Architecture* 54, no.3 (April 1964): 182–86.

21 Charles Abrams, "Downtown Decay and Revival," *Journal of the American Institute of Planners* 27, no.1 (February 1961): 4, 7.

22 Ibid., 8.

23 Ibid., 5.

24 Ibid., 9. Abrams cited both authors in a footnote.

25 Blanche Lemco Van Ginkel, "The Form of the Core," *Journal of the American Institute of Planners* 27, no.1 (February 1961): 57.

26 Ibid.

27 Ibid., 59.

28 George Sternlieb, " The Future of Retailing in the Downtown Core," *Journal of the American Institute of Planners* 29, no.2 (May 1963): 102.

29 Ibid., 111.

30 Ibid.

31 John Allpass, "Changes in the Structure of Urban Centers," *Journal of the American Institute of Planners* 34, no.3 (May 1968): 171.

32 Ibid.

33 Christopher Tunnard, "Cities by Design," *Journal of the American Institute of Planners* 17, no.3 (Summer 1951): 142–43.

34 Ibid., 143, 147.

35 Ibid., 143, 148, 150.

36 See Kevin Lynch and Alvin K. Lukashok, "Some Childhood Memories of the City," *Journal of the American Institute of Planners* 22, no.3 (Summer 1956): 142–52.

37 Kevin Lynch, "Urban Design," *American Society of Planning Officials, Annual Report, 1958,* 26.

38 Ibid., 29.

39 Kevin Lynch, *The Image of the City* (Cambridge, Mass.: MIT Press, 1960), 5, 9.

40 Ibid., 111–12

41 Ibid., 119.

42 Ibid.

43 Morton Hoppenfeld, "The Role of Design in City Planning," *Journal of the American Institute of Planners* 36, no.2 (May 1960): 100.

44 Ibid., 103.

45 Paul D. Spreiregen, "Making the Scene," *American Society of Planning Officials, Annual Report, 1966,* 194; Frank Hotchkiss, "Expanding Vistas for Urban Design," *American Society of Planning Officials, Annual Report, 1966,* 208.

46 *American Society of Planning Officials, Annual Report, 1968,* 189; Morton Hoppenfeld, "A Design for Change," *American Society of Planning Officials, Annual Report, 1968,* 195.

47 See Lynch, *The Image of the City.*

48 Thomas D. Schocken, "Must Our Cities Remain Ugly?" *Journal of the American Institute of Planners* 22, no.4 (Fall 1956): 218–26.

49 Stephen K. Bailey and Richard T. Frost, "Aesthetics and Metropolitan Growth," *Journal of the American Institute of Planners* 23, no.3 (Summer 1957): 111.

50 Grady Clay, "Anti-Uglies, Unite! A Proposal for an American Civic Trust," *Landscape Architecture* 52, no.4 (July 1962): 225.

51 Grady Clay, "B. . . . Is No Longer a Dirty Word," *Landscape Architecture* 55, no.3 (April 1965): 175.

52 Ibid; William Whyte, Jr., "Open Space—And Retroactive Planning," *American Society of Planning Officials, Annual Report, 1958,* 69.

53 Grady Clay, "What a Nice Park! Wasn't It?" *Landscape Architecture* 52, no.3 (April 1962): 145.

54 Grady Clay, "Genteel Strolls and Drunken Rolls or Time to Look at Your City Park," *Landscape Architecture* 54, no.3 (April 1964): 181.

55 Charles Eliot, "1961 Housing Act's Open-Space Provisions," *Landscape Architecture* 52, no.2 (January 1962): 112.

56 See Marion Clawson, "A Positive Approach to Open Space Preservation," *Journal of the American Institute of Planners* 28, no.2 (May 1962): 124–29; Daniel L. Mandelker, "What Open Space Where? How?" *American Society of Planning Officials, Annual Report, 1963,* 21–27; Lawrence Levine, "Land Conservation in Metropolitan Areas," *Journal of the American Institute of Planners* 30, no.3 (August 1964): 204–16.

57 Ann Satterthwaithe, "Open Space Is Not Enough," *Landscape Architecture* 55, no.2 (January 1965): 123.

58 Quoted in ibid.

59 Ibid.

60 David Lowenthal, "To Love at a Distance Is Not Enough," *Landscape Architecture* 59, no.1 (October 1968): 29.

61 Ibid.

62 See August Hecksher, *Open Spaces: The Life of American Cities* (New York: Harper and Row, 1977), 88–114, 243–77.

63 Ibid., 245.

64 Ibid., 247.

65 Norman J. Johnson, "A City Takes the First Step: An Experiment for Renewing a Central Business District," *Journal of the American Institute of Planners* 24, no.1 (Winter 1958): 11, 14.

66 Shirley F. Weiss, "The Downtown Mall Experiment," *Journal of the American Institute of Planners* 30, no.1 (February 1964): 66–68.

67 George Wickstead, "Critique: Fresno Mall's First 12 Months," *Landscape Architecture* 56, no.1 (October 1965): 44–46, 48.

68 *Los Angeles Times*, April 28, 1988, 1, 18.

69 Roger Martin, "Exciting Start with Nicollet Mall," *Landscape Architecture* 59, no.4 (July 1969): 300.

70 Ibid., 303–4.

71 See Robert L. Morris and S. B. Zisman, "The Pedestrian, Downtown, and the Planner," *Journal of the American Institute of Planners* 28, no.3 (August 1962): 152–58.

72 John Codman, "A Law for the Preservation of an Historic District," *American Society of Planning Officials, Annual Report*, 1964, 207–8.

73 Albert B. Wolfe, "Conservation of Historic Buildings and Areas," *American Society of Planning Officials, Annual Report*, 1964, 208–14.

74 See "Forecasts for Recreation," *American Society of Planning Officials, Annual Report*, 1966, 210–27.

75 "Planning for Leisure and Change: Programs of IFLA, ASLA, NCILA," *Landscape Architecture* 58, no.3 (April 1968): 184, 217.

76 See David Lowenthal, "The Environmental Crusade: Ideals and Realities," *Landscape Architecture* 60, no.4 (July 1970): 290–96; Maynard M. Hufschmidt, "Environmental Quality as a Policy and Planning Objective," *Journal of the American Institute of Planners* 37, no.4 (July 1971): 231–41; George Hagevik and Lawrence Mann, "The 'New' Environmentalism: An Intellectual Frontier," *Journal of the American Institute of Planners* 37, no.4 (July 1971): 274–78.

77 See Hufschmidt, "Environmental Quality," 231–41.

78 Quoted in Robert Paul Jordan, "Nebraska . . . The Good Life," *National Geographic* 145, no.3 (March 1974): 396.

79 John H. Mollenkopf, *The Contested City* (Princeton, N.J.: Princeton University Press, 1983), 12–46.

80 Ibid., 12, 40.

CHAPTER TWO

1 U.S. Bureau of the Census, *City and County Data Book*, 1952, 1962, 1972; Omaha City Planning Department, "Growth of the City Map" and "A Century of Progress Through Annexation," Report No.176 (1973), 7–8, 10. In 1970 the population was 347,328; 80,000 equals 23.03 percent of 347,328. Between 1950 and 1970 the population grew by 96,211; 80,000 equals 83.15 percent of 96,263. Nebraska law allows cities of the metropolitan class under certain circumstances (contiguous area, nonagricultural use) to annex territory by vote of the city council after a public hearing. Under this law, Omaha announces an annexation package nearly every year.

2 In the 1960s, Omaha's population grew by 45,739; 30,002 equals 65.59 percent of 45,739.

3 After 1973 the city adopted a development policy that restricted annexations to primarily commercial and industrial parcels with few or no residents. The policy was reversed after the 1980 census revealed that Omaha had fallen in rank among American cities. *Omaha World-Herald*, July 17, 1985; information provided by the Omaha City Planning Department.

4 Lawrence H. Larsen and Barbara J. Cottrell, *The Gate City: A History of Omaha* (Boulder, Colo.: Pruett Publishing Company, 1982), 250–51.

5 John C. Cunningham, "Education and Manpower in the Omaha SMSA" (University of Nebraska at Omaha, Center for Applied Urban Research, April 1971), 37.

6 Between 1951 and 1970, 69,450 jobs were added; in the service sector, 50,450 jobs were added; 50,450 equals 72.64 percent of 69,450.

7 U.S. Bureau of the Census, *City and County Data Book* 1962, 1972; Center for Applied Urban Research, "Omaha's Changing Profile," *Review of Applied Urban Research* 2, no.2 (February 1974): 3; U.S. Bureau of the Census, Seventeenth Census of the United States, 1950, Census of the Population, vol.2: *Characteristics of the Population*; Eighteenth Census of the United States, 1960, vol.1,

Characteristics of the Population; Nineteenth Census of the United States, 1970, vol. 1, *Characteristics of the Population*.

8 Alysia Smith, chief researcher, *Omaha Stockyards: A Century of Marketing, Commemorative Book, 1884–1984* (Omaha: Omaha Livestock Market, Inc., 1984), 21, 23–24.

9 Ibid., 25, 27, 30.

10 Omaha *Sun Newspapers*, July 15, 1965, 1-A, 2-A (Omaha Public Library, Social Science Department Clip File).

11 *Omaha World-Herald*, December 14, 1960, October 26, 1969 (Omaha Public Library, Business and Economics Department Clip File); Edd Bailey, "The Century of Progress: A Heritage of Service, Union Pacific, 1869–1969," address to the Newcomen Society, September 9, 1969 (Princeton University Press for the Newcomen Society, 1969), 13, 15.

12 *Sunday World-Herald Magazine*, "Mutual of Omaha Largest in Its Field," March 15, 1959 (Omaha Public Library, Social Science Department Clip File); Larsen and Cottrell, *Gate City*, 214.

13 Larsen and Cottrell, *Gate City*, 214, 252.

14 Ibid.

15 James C. Rippey, *The Diary of a Dream: Goodbye, Central; Hello, World; A Centennial History of Northwestern Bell* (Omaha: Northwestern Bell, 1975), 237–38, 244–46, 249–52, 279–80.

16 Ibid., 244–46, 272–73, 325; Dennis N. Mihelich, project director, "Omaha Profiles," River City Roundup Oral History Interviews: Alma F. Jacobson, Thomas S. Nurnberger, Jr. (Douglas County Historical Society).

17 *Northern, The First Fifty Years* (Omaha: Northern Natural Gas Company, 1983), 4–10.

18 Quoted in ibid., 14.

19 Ibid., 13–14.

20 Ibid., 17–18; *Omaha World-Herald, Magazine of the Midlands*, April 25, 1976, 28–29.

21 "An Uncommon Man," *Kie-ways* 35, no.4 (Peter Kiewit Sons', Inc.): 12; Harold B. Myers, "The Biggest Invisible Builder in the World," *Fortune* 74, no.4 (April 1966): 150.

22 PKS: A Past of Achievement. . . . A Future of Challenge (Peter Kiewit Sons', Inc.), 12; Myers, "Biggest Builder," 147–48.

23 *Omaha Sun Newspapers*, March 27, 1958; March 19, 1970 (Omaha Public Library, Social Science Department Clip File).

24 "Profile: Leo A. Daly, Jr." *The Alumnus: The Catholic University of America* (Winter 1966): 4–5; *Omaha World-Herald*, Feb. 18, 1973 (Omaha Public Library, Social Science Department Clip File).

25 Arvid E. Nelson, Jr., *The AK-SAR-BEN Story: A Seventy Year History of the Knights of AK-SAR-BEN* (Lincoln, Nebr: Johnsen Publishing Company, 1967), 384–85, 386–87.

26 *Omaha World-Herald*, April 17, 1966 (Omaha Public Library, Business and Economics Department Clip File); *Omaha Sun Newspapers*, March 5, 1965; April 7, 1966 (Omaha Public Library, Social Science Department Clip File); *Omaha World-Herald*, December 12, 1983 (Omaha Public Library, Social Science Department Clip File).

27 Omaha Chamber of Commerce, *Profile* 26, no.4 (February 14, 1966): 1, 3; *Profile* 30, no.4 (February 23, 1970): 1; U.S. Bureau of the Census, *City and County Data Book*, 1952, 1962, 1972.

28 The 1953 and 1956 employment breakdowns in *County Business Patterns* reported employment in medical and other health-related fields as under one thousand for Douglas County. The figure jumped to more than five thousand in 1959. Secondary material suggested no event or series of events that would explain the sudden increase. The earlier data were obviously collected under rules different from the later ones, making the figures incompatible.

29 The 1950 figure included only the number of students in public schools. No figures were given to indicate the number in private and parochial schools. The 1970 figure included students in all elementary and secondary schools; U.S. Bureau of the Census, *City and County Data Book*, 1962, 1972.

30 To obtain the figures listed in table 13, the number of Omaha city employees listed in the *City and County Data Books* was divided by the total number of government employees listed in Cunningham, "Education and Manpower." Those figures represent only an approximation. Official employment records do not list the number of government employees.

31 For a full account of the progressive-era reforms of city government, see Richard K. Wilson, "Business Progressivism in Omaha, 1900–1917" (Master's thesis, Creighton University, 1977); for discussion of the issue, see Garneth O. Peterson, "The Omaha City Council and Commission: A Profile 1888–1930"

(Master's thesis, University of Nebraska at Omaha, 1980); Glenn Cunningham, "Getting It Straight," radio address, April 9, 1951, station KOIL (transcripts in possession of the author).

32 "Omaha Home Rule Charter, 1956" (City of Omaha and the Charter Convention), i–v.

33 The inciting crisis came in 1947. In that year a court ordered the city to award its
police officers and firefighters a promised raise. The city did not have funds to
cover the expense. The business community, led by Robert Storz, responded,
going hat in hand to collect money from private sources to finance the raises. The
campaign succeeded, but the incident convinced the business and civic community of the necessity for reform in the tax system. *Sunday World-Herald Magazine*, October 23, 1949, 5-C; Omaha City Planning Department, "Growth of
the City Map"; Robert D. Miewald, ed., *Nebraska Government and Politics*
(Lincoln: University of Nebraska Press, 1984), 155–59.

34 Larsen, and Cottrell, *Gate City*, 261.

35 Paul Williams, "Twenty Top Omaha's Power Structure," *Omaha Sun Newspapers*, April 7, 1966; Paul Hammel, "Who Wields Power in Omaha?" *Omaha
Sun Newspapers*, July 22, 1981.

36 *Omaha World-Herald*, February 19, 1952 (Omaha Public Library, Social Science Department Clip File).

37 Robert Storz, declared "the man who gets things done" in 1949 and elected
King of Quivera in 1957, was leader of the business community in the 1950s.
After he sold the brewery to his brother he quietly faded from the forefront of
leadership, although he still remained somewhat active and civic leaders looked
to him for advice on occasion; Gilbert Swanson was one of two Swanson
brothers (the other, W. Clarke Swanson, died 1961), sons of Carl A. Swanson,
founder of C. A. Swanson and Sons. The Swanson company produced conve-
nience foods and developed the first frozen dinner, known as the Swanson TV
Dinner. The Swanson family fortune provided endowments for the Gilbert
Swanson Memorial Research Fund (Mayo Clinic), the Gilbert and W. Clarke
Swanson Memorial (Salvation Army), and the Carl and Caroline Swanson
Foundation, Inc. *Omaha World-Herald*, March 9, 1969 (Omaha Public Library,
Social Science Department Clip File).

38 W. Dale Clark headed the Omaha National Bank until 1962, when Morris
Miller succeeded him. Clark then directed the Omaha World-Herald Company

until 1966; Harold Andersen succeeded him. Clark remained very active in the business and civic community, especially in the effort to build a new main library, until his death in 1975. His continued involvement even after his retirement might have delayed the recognition of his successors as leaders in their own rights. Despite the lack of recognition, Miller and Andersen undoubtedly had influence because of their positions as heads of their respective businesses. They should be considered leaders by 1966 despite the absence of their names on the Williams list.

39 Nelson, *AK-SAR-BEN*, 373–74, 384–85, 386–87; *Omaha World-Herald*, April 8, 1967 (Omaha Public Library, Social Science Department Clip File).

40 See Williams, "Twenty Top Structure."

41 Both the Omaha City Planning Department and the Center for Applied Urban Research conducted economic surveys. These concentrated heavily on the manufacturing sector and how to expand it. Growth in other areas, including the service sector, received notice but was not deemed significant. As late as 1967 emphasis fell on manufacturing as an important growth sector and studies described the local economy as driven by transportation, processing, and distribution—very similar to the conclusions of studies conducted in the 1950s. Not until the 1970s did the service sector receive its share of attention and recognition. These surveys will be cited at greater length later. See Omaha City Planning Department, "An Economic Survey of Omaha, Nebraska: Section One, Master Plan," Report No.119 (May 1958); Carroll A. Stecklein, "The Economic Base and Community Multiplier for the SMSA of Omaha" (Master's thesis, University of Nebraska, 1960); Lawrence A. Danton, "Factors Influencing the Development of Omaha" (University of Omaha, Center for Applied Urban Research, March 1967); Center for Applied Urban Research, "The Economic Structure of the Omaha SMSA" (University of Omaha: April 1967); Lawrence A. Danton and Masoud Hariri, "Preliminary Projections of Growth of the Omaha SMSA to 1990" (University of Omaha, Center for Applied Urban Research, August 1967); Cunningham, "Education and Manpower"; David W. Hinton, "Manpower Needs in the Omaha SMSA: Employment and Occupational Projections" (University of Nebraska at Omaha, Center for Applied Urban Research, September 1975); Edward Houswald, "The Structure of Employment in the Omaha SMSA 1970, 1974, 1976–78 by Industry and Occupation" (University of Nebraska at Omaha, Center for Applied Urban

Research, November 1977); Omaha—Council Bluffs Metropolitan Area Planning Agency, "Regional Growth and Development: Conditions, Trends, Problems" (June 1978).

42 See Edward L. Ulman, "Amenities as a Factor in Regional Growth" *Geographical Review* 44, no.1 (January 1954).

43 *Omaha World-Herald*, August 30, 1970, 12-A.

44 Belkap Data Solutions, Ltd., "Facility Location Decisions: A *Fortune* Research Survey," *Fortune* (September 1977):1.

CHAPTER THREE

1 Kerwin Williams, *Grants-in-Aid Under the Public Works Administration: A Study in Federal-State-Local Relations* (New York: Columbia University Press, 1939), 41–43; Division of Information, Public Works Administration, *America Builds: The Record of PWA* (Washington D.C.: United States Government Printing Office, 1939), 95–97.

2 Arthur W. MacMahon, John D. Millett, and Gladys Ogden, *The Administration of Federal Work Relief*, Committee on Public Administration Social Science Research Council (Chicago: Public Administration Service, Studies in Administration, vol.12, 1941), 6, 11, 127.

3 C. W. Short and R. Stanley-Brown, *Public Buildings: Architecture Under the Public Works Administration, 1933 to 1939* (Washington, D.C.: United States Government Printing Office, 1939), xxiii.

4 For examples see Harold Ickes, *The First Three Years of PWA* (Washington, D.C.: United States Government Printing Office, 1936) and *PWA: A Four Year Record of the Construction of Permanent and Useful Public Works* (Washington, D.C.: United States Government Printing Office, 1937).

5 See PWA, *American Builds*.

6 Ibid., 195–205.

7 Ibid., 196.

8 Ibid., 198.

9 Ibid.

10 Ibid., 204–05.

11 Ibid., 200–1.

12 Ibid., 207–8.

13 Williams, *Grants-in-Aid*, 3–6.

14 Federal Works Agency, Works Progress Administration, *Reports on the Progress of the WPA Programs* (June 30, 1939), 21.

15 Federal Works Agency, Works Progress Administration, *Final Report on the WPA Program, 1935–43* (Washington, D.C.: United States Government Printing Office, 1946), 62, 65–66.

16 For examples of this literature see Carl Abbott, *The New Urban America: Growth and Politics in Sunbelt Cities* (Chapel Hill: University of North Carolina Press, 1981) and *Portland: Planning, Politics and Growth in a Twentieth Century City* (Lincoln: University of Nebraska Press, 1983) and Kirkpatrick Sale, *Power Shift: The Rise of the Southern Rim and Its Challenge to the Eastern Establishment* (New York: Random House, Vintage Books, 1975).

17 *Omaha World-Herald*, August 13, 1933, 1, 3; September 3, 1933, 1.

18 *Omaha World-Herald*, October 14, 1933, 18.

19 *Omaha World-Herald*, September 13, 1933. 2; Omaha Chamber of Commerce *Journal* 22, no.5 (June 1935): 8.

20 *Omaha World-Herald*, September 13, 1933, 2; Omaha Chamber of Commerce Minutes of Meetings, Public Works Committee, September 19, 1933, 778.

21 *Omaha World-Herald*, September 27, 1933, 1, 7; June 30, 1936, 1; Omaha Chamber of Commerce *Journal* 26, no.2 (February 1938), 8.

22 Omaha Chamber of Commerce *Journal* 26, no.2 (February 1938): 8; 26, no.8 (August 1938): 12; 27, no.3 (March 1939): 12; 26, no.6 (June 1938): 15. The total cost of the project was listed incorrectly in the June article. It was corrected in 26, no.7 (July 1938): 13.

23 Omaha City Planning Department, "A History of Omaha's Parks and Recreation System" [text by Garneth O. Peterson], Report No.214 (February 1984): 6; cited hereafter as "History of Parks and Recreation."

24 Omaha Chamber of Commerce *Journal* 25, no.8 (September 1937): 1, 4; 23 no.6 (July 1935): 7.

25 Ibid, 25, no.8 (September 1937): 4; 27, no.3 (March 1940): 3.

26 Ibid., 24, no.7 (August 1936): 7; 25, no.8 (September 1937), 1; Omaha Chamber of Commerce Minutes of Meetings, City Appearance Committee, October 16, 1934, 145; Omaha Chamber of Commerce *Journal* 23, no.7 (September 1935): 7. The Carter Lake Development Society announced a major improvement plan in March 1941, but nothing substantial came of it. After that point, no more reports appeared.

27 Omaha Chamber of Commerce *Journal* 23, no.7 (September 1935): 7.

28 Ibid., 24, no.2 (February 1936): 10. The city's other major university, Creighton, remained on the northwest edge of the downtown.

29 Omaha Chamber of Commerce Minutes of Meetings, Public Works Committee, October 28, 1933, 780; *Journal* 23, no.5 (June 1935): 8; *Omaha World-Herald*, August 5, 1936 (Special Collections, University of Nebraska at Omaha (cited hereafter as UNO: WPA Collection, Drawer 7, WPA-PWA File).

30 *Omaha World-Herald*, December 18, 1938 (Special Collections, UNO: WPA Collection, Drawer 7, WPA-PWA File); *Omaha World-Herald*, October 5, 1937, 2.

31 "History of Parks and Recreation," 4–6; City of Omaha, 1942: *Manual of Civic Improvements Sponsored by the Mayor and City Council of Omaha* (Omaha: Douglas Printing Company, 1942), 18. Whether the WPA added thirty miles to the system is not clear. The Planning Department's history of the system listed only one addition after 1920: Northridge Drive, finished in 1929. The WPA might have added thirty miles of paving to the boulevards.

32 *Omaha World-Herald*, August 13, 1933, 1, 3; Omaha Chamber of Commerce Minutes of Meetings, Public Works Committee, October 28, 1933; *Journal* 23, no.5 (June 1935): 8; *Omaha World-Herald*, November 4, 1935, 2; August 20, 1937 (Special Collections, UNO: WPA Collection, Drawer 7, WPA-PWA File); Omaha Chamber of Commerce *Journal* 23, no.5 (June 1935): 8.

33 *Omaha World-Herald*, October 5, 1937, 2.

34 Omaha Chamber of Commerce *Journal* 24, no.7 (August 1936): 7; *Omaha World-Herald*, August 5, 1936 (Special Collections, UNO: WPA Collection, Drawer 8, City Improvement Council File).

35 Omaha Chamber of Commerce *Journal* 24, no.7 (August 1936): 7; "History of Parks and Recreation," 12.

36 *Omaha World-Herald*, September 13, 1970 (Omaha Public Library, Social Science Department Clip File).

37 Omaha Chamber of Commerce Minutes of Meetings, City Improvement Council, August 21, 1935, 138; *Journal* 23, no.7 (September 1935): 11; *Omaha World-Herald*, August 25, 1937, 3.

38 Omaha Chamber of Commerce Minutes of Meetings, City Improvement Council, May 14, 1940, 87.

39 *Omaha World-Herald*, August 27, 1936 (Special Collections, UNO: WPA Col-

lection, Drawer 8, City Improvement Council File); *Omaha World-Herald*, June 20, 1938 (Special Collections, UNO: WPA Collection, Drawer 8, City Improvement Council File).

40 Omaha Chamber of Commerce Minutes of Meetings, City Appearance Committee, October 2, 1934, 141; January 2, 1935, 104; July 30, 1935, 128.

41 Ibid., September 26, 1934, 132.

42 T. Earl Sullenger, "An Ecological Study of Omaha" (Municipal University of Omaha, Bureau of Social Research, 1938), 13–20; Omaha Chamber of Commerce Minutes of Board of Directors, Executive Committee, Finance Committee, November 29, 1938, 78–79.

43 Omaha Chamber of Commerce Minutes of Meetings, Public Works Committee, June 30, 1933, 774.

44 Omaha Chamber of Commerce *Journal* 25, no.2 (February 1937): 4; *Omaha World-Herald*, October 1, 1938 (Special Collections, UNO: WPA Collection, Drawer 8, River-Traffic File).

45 *Omaha World-Herald*, September 9, 1938 (Special Collections, UNO: WPA Collection, Drawer 8, River-Traffic File); ibid., March 3, 1939 (Special Collections, UNO: WPA Collection, Drawer 8, River-Traffic File); Omaha Chamber of Commerce *Journal* 27, no.2 (February 1940): 3; 28, no.2 (February 1941): 14.

46 *Omaha World-Herald*, March 3, 1939 (Special Collections, UNO: WPA Collection, Drawer 8, River-Traffic File).

47 "History of Parks and Recreation," 9–10; Omaha Chamber of Commerce Minutes of Meetings, City Appearance Committee, August 8, 1935; *Omaha Post*, December 13, 1938 (Special Collections, UNO: WPA Collection, Drawer 8, River-Traffic File).

48 Omaha Chamber of Commerce *Journal* 23, no.7 (September 1935): 9; 23, no.8 (October 1935): 10.

49 Ibid., 27, no.8 (August 1940): 3–7.

50 Ibid., no.9 (September 1940): 4–5, 7.

51 Ibid., 27, no.12 (December 1940): 4.

52 Jacqueline McGlade, "The Zoning of Fort Crook: Urban Expansionism vs. County Home Rule," *Nebraska History* 65, no.1 (Spring 1983): 21–33.

53 *Omaha World-Herald*, July 18, 1937 (Special Collections, UNO: WPA Collection, Drawer 8, City Planning File).

54 Omaha Chamber of Commerce *Journal* 25, no.8 (September 1937): 7.

55 *Omaha World-Herald*, October 3, 1937 (Special Collections, UNO: WPA Collection, Drawer 8, City Planning File).

56 Ibid., July 18, 1937; Chamber of Commerce *Journal* 25, no.7 (July 1937): 6; *Omaha World-Herald*, August 26, 1937 (Special Collections, UNO: WPA Collection, Drawer 8, City Planning File); Omaha Chamber of Commerce *Journal* 25, no.8 (September 1937): 7; no.9 (October 1937): 9.

57 *Omaha World-Herald*, June 20, November 13, 1938 (Special Collections, UNO: WPA Collection, Drawer 8, City Planning File); Omaha Chamber of Commerce *Journal* 26, no.12 (December 1938): 3; Omaha Chamber of Commerce Minutes of Meetings, City Improvement Council, April 5, 1940, 78, 82.

58 See 1942: *Manual of Civic Improvements*; Omaha Chamber of Commerce, *Bulletin* 2, no.8 (January 5, 1943): 1.

59 Omaha Chamber of Commerce *Bulletin* 2, no.30 (August 1943): 3; 3, no.6 (October 8, 1943): 1–3, 3; 3, no.26 (February 24, 1944): 3; 3, no.8 (October 22, 1943): 1; 3, no.2 (September 1943): 3; 3, no.29 (March 16, 1944): 3.

60 Omaha Chamber of Commerce Minutes of Meetings, City Improvement Council, July 29, 1943, 84; *Bulletin* 2, no.29 (July 1943): 3; Minutes of Meetings, Postwar Planning Committee, October 18, 1943, 665, 667.

61 Omaha Chamber of Commerce *Bulletin* 3, no.11 (November 12, 1943): 1; 3, no.12 (November 19, 1943): 1; Minutes of Meetings, City Improvement Council, November 9, 1943, 89; *Bulletin* 3, no.21 (January 20, 1944): 3.

62 Omaha Chamber of Commerce *Bulletin* 3, no.28 (March 10, 1944): 3.

CHAPTER FOUR

1 Omaha Chamber of Commerce *Bulletin* 2, no.8 (January 15, 1943): 1.

2 Ibid., 3, no.12 (November 19, 1943): 1; Omaha City Planning Board Minutes, December 1, 1943, 174.

3 Planning Board Minutes, January 12, 1944, 176–78.

4 Ibid., 179–80; Omaha Chamber of Commerce Minutes of Meetings, City Improvement Council, August 1, 1944, 130.

5 Omaha City Planning Department, "A History of Omaha's Parks and Recreation System," 14; Omaha Chamber of Commerce *Bulletin* 3, no.28 (March 10, 1944): 3.

6 Omaha Chamber of Commerce Minutes of Meetings, City Improvement Council, September 27, 1944, 132.

7 Ibid., April 10, 1945, 145.

8 *Omaha World-Herald*, April 17, 1945, 13; April 18, 1945, 1.

9 Mayor's City-Wide Planning Committee, "Improvement and Development Program Recommended for the City of Omaha by the Mayor's City-Wide Planning Committee," March 15, 1946, 299–302.

10 Omaha Chamber of Commerce *Bulletin* 5, no.1 (September 14, 1945): 3; 6, no.3 (September 20, 1946): 2; "Improvement and Development Program," 299–302.

11 "Improvement and Development Program," 299–302.

12 "History of Parks and Recreation," 14.

13 "Improvement and Development Program," 290.

14 Ibid., 9–21.

15 Ibid., 17.

16 Ibid., 160–64, 302; *Omaha World-Herald*, January 12, 1949 (Omaha Public Library, Social Science Department Clip File). The National Association of Real Estate Boards elected Maenner president in 1949. He spent the next year campaigning against what he called socialized housing.

17 "Improvement and Development Program," 122–23, 128.

18 Ibid., 134, 136.

19 *Omaha World-Herald*, March 23, 1946, 1.

20 Ibid., March 30, 1946, 1, 3.

21 "Improvement and Development Program", 195.

22 *Omaha World-Herald*, April 8, 1946, 1–2.

23 Ibid., 2; "Improvement and Development Program," 248.

24 *Omaha World-Herald*, November 6, 1946, 8.

25 Ibid. The home-rule charter adopted in 1957 abolished the last temporary committee. Subsequently, a new, independent park board and airport authority were created. The improvement commission disbanded in 1961, on schedule.

26 *Omaha World-Herald*, August 11, 1946, 1.

27 Ibid., March 31, 1946, 1.

28 Ibid., September 8, 1946, 1.

29 Ibid., September 24, 1951 (Omaha Public Library, Social Science Department Clip File).

30 Omaha Chamber of Commerce Bulletin 7, no.8 (October 24, 1947): 1; *Omaha World-Herald*, April 12, 1950, 1; November 3, 1950, 8.

31 *Congressional Record—House*, December 30, 1970, H12531–H12534. The

Congressional Record cited a biographical article on Congressman Cunningham; *Omaha World-Herald*, May 9, 1950 (Omaha Public Library, Social Science Department Clip File); interview with Glenn Cunningham, August 5, 1985 (transcript in possession of the author); *Omaha World-Herald*, November 11, 1950, 1.

32 See B. F. Sylvester, "Omaha's Flood, 1952," *Nebraska History* 35, no.1 (March 1954): 45–59.

33 Omaha Chamber of Commerce Minutes of Meetings, Program of Work Committee, August 28, 1951, 392; *Omaha World-Herald*, January 31, 1973, 13. The article presented a history of the OIF.

34 *Omaha World-Herald*, January 31, 1973, 13.

35 Ibid.

36 State-Wide Highway Planning Survey, Nebraska Department of Roads and Irrigation, Iowa State Highway Commission, Federal Works Agency, Public Roads Administration, "A Traffic Survey of the Omaha–Council Bluffs Metropolitan Area" (1946), 19. As late as 1968 a spokesman for the OIF hoped that manufacturing employment in Omaha would rise to 20 percent of the work force. In 1968 it stood at 17 percent, although the article said it stood at only 10 percent. *Omaha World-Herald*, November 17, 1968; Cunningham, "Getting It Straight," 37.

37 Omaha Chamber of Commerce *Bulletin* 14, no.23 (June 10, 1955): 3.

38 For a full account of the charter convention election and the prominence of A. V. Sorensen, see Harold T. Muir, "The Formation and Adoption of the 1956 Omaha Home Rule Charter, 1954–1956" (Master's thesis, University of Nebraska at Omaha, 1969), 30–51.

39 Rene Beauchesne, "The Political Impact of the Omaha Home Rule Charter" (typed, Xeroxed photocopied manuscript, June 1, 1961).

40 Ibid., 6, 9, 11.

41 Ibid., 15–32.

42 Ibid., 33–38.

43 City of Omaha and Charter Convention, "Omaha Home Rule Charter, 1956," 52–57.

44 Ibid., 55; Donald Louis Stevens, Jr., "The Urban Renewal Movement in Omaha, 1954–1970" (Master's thesis, University of Nebraska at Omaha, 1981), 41–42.

45 Omaha Chamber of Commerce Minutes of Meetings, Municipal Affairs Committee, December 13, 1954, 332–33; Omaha Chamber of Commerce *Bulletin* 14, no.24 (June 24, 1955): 1–3; Mayor's City-Wide Planning and Development Committee, "Omaha Plan, 1957" (Omaha, Neb., 1957), 1.

46 See Abbott, *The New Urban America*, 241–56; John Mollenkopf, "The Post War Politics of Urban Development," *Politics and Society* 28 (September 1976): 245–95; Herbert Molotch, "The City as a Growth Machine: Towards a Political Economy of Place," *American Journal of Sociology* (September 1976): 290–331.

47 *Omaha Sun Newspapers*, May 25, 1961, 1, 22 (Omaha Public Library, Social Science Department Clip File).

48 Omaha Chamber of Commerce Minutes of Meetings, Municipal Affairs Committee, December 22, 1952, 358; January 12, 1953, 359; January 26, 1953, 360.

49 See Omaha City Planning Department, "Growth of the City Map"; Omaha Chamber of Commerce Minutes of Meetings, Urban Development and Planning Committee, October 11, 1956, 480; October 10, 1957, 474.

50 Omaha Chamber of Commerce *Bulletin* 12, no.8 (October 10, 1952): 1, 2; 12, no.9 (October 17, 1952): 3.

51 Ibid., 17, no.4 (September 19, 1958): 4.

52 "Omaha Plan 1957," 223–24.

53 Ibid., 232–35, 237–43, 245–46; Omaha Chamber of Commerce *Bulletin* 16, no.4 (September 21, 1956): 1, 4.

54 "Omaha Plan, 1957," 224–30.

55 For examples of boosterism see the various project committee reports in "Omaha Plan, 1957" and the Omaha Public Library Social Science Department Clip File on the Omaha Plan.

56 Omaha Chamber of Commerce *Bulletin* 13, no.21 (March 9, 1954): 1; 16, no. 18 (April 5, 1957): 1; *Bulletin* 13, no.21 (March 9, 1954): 1, 3.

57 *Omaha World-Herald*, October 31, 1955.

58 "Omaha Plan, 1957," 37–41.

59 Ibid., 37.

60 U.S. Bureau of the Census, 1954 Census of Business, vol.2, *Retail Trade Area Statistics*; 1963 Census of Business, 1963, vol.2, *Retail Trade Area Statistics*; 1967 Census of Business, vol.2, *Retail Trade Area Statistics*.

61 "Omaha Plan, 1957," 4, 6, 7.

62 The Omaha Plan reports included one from the Civic Center and City Hall Committee. That committee seemed to endorse the plan of the Public Educational and Cultural Facilities Committee. It then made a number of suggestions for a new or remodeled city hall, including the remodeling of the old post-office building. "Omaha Plan, 1957," 43–45, 165–75.

63 *Omaha Sun Newspapers*, March 5, 1959 (Omaha Public Library, Social Science Department Clip File); Barry D. Karl, *Charles E. Merriam and the Study of Politics* (Chicago: University of Chicago Press, 1974); Chamber of Commerce *Bulletin* 9, no.46 (June 23, 1950).

64 *Omaha Sun Newspapers*, March 5, 1959 (Omaha Public Library, Social Science Department Clip File).

65 "Omaha Plan, 1957," 166, 172.

66 Ibid., 172.

67 Ibid., 197, 199–200.

68 Stevens, "Urban Renewal," 15–16, 31, 46, 51. In 1957 the state legislature passed a bill requiring that all urban-renewal proposals be submitted to the people. "Omaha Plan, 1957," 225. Charles Davis, an attorney, was associated with the Urban League. George Robinson, head of the Omaha Urban League, still tentatively supported urban renewal as late as 1961. However, as early as 1959 the league began to focus its attention on the open-housing issue, which began to take center stage in 1961–62. *Omaha World-Herald*, November 15, 1959, A.M. edition; *Omaha Star*, March 31, 1961; *Omaha Star*, June 30, 1961. Even though it did lend its support to housing measures, throughout most of the postwar period, up through the mid-1960s, jobs remained the league's primary concern. See Dennis N. Mihelich, "World War II and the Transformation of the Urban League," *Nebraska History* 60, no.3 (Fall 1979): 401–23.

69 Stevens, "Urban Renewal," 28–29, 42–44; "Omaha Plan, 1957," 24.

70 Ibid., 25

71 *Omaha World-Herald*, April 26, June 4, 1958 (Omaha Public Library, Social Science Department Clip File).

72 Stevens, "Urban Renewal," 51; Beauchesne, "Political Impact," 34. While neither Stevens nor Beauchesne linked the municipal elections and the plan vote directly, the similarity between the voting patterns was quite evident.

73 The *Omaha World-Herald's All-American City Magazine*, March 1958, con-

tained a map of the proposed Interstate system, including the downtown and the South Omaha links that cut across the renewal area. See also *Omaha World-Herald*, April 21, 1959 (Omaha Public Library, Social Science Department Clip File).

74 Stevens, "Urban Renewal," 51.

75 Arthur W. Baum, "Omaha," *Saturday Evening Post* no.222 (September 10, 1949): 24–25, 123–34, 127, 129–30.

76 Ibid., 123–24.

77 Ibid., 25.

78 Omaha Chamber of Commerce Bulletin 11, no.21 (December 21, 1951): 3; 15, no.18 (March 30, 1956): 1.

79 *Omaha World-Herald, All-American City Magazine*, March 2, 1958, 14-I, 40-I.

80 Ibid., 3-I, 7-I, 24-I.

81 Ibid., 8-I, 29-I, 39-I.

82 Cunningham, "Getting It Straight," 37; Omaha City Planning Department, "Economic Survey of Omaha," 11. A service sector as such was not identified, but its various components were dealt with as a related group of employment sources. "Omaha Plan, 1957," 241–44.

CHAPTER FIVE

1 Omaha Chamber of Commerce *Profile* 19, no.18 (April 11, 1960): 4. For examples of such areas refer to the "Growth of the City Map." Several areas north of Ames Avenue between Forty-Eighth streets and Seventy-Second streets were not annexed until the late 1960s or early 1970s.

2 Fifteen divided by forty-one equals 37 percent.

3 Omaha Chamber of Commerce *Profile* 20, no.4 (October 3, 1960): 1; 23, no.20 (November 4, 1963): 5; 26, no.6 (March 28, 1966): 5.

4 *Omaha World-Herald*, April 21 and April 12, 1959 (Omaha Public Library, Social Science Department Clip File). For examples of such a sentiment see *Omaha World-Herald*, April 23, 1959; December 9, 1962 (Omaha Public Library, Social Science Department Clip File).

5 *Omaha World-Herald*, April 21, April 23, 1961 (Omaha Public Library, Social Science Department Clip File); ibid., July 12, 1945. The battle over parks also involved people wishing to save homes, but in a negative way. Park supporters endorsed a rerouting of the Interstate that would result in the demolition of

many homes but save parkland. Thus the battle lines were drawn for parks vs. homes.

6 *Omaha Sun Newspapers*, October 29, 1959 (Omaha Public Library, Social Science Department Clip File); see Gordon E. Baker, *Rural Versus Urban Political Power* (New York: Random House, 1955), 17. The still rural-dominated state legislature was traditionally wary of and hostile to Omaha. This was especially true as Omaha grew and began to demand an ever larger share of state funds. For more detailed information on the funding-formula battle, see *Omaha World-Herald*, January 12, 1960 (Omaha Public Library, Social Science Department Clip File); ibid., February 3, 1960; March 17, 1962; March 22, 1962; August 14, 1962; January 16, 1967.

7 Omaha Chamber of Commerce *Profile* 19, no.18 (April 11, 1960): 4; *Omaha World-Herald*, September 26, 1965; June 7, 1967 (Omaha Public Library, Social Science Department Clip File).

8 Omaha Chamber of Commerce Minutes of Meetings, Urban Planning and Development Committee, September 15, 1960, 399; *Profile* 20, no.4 (October 3, 1960): 4; Stevens, "Urban Renewal," 85.

9 Omaha Chamber of Commerce *Profile* 21, no.19 (April 23, 1962): 1, 2; Stevens, "Urban Renewal," 15–16, 44–47.

10 Before each election in 1961 and 1965, the *Omaha World-Herald* published short profiles of council candidates. They ran between April 16, and April 29, 1961 and April 25 and May 6, 1965, one profile each day. According to the articles, the council members had many occupations. Although several owned or operated businesses, none could be considered a big businessman. Their occupations ranged from insurance broker–agent (three members) and real-estate agent (two members) to president of a laundry firm, president of a building-supply firm, owner of a grocery store, attorney, musician, television announcer, and a former council administrative assistant.

11 That area was a part of a larger territory referred to as a "twilight zone" west of the downtown in the 1930s. Omaha Chamber of Commerce Minutes of the Board of Directors, Executive Committee, Finance Committee, November 29, 1938, 78–79; *Profile* 21, no.6 (October 23, 1961): 3.

12 Stevens, "Urban Renewal," 75; Beauchesne, "Political Impact," 37–38.

13 *Omaha World-Herald*, July 10, 1975; October 26, 1983 (Omaha Public Library, Social Science Department Clip File).

14 Ibid., October 26, 1983; *Omaha Sun Newspapers*, April 1966; Williams, "Twenty Top Structure"; *Omaha World-Herald*, May 13, 1982 (Omaha Public Library, Social Science Department Clip File).

15 City of Omaha Budget, 1959–1966. Beginning in 1959, the city published an annual budget report. The figures were drawn from those reports.

16 Interview with James Kelly, August 7, 1985 (tape recording in possession of the author); interview with Alden Aust, August 12, 1985 (tape recording in possession of the author).

17 Omaha Chamber of Commerce *Profile* 19, no.11 (January 4, 1960): 3, 4.

18 Ibid., 20, no.19 (May 15, 1961): 5.

19 Ibid., 24, no.7 (April 6, 1964): 1, 5.

20 Ibid., 5.

21 *Omaha World-Herald*, October 11, 1959, 42.

22 Ibid., December 11, 1960, B-1.

23 Ibid., November 19, 1961, B-1; November 26, 1961, B-1.

24 U.S. Bureau of the Census, 1958 Census of Business, vol.2, *Retail Trade Area Statistics*; 1963. Census of Business, vol.2, *Retail Trade Area Statistics*; 1967. Census of Business, vol.2, *Retail Trade Area Statistics*.

25 The *Omaha World-Herald* began conducting market surveys in 1951 but did not begin to ask questions about shopping habits until 1963. *Omaha World-Herald, Profile of a Prosperous Market*, 1963, 1964, 1965, 1966, 1967, 1968, 1969, 1970, 1972, 1973.

26 Burroughs Corporation, "A History of the Omaha Women's Job Corps Center" (Omaha, Nebr., n.d.), appendix; Omaha Chamber of Commerce *Profile* 29, no.8 (April 14, 1969): 1, 4.

27 *Omaha World-Herald*, October 30, 1979 (Omaha Public Library, Social Science Department Clip File).

28 Omaha Chamber of Commerce *Profile* 21, no.17 (March 26, 1962): 6; *Omaha World-Herald*, May 11, 1958, 1-B, 4-B; for examples, see *Profile* 19, no.19 (April 25, 1960): 4; 24, no.17 (September 28, 1964): 5; 24, no.14 (July 20, 1964): 1, 3; Interview with Alden Aust.

29 *Omaha World-Herald*, September 7, 1962, 1, 2; October 2, 1962, 1.

30 *Omaha World-Herald*, November 15, 1962, 1; November 17, 1962, 2; December 13, 1962, 8; December 19, 1962, 1; February 12, 1963, 20; August 2, 1963, 8.

31 Omaha Chamber of Commerce Minutes of Meetings, Central Omaha Committee, March 8, 1962, 36–37; August 16, 1962, 51.

32 Ibid., May 17, 1963, 64. Opponents of the Interstate and urban renewal often referred to proponents of those programs negatively as "chamber of commerce types." Omaha Chamber of Commerce Minutes of Meetings, Central Omaha Committee, May 17, 1963, 64.

33 Omaha Chamber of Commerce *Profile* 23, no.12 (June 10, 1963): 6; Omaha City Planning Department, "Previous Planning History" (unpublished typed manuscript, 1985), 5–6; *Omaha World-Herald*, January 10, 1965, 3-J.

34 Omaha Chamber of Commerce Profile 26, no.23 (December 19, 1966): 1, 6; City of Omaha and Central Omaha Committee, "Central Omaha Plan" (City of Omaha, 1966), 5.

35 Ibid., 8, 12.

36 Ibid., 13.

37 Ibid., 14–17.

38 The research was conducted primarily in 1963. "Central Omaha Plan," 19–21.

39 Ibid., 23–28; *Omaha World-Herald,* December 6, 1963 (Omaha Public Library, Social Science Department Clip File).

40 "Central Omaha Plan," 29–55.

41 Ibid., 55.

42 Ibid., 71–73; Omaha Chamber of Commerce *Profile* 25, no.3 (February 1, 1965): 5; *Omaha World-Herald,* March 25, 1965, 6. Every time Congress voted to build a federal office building or new post office in Omaha, the Old Post Office block received mention as the preferred site. The civic and business community first expressed such an idea in the 1930s and repeated it frequently thereafter.

43 "Central Omaha Plan," 70, 73. The Eighteenth Street Mall project was described, briefly, as a pedestrian mall. It was not as extensive as the Sixteenth Street Mall project and was not described in great detail.

44 Ibid., 75–78.

45 Ibid., 79.

46 Ibid., 78, 89–90.

47 Ibid., 80–82.

48 *Omaha World-Herald*, September 26, 1954; July 4, 1956 (Omaha Public Library, Social Science Department Clip File).

49 Ibid., October 1, 18, 1959 (Omaha Public Library, Social Science Department Clip File).

50 Omaha Chamber of Commerce *Profile* 20, no.4 (October 3, 1960): 5; 20, no.15 (March 6, 1961): 4; 20, no.16 (March 20, 1961): 5.

51 *Omaha World-Herald*, April 25, 1963 (Omaha Public Library, Social Science Department Clip File).

52 Ibid.

53 Ibid., May 22, 1963.

54 Ibid., April 19, 1964; February 3, 1965.

55 Omaha Chamber of Commerce *Profile* 24, no.18 (October 12, 1964): 3.

56 Ibid.

57 Omaha Chamber of Commerce Minutes of Meetings, memorandum, May 25, 1966, 36.

58 Ibid., Central Omaha Committee, July 24, 1962, 46.

59 Omaha Chamber of Commerce *Profile* 23, no.6 (March 18, 1963): 4; Minutes of Meetings, Central Omaha Committee, January 15, 1964, 414.

60 Omaha Chamber of Commerce *Profile* 24, no.3 (February 10, 1964): 5; Minutes of Meetings, Central Omaha Committee, July 21, 1965, 16.

61 *Omaha Sun Newspapers*, July 15, 1965 (Omaha Public Library, Social Science Department Clip File).

62 Ibid.; "Central Omaha Plan, 1966," 79.

63 Omaha Chamber of Commerce *Profile* 25, no.18 (September 27, 1965): 6; "Central Omaha Plan," 79; *Omaha World-Herald*, June 15, 1965 (Omaha Public Library, Social Science Department Clip File).

64 Omaha Chamber of Commerce *Profile* 20, no.19 (May 1, 1961): 3; 20, no.20 (May 15, 1961): 3; 20, no.19 (May 1, 1961): 3.

65 Joslyn Art Museum, Annual Report, 1962, 10 (available in the Joslyn Art Museum library).

66 Ibid., 1966.

67 *Omaha World-Herald*, October 13, 1955; January 6, 1957; July 8, 1960; June 28, 1969 (Omaha Public Library, Social Science Department Clip File).

68 Omaha Chamber of Commerce *Profile* 23, no.8 (April 15, 1963): 6.

69 Ibid., 23, no.9 (April 29, 1963): 5–6.

70 U.S. Bureau of the Census, Seventeenth Census of the United States, 1950, Census of the Population, vol.2, *Characteristics of the Population*; Eighteenth

Census of the United States, 1960, Census of the Population, vol. 1, *Characteristics of the Population*; Nineteenth Census of the United States, 1970, Census of the Population, vol. 1, *Characteristics of the Population*.

71 Chamber of Commer *Profile* 26, no. 18 (October 10, 1966): 5.

72 Ibid., 23, no. 14 (July 22, 1963): 1, 2; 24, no. 4 (February 24, 1964): 1.

73 Ibid., 25, no. 18 (September 27, 1965): 1, 5.

74 Ibid., 5.

75 Cunningham, "Education and Manpower," 37.

76 *Omaha World-Herald*, April 23, 1959 (Omaha Public Library, Social Science Department Clip File).

CHAPTER SIX

1 Jordan, "Nebraska," 396.

2 Omaha Chamber of Commerce *Profile* 28, no. 20 (November 4, 1968): 3.

3 Larsen and Cottrell, *The Gate City*, 251.

4 Ibid.

5 Cunningham, "Education and Manpower," 37.

6 See Danton, "Factors"; Center for Applied Urban Research, "Economic Structure"; Danton and Hariri, "Preliminary Projections"; Hinton, "Manpower Needs."

7 U.S. Bureau of the Census, Seventeenth Census of the United States, 1950, Census of the Population, vol. 2, *Characteristics of the Population*; Eighteenth Census of the United States, 1960, Census of the Population, vol. 1, *Characteristics of the Population*; Nineteenth Census of the United States, 1970, Census of the Population, vol. 1, *Characteristics of the Population*.

8 U.S. Bureau of the Census, *City and County Data Book*, 1962, 1972.

9 The material on leadership and the companies came from files available in the Omaha Public Library's Social Science and Business and Economics departments' clip files. For more details see notes on leadership in chapter 2 and table 15.

Retired: Morris Jacobs, John F. Merriam, Frank Fogarty, John F. Davis, Edd Bailey. Died: Gilbert Swanson, Melvin Bekins. Promoted: A. F. Jacobson. Other: A. W. Gordon, Erhard Edquist, Kenneth C. Holland, Richard Walker.

10 Succeeding the departing chairmen and presidents were Morris Miller, Harold Andersen, Charles Peebler, Thomas J. Nurnberger, Jr., John Lauritzen, John

Kennefick, and Nick Newberry. Up-and-comers by the middle 1960s were William A. Fitzgerald, Ed Owen, J. Allan Mactier, and Nick Newberry. *Omaha Sun Newspapers*, March 5, 1964 (Omaha Public Library, Social Science Department Clip File).

11 Examples: Cudahy Meats closed; Storz Brewing's new leader, Arthur Storz, did not have the prestige of his brother Robert; Swanson sold out to Campbell Soups; Fairmont Foods closed local operations; Byron Reed faded as a strong contender in the highly competitive real-estate market.

12 After leaving the mayor's office, Leahy held no further public office and ceased to participate much in local politics in any high-profile way.

13 *Omaha World-Herald, Magazine of the Midlands*, December 31, 1972 (Omaha Public Library, Social Science Department Clip File); *Omaha Sun Newspapers*, December 28, 1972 (Omaha Public Library, Social Science Department Clip File).

14 *Omaha Sun Newspapers*, December 28, 1972 (Omaha Public Library, Social Science Department Clip File).

15 Omaha Chamber of Commerce Profile, 26, no.31 (April 17, 1967): 2.

16 Ibid., 27, no.2 (May 1, 1967): 1, 7.

17 Ibid., 28, no.4 (March 11, 1968): 7; *Omaha World-Herald*, June 7, 1970 (Omaha Public Library, Social Science Department Clip File).

18 The advertisements appeared periodically as inserts in 1968 in the Chamber of Commerce newsletter *Profile*.

19 The advertisements appeared periodically as inserts in 1969 in the Chamber of Commerce newsletter *Profile*.

20 Omaha Chamber of Commerce Profile 30, no.5 (March 9, 1970): 1; 30, no.17 (September 28, 1970): 1, 6.

21 *Omaha Sun Newspapers*, March 4, 1971 (Omaha Public Library, Social Science Department Clip File).

22 Ibid.

23 Quoted in ibid.

24 Omaha Chamber of Commerce *Profile* 29, no.13 (June 23, 1969): 1, 4, 5.

25 Ibid., 29, no.19 (October 14, 1969): 2; Larsen and Cottrell, *The Gate City*, 251, 252.

26 Omaha Chamber of Commerce *Profile* 3, no.16 (September 7, 1971): 4–5.

27 Ibid.

28 Quoted in *Omaha World-Herald*, August 30, 1970, 12-A; Belkap Data Solutions, "Facility Location Decisions," 1; *Fortune* 90, no.1 (July 1974): 25–35.

29 *Fortune* 90, no.1 (July 1974): 27.

30 Ibid., 29.

31 Ibid., 29, 31, 33, 34.

32 Omaha Chamber of Commerce *Profile* 30, no.9 (May 4, 1970): 3, 7; *Omaha World-Herald, Profile of a Prosperous Market*, 1973, 7.

33 For examples see *Omaha World-Herald*, October 10, 1968; October 8, 1970; March 21, 1971; April 5, 1971; August 20, 1972 (Omaha Public Library, Social Science Department Clip File); ibid., December 22, 1968, 1-B, 2-B; October 5, 1969, 22-A.

34 U.S. Bureau of the Census, 1967 Census of Business, vol.2, *Retail Trade Area Statistics*; 1972 Census of Retail Trade, vol.3, *Major Retail Center Statistics*.

35 See *Omaha World-Herald* annual market surveys, 1966–70, 1972–73.

36 *Omaha World-Herald*, December 22, 1968, 1-B, 2-B.

37 Ibid., January 10, 1968 (Omaha Public Library, Social Science Department Clip File); October 5, 1969, 22-A.

38 Quoted in ibid., November 6, 1970 (Omaha Public Library, Social Science Department Clip File).

39 Ibid., March 21, 1971 (Omaha Public Library, Social Science Department Clip File); January 10, 1971, 12-J; July 23, 1972 (Omaha Public Library, Social Science Department Clip File); August 9, 1970, 2-B; January 10, 1971, 2-B; quoted in ibid., June 1, 1972 (Omaha Public Library, Social Science Department Clip File).

40 Omaha Chamber of Commerce *Profile* 25, no.13 (June 21, 1965); 25, no.19 (October 11, 1965): 1; 26, no.1 (January 3, 1966): 1.

41 See Mayor's Committee, "Program" and "Central Omaha Plan," 79.

42 Omaha City Planning Department, "Central Business District Plan; Riverfront Development Area, Omaha, Nebraska" (Omaha–Council Bluffs Metropolitan Area Planning Agency: Missouri Riverfront Development Program, Subelement 905, n.d.), 74; Omaha Chamber of Commerce, Minutes of the Board of Directors, Executive Committee, Finance Committee, March 22, 1968, 25.

43 Nebraska State Historical Society, "Historic Preservation in Nebraska" (Preservation Series, Report No.1, 1971), 30–34; Omaha Chamber of Commerce *Profile* 30, no.14 (July 20, 1970): 7.

44 Omaha City Planning Department, "An Opportunity for the Union Station" (Report No.175, 1973), 2; Larsen and Cottrell, *The Gate City*, 284, 286.

45 *Omaha World-Herald*, November 11, 1968; September 15, 1969; October 26, 1969 (Omaha Public Library, Social Science Department Clip File).

46 *Omaha Sun Newspapers*, October 8, 1970 (Omaha Public Library, Social Science Department Clip File).

47 *Omaha World-Herald*, January 10, 1971, 4-J.

48 Quoted in *Omaha World-Herald*, May 14, 1972 (Omaha Public Library, Social Science Department Clip File); July 23, 1972, 1-F, 2-F.

49 Omaha City Planning Department, "Beautification Master Plan for Omaha Nebraska" (Report No.160, 1968), 5.

50 Ibid., 23–24.

51 Ibid., 26; Omaha City Planning Department, "Neighborhood Planning Guide" (Report No.171, 1971). The booklet was published without pagination.

52 "Neighborhood Planning Guide."

53 "Beautification Master Plan," 34.

54 Ibid., 30; *Omaha World-Herald*, January 26, 1968 (Omaha Public Library, Social Science Department Clip File).

55 "Beautification Master Plan," 25, 29.

56 Ibid., 33.

57 Ibid., 31.

58 Ibid., 36.

59 Ibid., 32.

60 *Omaha World-Herald*, June 2, 1967 (Omaha Public Library, Social Science Department Clip File).

61 Omaha Chamber of Commerce Minutes of Meetings, Special Subcommittee, Tourism, June 26, 1967, 252–53.

62 Omaha Chamber of Commerce Minutes of Meetings, Tourism Committee, January 24, 1968, 382.

63 Larsen and Cottrell, *The Gate City*, 273–74, 275.

64 Interview with Alden Aust, August 12, 1985.

65 *Omaha World-Herald*, January 19, 1971 (Omaha Public Library, Social Science Department Clip File).

66 Ibid.

67 Ibid.

68 *Omaha World-Herald, Magazine of the Midlands*, February 18, 1973 (Omaha Public Library, Social Science Department Clip File); League of Women Voters, "The Omaha-Council Bluffs Metropolitan Area Planning Agency" (Publication No.73–1), 1, 3; *Omaha World-Herald*, "Magazine of the Midlands," February 18, 1973 (Omaha Public Library, Social Science Department Clip File).

69 *Omaha World Herald*, January 31, 1973, 13.

70 Omaha–Council Bluffs Riverfront Development Committee and Omaha City Planning Department, "A Proposal for a Model River Project Concerning 'Riverfront Beautification and Utilization in Metropolitan Areas'" (May 20, 1971), 12.

71 Omaha-Council Bluffs Metropolitan Area Planning Agency, "Open Space Plan and Program" (Report No.106, adopted October 26, 1972), 47–48.

72 Ibid.; League of Women Voters, "Metropolitan Area Planning Agency," 21.

73 Omaha–Council Bluffs Metropolitan Area Planning Agency, "Open Space," 39, 50.

74 Ibid., 82.

75 Omaha City Planning Department, "Central Business District Plan," 6.

76 *Omaha World-Herald*, November 15, 1973 (Omaha Public Library, Social Science Department Clip File).

77 Ibid.; Omaha City Planning Department, "Central Business District Plan," 16–17, 21.

78 Omaha City Planning Department, "Central Business District Plan," 3, 21.

79 Ibid., 18, 23.

80 Ibid., 24; see *Omaha World-Herald*, May 14, 1972 (Omaha Public Library, Social Science Department Clip File), and July 23, 1972, 1-F.

81 *Omaha World-Herald*, November 11, 1973 (Omaha Public Library, Social Science Department Clip File); Omaha City Planning Department, "Central Business District Plan," 26–27; *Omaha World-Herald*, July 25, 1973 (Omaha Public Library, Social Science Department Clip File).

82 *Omaha World-Herald*, April 17, 1971, 1; Larsen and Cottrell, *The Gate City*, 266, 284; Omaha City Planning Department, "Central Business District Plan," 29.

83 Omaha City Planning Department, "Central Business District Plan," 74, 76, 77.

84 *Omaha World-Herald, Magazine of the Midlands*, July 21, 1985, 25.

85 *Omaha World-Herald*, January 8, 1984, 1-M, 6-M, 7-M.

EPILOGUE

1 *Omaha World-Herald*, January 8, 1985, 1-M, 6-M, 7-M; ibid., *Discover Downtown*, June 23, 1985, 1-K; *MetroGuide*, June 16, 1985.

2 *Omaha World-Herald*, January, 8, 1985, 6-M, 7-M.

3 *Omaha World-Herald, Discover Downtown*, June 23, 1985, 1-K.

4 Ibid., 2-K, 6-K, 7-K.

5 *Omaha World-Herald, MetroGuide*, June 16, 1985, 3-L.

6 Ibid., 30-L, 31-L.

7 *Omaha World-Herald*, December 14, 1989, 53–54.

Bibliography

Books and Articles

Abbott, Carl. *The New Urban America: Growth and Politics in Sunbelt Cities*. Chapel Hill: University of North Carolina Press, 1981.

————. *Portland: Planning, Politics and Growth in a Twentieth Century City*. Lincoln: University of Nebraska Press, 1983.

Abell, T. H. "A Shoreline Master Plan for Los Angeles." *Journal of the American Institute of Planners* 12, no.3 (Summer 1946).

Abrams, Charles. "Downtown Decay and Revival." *Journal of the American Institute of Planners* 27, no.1 (February 1961).

Allpass, John. "Changes in the Structure of Urban Centers." *Journal of the American Institute of Planners* 34, no.3 (May 1968).

American Society of Planning Officials, Annual Report for the years 1958, 1963, 1964, 1966, 1968.

"An Uncommon Man." *Kie-ways* 35, no.4 (published by Peter Kiewit Sons' Inc.).

Bailey, Stephen K., and Richard T. Frost. "Aesthetics and Metropolitan Growth." *Journal of the American Institute of Planners* 23, no.3 (Summer 1957).

Baker, Gordon E. *Rural Versus Urban Political Power*. New York: Random House, 1955.

Baum, Arthur W. "Omaha." *Saturday Evening Post* no.222 (September 10, 1949).

Clawson, Marion. "A Positive Approach to Open Space Preservation." *Journal of the American Institute of Planners* 28, no.2 (May 1962).

Clay, Grady. "Anti-Uglies Unite! A Proposal for an American Civic Trust." *Landscape Architecture* 52, no.4 (July 1962).

———. "B. . . . Is No Longer a Dirty Word." *Landscape Architecture* 55, no.3 (April 1965).

———. "Genteel Strolls and Drunken Rolls or Time to Look at Your City Park." *Landscape Architecture* 54, no.3 (April 1964).

———. "What a Nice Park! Wasn't It?" *Landscape Architecture* 52, no.3 (April 1962).

Codman, John. "A Law for the Preservation of an Historic District." *American Society of Planning Officials, Annual Report, 1964.*

Division of Information, Public Works Administration. *America Builds: The Record of PWA*. Washington, D.C.: United States Government Printing Office, 1939).

Eliot, Charles. "1961 Housing Act's Open-Space Provisions." *Landscape Architecture* 52, no.2 (January 1962).

Federal Works Agency, Works Progress Administration. *Reports on the Progress of the WPA Programs.* June 30, 1939.

———. *Final Report on the WPA Program, 1935–43.* Washington, D.C.: United States Government Printing Office, 1946.

"Forecasts for Recreation." *American Society of Planning Officials, Annual Report, 1966.*

Haar, Charles. "The Content of the General Plan: A Glance at History." *Journal of the American Institute of Planners* 21, nos.2–3 (Spring–Summer 1955).

Hagevik, George, and Lawrence Mann. "The 'New' Environmentalism: An Intellectual Frontier." *Journal of the American Institute of Planners*, 37, no.4 (July 1971).

Hecksher, August. *Open Spaces: The Life of American Cities*. New York: Harper and Row, 1977.

Hammel, Paul. "Who Wields Power In Omaha?" *Omaha Sun Newspapers*, July 22, 1981.

Hoppenfeld, Morton. "A Design for Change." *American Society of Planning Officials, Annual Report, 1968.*

———. "The Role of Design in City Planning." *Journal of the American Institute of Planners* 36, no.2 (May 1960).

Hotchkiss, Frank. "Expanding Vistas for Urban Design." *American Society of Planning Officials, Annual Report, 1966.*

Hufschmidt, Maynard M. "Environmental Quality as a Policy and Planning Objective." *Journal of the American Institute of Planners* 37, no.4 (July 1971).

Ickes, Harold. *The First Three Years of PWA*. Washington, D.C.: United States Government Printing Office, 1936.

――――. *PWA: A Four Year Record of the Construction of Permanent and Useful Public Works*. Washington. D. C.: United States Government Printing Office, 1937.

Johnson, Norman J. "A City Takes the First Step: An Experiment for Renewing a Central Business District." *Journal of the American Institute of Planners* 24, no.1 (Winter 1958).

Jordan, Robert Paul. "Nebraska . . . The Good Life." *National Geographic* 145, no.3 (March 1974).

Karl, Barry D. *Charles E. Merriam and the Study of Politics*. Chicago: University of Chicago Press, 1974.

Larsen, Lawrence H., and Barbara J. Cottrell. *The Gate City: A History of Omaha*. Vol.4 in the Western Omaha Urban History Series. Boulder, Colo. Pruett Publishing Company, 1982.

Layton, Ruth. "St. Louis Riverfront Revisited, 1933–1964." *Landscape Architecture* 54, no.3 (April 1964).

Levine, Lawrence. "Land Conservation in Metropolitan Areas." *Journal of the American Institute of Planners* 30, no.3 (August 1964).

Lowe, Jeanne R. *Cities in a Race With Time*. New York: Random House, 1967.

Lowenthal, David. "The Environmental Crusade: Ideals and Realities." *Landscape Architecture* 60, no.4 (July 1970).

――――. "To Love at a Distance Is Not Enough." *Landscape Architecture* 59, no.1 (October 1968).

Lynch, Kevin. "Urban Design." *American Society of Planning Officials, Annual Report, 1958*.

――――. *The Image of the City*. Cambridge, Mass.: MIT Press, 1960.

―――― and Alvin K. Lukashok. "Some Childhood Memories of the City." *Journal of the American Institute of Planners* 22, no.3 (Summer 1956).

McGlade, Jacqueline. "The Zoning of Fort Crook: Urban Expansionism vs. County Home Rule." *Nebraska History* 65, no.1 (Spring 1983).

MacMahon, Arthur W., John D. Millett, and Gladys Ogden. *The Administration of Federal Work Relief*. Committee on Public Administration Social Science Research Council. Chicago: Public Administration Service, Studies in Administration, vol.12, 1941.

Mandelker, Daniel L. "What Open Space Where? How?" *American Society of Planning Officials, Annual Report, 1963*.

Martin, Roger. "Exciting Start with Nicollet Mall." *Landscape Architecture* 59, no.4 (July 1969).

Miewald, Robert D., ed. *Nebraska Government and Politics*. Lincoln, Nebraska: University of Nebraska-Lincoln Press, 1984.

Mihelich, Dennis. "World War II and the Transformation of the Urban League." *Nebraska History* 60, no.3 (Fall 1979).

Mollenkopf, John. H. *The Contested City*. Princeton, N.J.: Princeton University Press, 1983.

———. "The Post War Politics of Urban Development." *Politics and Society* 28 (September 1976).

Molotch, Herbert. "The City as a Growth Machine: Towards a Political Economy of Place." *American Journal of Sociology* (September 1976).

Morris, Robert L., and S. B. Zisman, B. "The Pedestrian, Downtown, and the Planner." *Journal of the American Institute of Planners* 28, no.3 (August 1962).

Myers, Harold B. "The Biggest Invisible Builder in the World." *Fortune*, 74, no.4 (April 1966).

Nelson, Arvid E., Jr. *The AK-SAR-BEN Story: A Seventy Year History of the Knights of AK-SAR-BEN*. Lincoln, Nebr.: Johnsen Publishing Company, 1967.

Northern, The First Fifty Years. Omaha: Northern Natural Gas Company, 1983.

PKS: A Past of Achievement. . . . A Future of Challenge. Peter Kiewit Sons', Inc.

"Planning for Leisure and Change: Programs of the IFLA, ASLA, NCILA." *Landscape Architecture* 58, no.3 (April 1968).

"Profile: Leo A. Daly, Jr." *The Alumnus: The Catholic University of America* (Winter 1966).

Rippey, James C. *The Diary of a Dream: Goodbye, Central; Hello, World; A Centennial History of Northwestern Bell*. Omaha: Northwestern Bell, 1975.

Sale, Kirkpatrick. *Power Shift: The Rise of the Southern Rim and Its Challenge to the Eastern Establishment*. New York: Random House, Vintage Books, 1975.

Satterthwaithe, Ann. "Open Space Is Not Enough." *Landscape Architecture* 55, no.2 (January 1965).

Schocken, Thomas. "Must Our Cities Remain Ugly?" *Journal of the American Institute of Planners* 22, no.4 (Fall 1956).

Scott, Mel. *American City Planning since 1890*. Berkeley: University of California Press, 1969.

Short, C. W., and R. Stanley-Brown. *Public Buildings: Architecture Under the Public*

Works Administration, 1933 to 1939. Washington, D.C.: United States Government Printing Office, 1939.

Smith, Alysia, chief researcher. *Omaha Stockyards: A Century of Marketing, Commemorative Book, 1884–1984.* Omaha: Omaha Livestock Market, Inc., 1984.

Spreiregen, Paul D. "Making the Scene." *American Society of Planning Officials, Annual Report, 1966.*

Sternlieb, George. "The Future of Retailing in the Downtown Core." *Journal of the American Institute of Planners* 29, no.2 (May 1963).

Sylvester, B. F. "Omaha's Flood, 1952." *Nebraska History* 35, no.1 (March 1954).

Tunnard, Christopher. "Cities by Design." *Journal of the American Institute of Planners* 17, no.3 (Summer 1951).

Ulman, Edward. "Amenities as a Factor in Regional Growth." *Geographical Review* 44, no.1 (January 1954).

Van Ginkel, Blanche Lemco. "The Form of the Core." *Journal of the American Institute of Planners* 27, no.1 (February 1961).

Weiss, Shirley F. "The Downtown Mall Experiment." *Journal of the American Institute of Planners* 30, no.1, (February 1964).

Whyte, William, Jr. "Open Space—And Retroactive Planning." *American Society of Planning Officials, Annual Report, 1958.*

Wickstead, George. "Critique: Fresno Mall's First 12 Months." *Landscape Architecture* 56, no.1 (October 1965).

Williams, J. Kerwin. *Grants-in-Aid Under the Public Works Administration: A Study in Federal-State-Local Relations.* New York: Columbia University Press, 1939.

Williams, Paul. "Twenty Top Omaha's Power Structure." *Omaha Sun Newspapers,* April 7, 1966.

Wolfe, Albert B. "Conservation of Historic Buildings and Areas." *American Society of Planning Officials Annual, Report, 1964.*

Zeitlen, Samuel. "Waterfront Planning and the Master Plan." *Journal of the American Institute of Planners* 11, no.3 (Summer 1945).

Theses

Muir, Harold T. "The Formation and Adoption of the 1956 Omaha Home Rule Charter, 1954–1956." Master's thesis, University of Nebraska at Omaha, 1969.

Peterson, Garneth O. "The Omaha City Council and Commission: A Profile 1888–1930." Master's Thesis, University of Nebraska at Omaha, 1980.

Stecklein, Carroll A. "The Economic Base and Community Multiplier for the SMSA of Omaha. Master's Thesis, University of Nebraska, 1960.

Stevens, Donald Louis, Jr. "The Urban Renewal Movement in Omaha, 1954–1970." Master's thesis, University of Nebraska at Omaha, 1981.

Wilson, Richard K. "Business Progressivism in Omaha, 1900–1917." Master's thesis, Creighton University, 1977.

Center for Applied Urban Research Publications

Center for Applied Urban Research. "The Economic Structure of the Omaha SMSA." University of Omaha, April 1967.

———. "Omaha's Changing Profile." *Review of Applied Urban Research* 2, no.2 (February 1974).

Cunningham, John C. "Education and Manpower in the Omaha SMSA." University of Nebraska at Omaha, April 1971.

Danton, Lawrence A. "Factors Influencing the Development of Omaha." University of Omaha, March 1967.

Danton, Lawrence A., and Masoud Hariri. "Preliminary Projections of Growth of the Omaha SMSA to 1990." University of Omaha, August 1967.

Hinton, David W. "Manpower Needs in the Omaha SMSA: Employment and Occupational Projections." University of Nebraska at Omaha, September 1975.

Houswald, Edward. "The Structure of Employment in the Omaha SMSA 1970, 1974, 1976–78 by Industry and Occupation." University of Nebraska at Omaha, November 1977.

Omaha City Planning Documents

City of Omaha. 1942: *Manual of Civic Improvements Sponsored by the Mayor and City Council of Omaha*. Omaha: Douglas Printing Company, 1942.

City of Omaha and Central Omaha Committee. "Central Omaha Plan, 1966." City of Omaha, 1966.

Mayor's City-Wide Planning Committee. "Improvement and Development Program Recommended for the City of Omaha by the Mayor's City-Wide Planning Committee." Omaha, Nebr., March 15, 1946.

Mayor's City-Wide Planning and Development Committee. "Omaha Plan, 1957." Omaha, Nebr., 1957.

Omaha City Planning Board Minutes.

Omaha City Planning Department. "A Century of Progress Through Annexation."
    Report No.176, 1973.

———. "A History of Omaha's Parks and Recreation System" [text by Garneth O.
    Peterson]. Report No.214, February 1982.

———. "An Economic Survey of Omaha, Nebraska: Section One, Master Plan."
    Report No.119, May 1958.

———. "An Opportunity for the Union Station." Report No.175, 1973.

———. "Beautification Master Plan for Omaha Nebraska." Report No.160, 1968.

———. "Central Business District Plan; Riverfront Development Area, Omaha,
    Nebraska." Omaha–Council Bluffs Metropolitan Area Planning Agency: Mis-
    souri Riverfront Development Program, Subelement 905, n.d.

———. "Growth of the City Map."

———. "Neighborhood Planning Guide." Report No.171, 1971.

———. "Previous Planning History." Unpublished typed manuscript, 1985.

Omaha–Council Bluffs Metropolitan Area Planning Agency, "Open Space Plan
    and Program." Report No.106, adopted October 26, 1972.

———. "Regional Growth and Development: Conditions, Trends, Problems."
    June 1978.

Omaha–Council Bluffs Riverfront Development Committee and Omaha City
    Planning Department. "A Proposal for a Model River Project Concerning
    'Riverfront Beautification and Utilization in Metropolitan Areas.'" May 20,
    1971.

Chamber of Commerce Documents

NEWSLETTERS
Bulletin.
Profile.
Journal.

ARCHIVAL RECORDS
Minutes of the Board of Directors, Executive Committee, Finance Committee.

Minutes of Meetings. Central Omaha Committee, City Improvement Council,
    Municipal Affairs Committee, Postwar Planning Committee, Program of Work
    Committee, Public Works Committee, Special Subcommittee Tourism, Tourism
    Committee, and Urban Development and Planning Committee.

Newspapers and Related Publications

Los Angeles Times.

Omaha Post.

Omaha Star.

Omaha Sun Newspapers.

Omaha World-Herald.

Omaha World-Herald, All-American City Magazine.

Omaha World-Herald, Discover Downtown.

Omaha World-Herald, Magazine of the Midlands.

Omaha World-Herald, MetroGuide.

Omaha World-Herald, Profile of a Prosperous Market, 1963, 1964, 1965, 1966, 1967, 1968, 1969, 1970, 1972, 1973.

Omaha World-Herald, Sunday World-Herald Magazine.

Additional newspaper material available in the Omaha Public Library's Business and Economic Department and Social Science Department clip files. The material is organized by subject.

Census Documents

CENSUS OF BUSINESS

1948 Census of Business, vol. 3, *Retail Trade Area Statistics.*

1954 Census of Business, vol. 2, *Retail Trade Area Statistics.*

1958 Census of Business, vol. 2, *Retail Trade Area Statistics.*

1963 Census of Business, vol. 2, *Retail Trade Area Statistics.*

1967 Census of Business, vol. 2, *Retail Trade Area Statistics.*

CENSUS OF THE POPULATION

Seventeenth Census of the United States, 1950, Census of the Population, vol. 2, *Characteristics of the Population.*

Eighteenth Census of the United States, 1960, Census of the Population, vol. 1, *Characteristics of the Population.*

Nineteenth Census of the United States, 1970, Census of the Population, vol. 1, *Characteristics of the Population.*

CENSUS OF RETAIL TRADE

1972 Census of Retail Trade, vol. 3, *Major Retail Trade Area Statistics.*

City and County Data Book. Washington: Government Printing Office, 1952, 1956, 1962, 1967, 1972.

County Business Patterns. Washington: Government Printing Office, 1959, 1962, 1964–73.

State, Local and Federal Government Documents

STATE

Nebraska State Historical Society. "Historic Preservation in Nebraska." Preservation Series, Report No.1, 1971.

State-Wide Highway Planning Survey, Nebraska Department of Roads and Irrigation, Iowa State Highway Commission, Federal Works Agency, Public Roads Administration. "A Traffic Survey of the Omaha–Council Bluffs Metropolitan Area." 1946.

LOCAL

City of Omaha. Budget, 1959–1966.

City of Omaha and Charter Convention. "Omaha Home Rule Charter, 1956."

FEDERAL

Congressional Record—House, December 30, 1970.

INTERVIEWS

Mihelich, Dennis N., project director. "Omaha Profiles." River City Roundup Oral History Interviews. Douglas County Historical Society and the *Omaha World-Herald.*

Interview with Alden Aust, August 12, 1985. Tape recording in possession of the author.

Interview with Glenn Cunningham, August 5, 1985. Transcript in possession of the author.

Interview with James Kelly, August 7, 1985. Tape recording in possession of the author.

Miscellaneous

Bailey, Edd. "The Century of Progress: A Heritage of Service, Union Pacific, 1869–1969." Address to the Newcomen Society, September 9, 1969. Princeton University Press for the Newcomen Society, 1969.

Beauchesne, Rene. "The Political Impact of the Omaha Home Rule Charter." Typed, photocopied manuscript, June 1, 1961. Available in Creighton University's Reinert Memorial Library.

Belkap Data Solutions, Ltd. "Facility Location Decisions: A *Fortune* Research Survey." *Fortune* (September 1977).

Burroughs Corporation. "A History of the Omaha Women's Job Corps Center." Omaha, Nebr., n.d.

Cunningham, Glenn. "Getting It Straight." Radio address, April 9, 1951, station KOIL. Transcripts in possession of the author.

Joslyn Art Museum. Annual Report. 1963, 1966. Available in the Joslyn Art Museum library.

League of Women Voters. "The Omaha–Council Bluffs Metropolitan Area Planning Agency." Publication No.73–1.

PWA-WPA Papers. Special Collections, University of Nebraska at Omaha.

Sullenger, T. Earl. "An Ecological Study of Omaha." Municipal University of Omaha, Bureau of Social Research, 1938.

Index